Flying the Hump

TEXAS A&M UNIVERSITY

25

MILITARY HISTORY SERIES

FLYING THE HUMP

Memories of an Air War

Otha C. Spencer

Texas A&M University Press
College Station

The paper used in this book meets the minimum requirements
of the American National Standard for Permanence
of Paper for Printed Library Materials, Z39.48-1984.
Binding materials have been chosen for durability.

Library of Congress Cataloging-in-Publication Data

Spencer, Otha Cleo, 1920–
    Flying the Hump : memories of an air
war / Otha C. Spencer.— 1st ed.
       p.   cm.— (Texas A&M University mili-
tary history series ; no. 25)
    Includes bibliographical references and
index.
    ISBN 0-89096-513-7 (alk. paper);
0-89096-624-9 (pbk.)

    1. World War, 1939–1945 — Aerial opera-
tions, American.   2. Airlift, Military —
United States — History.   3. World War,
1939–1945 — Campaigns — Himalaya Mountains.   4. World War, 1939–1945 — Campaigns — China.   5. World War, 1939–1945 —
Campaigns — Burma.   6. World War, 1939–
1945 — Campaigns — India.   7. Himalaya
Mountains — History, Military.   8. China —
History, Military.   I. Title.   II. Series:
Texas A&M University military history
series ; 25.
D790.S625   1992
940.54′4373 — dc20   91-48253
                                       CIP

To members of my flight crew
who were with me through the hurricanes
of the South Atlantic
and the storms of the CBI Hump:

John C. Bortz, navigator
Arthur Lincks, copilot
George Abersole, weather officer
Michael Dezazzo, crew chief
John Terrell, flight engineer
Raymond Merritt, radio operator

Contents

Illustrations

MAPS

Preface

This book, very simply, tells a story of a military miracle, halfway around the world in a strange, weather-tortured land, that in World War II saved one-fifth of the world's people.

This is the story of the China-Burma-India (CBI) Hump, the great airlift of World War II over the mighty Himalayas from India across Burma into China—the most dangerous air routes in all of the operations of the Allied Air Forces.

The Hump was a major battle of World War II—a three-year siege of the Himalayas. Slow, clumsy unarmed cargo planes carried the freight of war to the Chinese; their crewmen were the aerial "quartermasters" who flew through rain, ice, wind, and clouds twenty thousand feet above the jungles of Burma and the snow-laden passes of China.

This narrative tells only the story of the Hump airlift of the U.S. Air Transport Command (ATC) and the other air crews that crossed and crisscrossed the Himalayas during the CBI campaign. The struggles of the foot soldier and the sailors of the sea are omitted. I do not want to disparage their roles as they fought disease, leeches, snakes, starvation, head-hunting natives, and the Japanese. Their story has been told many times, but the story of the air war over the great Himalayas has never been completely told.

Wars and struggles for power are not always limited to or decided on the battlefields—in the jungles, on the sea, or in the air. Generals, admirals, and other leaders of the various countries involved have their individual wills, desires, egos, ambitions, local concerns, and, too often, their downright "cussedness" which influence their actions.

War is the back alley of politics. Men who fight are sometimes the pawns of powerful, greedy, and corrupt interests. War is a drama of mistakes, inefficiency, and stupidity in addition to heroism and courage. Mountains and weather were not the only hazards that the Hump airmen had to battle.

I was a pilot in the CBI for the Tenth Weather Squadron at Barrackpore, near Calcutta, India. My crew and I had flown together for over a year in weather and hurricane reconnaissance over the North and South Atlantic. In India, our job was flying weather reconnaissance over the Bay of Bengal and across the Hump into China. We also flew supplies, equipment, and personnel to weather stations throughout India, Burma and China.

The real day-and-night, weather-be-damned flights over the Hump were by the ATC, an outfit of some of the bravest and most skilled crews in the world. Their job was to keep China in the war, bringing supplies, troops, high-octane gasoline, guns, and whatever else a war needed in a 'round-the-clock airlift operation. Without their daring flights, the machinery of war could not operate. Their story was the main act in this drama in the backwaters of World War II. Their war was the Hump.

Theodore White and Annalee Jacoby, in *Thunder Out of China*, wrote, "The Hump drove men mad, killed them, sent them back to America wasted with tropical fevers and broken for the rest of their lives. Some of the boys called it The Skyway to Hell; it was certainly the most dangerous, terrifying, barbarous aerial transport run in the world."[1]

The Hump was also called "the greatest effort of its kind in the war."[2] The Hump was President Franklin D. Roosevelt's special project in World War II, for his beloved China.

Almost every history of World War II mentions the Hump airlift — a page or a paragraph — usually with a series of dramatic pictures of transport planes crossing the treacherous mountains. Historians have stressed the heroism of Vinegar Joe Stilwell, Merrill's Marauders, and Brigadier Orde Wingate, and the world responded to the glamour of the shark-nosed planes of Chennault's Flying Tigers. Together they make a dramatic story of the Chinese struggle against Japan, and they deserve every word of praise written about them. But they were heroes only because the Hump crews of the ATC were there to bring supplies over the great mountains of the Himalaya.

The author's B-25 flight crew sent to the CBI in 1945 for weather reconnaissance over the Hump. *Left to right, standing:* 1st Lt. John Bortz, navigator; 1st Lt. Otha Spencer, pilot; 1st Lt. George Abersold, weather officer; 2nd Lt. Arthur Lincks, copilot; *left to right, front row:* T. Sgt. Michael Dezazzo, crew chief; T. Sgt. Raymond Merritt, radio operator; S. Sgt. John Terrell, flight engineer.

Through the years the famous Flying Tigers have symbolized the air war against the Japanese and dominated the lore of the Hump. After the war when my friends learned that I flew the Hump, they would say, "Oh, the Flying Tigers?" "No, I flew transports over the Hump." "Oh," was their answer, with obvious disappointment.

China's critical situation in World War II was described by Gen. Y. T. Loh, president of the Chinese Air Force Veterans' Association, in a speech at a reunion of former Hump pilots in Little Rock, Arkansas, in 1986: "When we go to the war in 1937, the Japanese took all our ports. We have two supply routes to China. One is Burma Road, but the Japanese took it. We can't do anything . . . we have nothing, not even a drop of gasoline. Later comes the Hump pilots. We can never forget. . . . the U.S. have its big army, yes, very good. But . . . most important factor was you have some young wonderful Hump pilots to bring supplies over there. Otherwise we wouldn't make it."[3]

The Hump airlift does not have its own history because historians have never recognized transport planes as a major part of war. In the air battles of World War II, fighters and bombers were the heroes. The role of the slow, unglamorous, and unarmed cargo plane was never recognized until the determined ATC Hump crews gave flesh and blood and scattered aluminum across India and Burma to help China fight Japan.

Air crews of the Hump perfected a new idea in warfare: airlifting supplies and men on a grand scale. What was learned in the CBI later saved Berlin with its airlift, and taught the army how to move troops and evacuate the wounded by air in the Korean and Vietnam wars.

Over forty-five years ago, I was one of the young, inexperienced, eager pilots who shuttled back and forth across the Himalayas, flying the C-47 "Gooney Bird" and "Old Dumbo," the great C-46, through rain, ice, and turbulence. It is an experience that can never be forgotten.

Acknowledgments

I learned quickly in World War II that no one person can fly a combat airplane alone. There was always a support crew, and the mission succeeded or failed depending on how well the crew members did their job. Those very important people went unrecognized, unremembered, and, except to the pilot, often unappreciated. The same is true in writing a book. A book can never be the work of one person—there is always a support crew. Their names do not appear on the dust jacket or the title page, but without their help, the book might not have been published. I wish to thank my support crew.

George Larson, an unsuspecting editor of *Air & Space* magazine, after reading a long rambling article I had written on the CBI Hump in 1986, wrote, "People write books about that, Otha!" I thank you, George, for this idea. I discussed the subject with Lloyd Lyman, then director of the Texas A&M University Press, and he said, "Let's try for the book." That was in 1987. Lloyd was my most encouraging booster.

Dr. William Leary, professor of history of the University of Georgia, an authority on Chinese aviation, made a few comments that got the book under way. That was in late 1987.

There followed three years of the most rewarding research I have ever done. My own experiences came back to me, and I met friends and fellow air crewmen from all parts of the world who were interested in a history of the Hump. I want to acknowledge staff members of the Hump Pilots Association (HPA), Mrs. Jan Thies, executive secretary; John K. Troster, secretary; Frank Roth, editor of the HPA news-letter; and Dr. John Martin, HPA historian, who has written two books on the Combat Cargo of the CBI.

Individual members of HPA who sent photographs and personal experiences were Richard "Sahib" Foster, Don Carlson, Jack Corns, Edgar Crumpacker, Wu Ziden, General Konsin C. Shah, Mrs. "Chick" Marrs Quinn, Robert Boody, and Gene Leslie. Don Van Cleve, Dick Maddox, Dick Rossi and Milton Miller of the Flying Tigers of the Fourteenth Air Force Association were helpful with information, pictures, and personal experiences.

My own family, Billie, John, and Mary, made the three years of research and writing possible by simply putting up with me and reading and rereading the manuscript. Their chief comments were, "Rewrite this part." Friends, Dr. Ernestine Sewell Linck, and Dr. Charles Linck, helped with the manuscript.

With the help of this support group, I hope our mission is a success. "No man is an island."

Flying the Hump

Prologue

Gusty rain lashed the flight line in the steamy blackness at Chabua Air Field, in India's Upper Assam Valley. There is no other dark like the dark of a night in India, when the rain is sharp and the clouds push down on you. Our flight was to Kunming, China, 561 miles to the southeast, across the Himalaya Mountain range — the great China-Burma-India Hump.

This was June 1945, in World War II. My crew and I were on temporary duty with the Air Transport Command (ATC) for a big push during June and July to fly as much cargo into China as possible. We were flying out of a strange field over a strange air route to a strange country, and the rain and darkness provided an ominous beginning. Rain continued to come down. The darkness grew darker.

Juggling a battered map case, parachute, loaded 45-caliber pistol, and a hunting knife in a shoulder holster, I swung out of the jeep at the operations hut and ducked into the door. The weather forecast was terrible; weather over the Hump was almost always bad — a constant plague. But in the terrible reality of war, weather had to be ignored — we had to get the cargo to China.

In the operations hut, a new copilot and my regular radio operator, Raymond Merritt, were waiting. Crew chief Michael Dezazzo and flight engineer John Terrell were already at the plane — C-46-702 — that had just returned from China two hours before. We met Lt. Ken Jensen, the copilot, for the first time. We almost always had new copilots getting Hump experience so they could become first pilots.

"Bad night," the operations officer said. He handed us the clearance with the little weather information he had.

I signed out, and Jensen, Merritt, and I rode the jeep through the rain out to a C-46 bathed in lights. Ground crewmen were making last-minute checks. Flight engineer Terrell was on the wings peeping into the tanks to see if they were full. We got full tanks when the weather was bad. Terrell was hell on ground crews if he couldn't get enough gas. As we drove under the wing of the C-46, I was not quite ready for the huge size of the aircraft. I never was—I was constantly awed.

"Ready to go, captain," the crew chief yelled, against the noise of the flight line. "She'll get you there." Crew chiefs had a personal feeling for their planes. "Be damned sure you bring her back."

"Just so it gets us back. Next trip's yours." Sometimes the crew chief would go on a flight. It was a matter of honor that a crew chief would fly in his own plane at any time.

Inside the cargo bay of the huge aircraft, the air was hot and heavy with the smell of high-octane gasoline—twenty-five fifty-five-gallon drums were lashed to the floor. Four and a half tons of gasoline— what a bloody bonfire. Add a ton for the drums and a couple of tons of equipment and you have an overloaded airplane. And we had passengers. Up front, near the crew compartment, were three serious-faced Chinese officers with their equipment. They had no parachutes and I felt embarrassed as I carried my own 'chute to the cockpit.

"Can't we get these men 'chutes?" I yelled to the crew chief. I knew the answer would be "no," but I asked anyway.

The cockpit was a busy, no-nonsense place. Small lights were blinking, and the hum of the gyro instruments and the sharp crackling of the radio were welcome sounds to a pilot who really liked to fly. I liked the smell of these old GI airplanes—greasy aluminum with the heavy ozone odor from the old tube radios. Slipping into the seat, buckling the 'chute straps, tightening the safety belt, I was pleased that I had the most dangerous and best job in the army.

The adventure of a far-away destination and the threatening weather hung heavy in the cockpit. The oriental intrigue of China was always there, and flight had its own mystery. Copilot Jensen and radio operator Merritt were already in their places, listening to a weather report from a pilot somewhere in the muck, coming in from China.

"Pilot report, captain. Weather's bad to Paoshan . . . clearing to

Tsuyung. Kunming zero, lifting," Merritt reported. "That was six hours ago."

I thanked him and added, "Keep talking to anyone you can raise."

The new copilot knew what he was doing—quickly he had the two engines running smoothly. Rain was streaming down the cockpit windows and it was almost impossible to see. Suddenly, lights from a jeep swung around the left wing and someone threw three parachutes through the closing cargo door.

"I'll be damned," the flight engineer muttered as he locked the door and took the 'chutes to the Chinese officers. "A damned miracle." 'Chutes for the Chinese. It was a good omen. I always looked for good omens.

Engines revved up, brakes released, the huge plane came to life. We followed a lighted "FOLLOW ME" jeep to the takeoff runway. Rain sprayed in from the open window. The rotating beacon atop the tower showed clouds almost to the ground. A theodolite from the weather shack lighted the bottom of the overcast, not more than three hundred feet high. Planes coming in from China dropped out of the clouds about every ten minutes.

"CBI takeoff—if you can see the end of the runway, it's OK to take off," I yelled to the copilot. The tower cleared our flight. "Circle to ten thousand before heading to LX; altimeter, 2930; time, 2006; visibility, one mile; ceiling, three hundred; give it the gas!"

"Kick it in the ass!" Terrell yelled just behind my ear. That was our normal takeoff procedure. Jensen smiled.

"Roger, VG, thanks and good night." The jeep had driven down the runway and was waiting at the far end for the takeoff. This was a procedure at night, to get cows or people off the runway. I squirmed to get comfortable on the hump of my seat parachute. Jensen gave a big smile—another good omen—as he put on his oxygen mask; night flights required oxygen from the ground up.

With fuel mixture in full rich, props at highest RPM, I slowly pushed the throttles forward and the sudden surge of power snapped us back against the seats. The pull from the engines made us feel invincible. Feel that power! Our lives were in those engines. If our engines die, we die.

The roar of the engines was good—a good flight feels and sounds good. At the right instant, copilot Jensen grabbed the throttles and held them in place. Copilots never locked the throttles in case the pilot had to suddenly abort the takeoff. Two 2,000-horsepower engines grabbed 702 and firmly pulled it down the white stripe in the middle of the black path between the runway lights—toward the lights of the jeep a mile away.

The runway was bumpy, the load was heavy; the plane strained to stay on the ground, bumped a little, left the runway, settled back, and with one sharp bump, sluggishly lifted into the night—yawing sharply to correct for crosswind. I could feel the weight of the load as the C-46 groaned and wallowed in the rain. We were literally hanging on the props—a normal CBI procedure.

Immediately, we were in the clouds—the beginning of a five-hour flight to Kunming. We were about to match our skill against weather. The C-46 was overloaded; cargo flights usually were. We handled the fear on the Hump flights by ignoring the danger. This would be a good flight: the Chinese had 'chutes and Jensen had smiled. My stomach was knotted in anxiety. I was always scared, but loved every minute of it.

Flying from Chabua was like flying out of a hole in the mountains. We had to circle the field to ten thousand feet before heading out across the Hump. We slowly climbed—three hundred feet per minute—air speed about 120, engines roaring in agony. The heavy plane bounced and pitched, pulling the crew against the seat belts. In the clouds, the wing-tip lights created small rainbows in the mist. With landing lights on during the climb, rain was coming at the plane in horizontal sheets as we slowly spiraled upward.

In my concentration during a flight, I am the aircraft; the plane and I are one. Flying in weather is a limbo of "no-being"—my own being submerged in an existence of perfect harmony of plane, pilot, the air, and weather. I am happy—there is no danger—we are one, at home in the air. Weather, good or bad, is just a part of air we fly in.

As we continued the climb, I watched Jensen staring at the instruments. He leaned over to me. "Captain?" He hesitated. "This is my first time in real weather. Lotsa hood—lotsa Link—no weather. But I can fly hell outa the gauges."[1]

It is now forty-five years later, and I still remember those words. A copilot who has never flown weather—a sailor who has never been to sea.

"Hell, Jensen, you're in real weather now! Fly the damned plane! Take over and I'll fill in the gaps. Climb to ten thousand . . . forty minutes, cross VG, keep climbing, head 214 to Moran . . . ten minutes . . . need twenty thousand after Moran to cross Naga Hills, if we can get it. Keep an eye on the radio compass for drift. Welcome to the Hump!"

The Naga Hills had peaks to 12,500 feet, but not far north were 18,000- and 20,000-foot peaks. Stormy turbulence kept the crew buckled in, and the rain changed to light snow. Sometimes, through a break in the clouds, we could see a moon and towering black thunderstorms. But we couldn't climb over the storm, and head-on was the threatening buildup over Naga. Lightning outlined the boiling clouds. Winds striking the mountains glanced upward, and the storm would build up to forty or fifty thousand feet. There was no way except straight through. So far, this was a good flight; copilot doing well.

Thumbs up to Jensen. He could still smile and, by-damned, he knew how to fly instruments.

As the clouds cleared, the air was smoother, and I trusted Jensen enough to leave my seat and check the back of the plane. The Chinese officers were quiet but smiling. Terrell, the flight engineer, had given them oxygen masks. The gasoline drums were riding well—no leaks.

Suddenly the weather changed again. I knew instantly. Turbulence was sharper. We were getting into thunderstorms.

"Captain," the flight engineer yelled back. "Ice!" Back on the flight deck, I watched the ice begin a slow buildup on the wings. Our C-46, Old Dumbo, was one small speck in the black sky, high above the jungles of Burma—alone, in the clutches of an ice storm.

Copilot Jensen jumped when he heard a loud crash against the fuselage, just behind the pilots' seats. As many times as I had heard it, I jumped, too. Ice was breaking off the propellers and hitting the plane. It is a chilling sound, but a good sound, since it tells us that the ice is being broken loose.

"Tell the men things are OK," I yelled to the engineer. I wished I could be sure of that. Ten minutes of severe icing can transform a plane into an iceberg. Icebergs don't fly.

Ice is broken off the wings and control surfaces with rubber boots that can be inflated and swelled out. This breaks the glaze and the violent wind rushing over the wings tears the ice off—if the system is working. We were lucky, the deicing system of 702 was working. I liked the C-46. It had the best engines in the world. If you can't have faith in your airplane, you might as well try to cross the Himalayas in a rowboat.

Suddenly the plane shuddered and almost rolled over. We were over the east side of the Naga range. Fifty- and sometimes hundred-mile-an-hour winds created violent updrafts from the mountains. We were thrown five hundred feet upward. Jensen and I fought the controls and, just as suddenly, a downdraft dropped the plane back down to twenty thousand. The clouds were a mass of anger. I had fought this turbulence on almost every flight and it was always a miracle that the plane was not torn apart. Sometimes planes were broken in two and we read about it on the operations bulletin board.

This violent turbulence was from the storm we had seen over the Naga Hills. The ice turned to sleet, and the sleet pellets battered the crew compartment like rocks in the clouds. Sleet is better than ice — sleet doesn't build up.

For the next ten minutes both Jensen and I worked to keep the plane right side up and somewhere near the right altitude. The giant C-46 was pitching and rolling like an angry dragon.

Lightning flashes made the black night seem like a scene from Dante's Inferno, and suddenly the crew experienced one of the most frightening, but harmless, phenomena of weather flight — Saint Elmo's fire.

As the battered C-46 flew through electrically charged clouds, balls of fire edged along the wingtips; the propellers created huge circles of flame, and dancing tongues of electrical energy entered the cockpit and tripped along the instrument panel, tickling the pilots' hands or neck. Saint Elmo's fire is an unearthly encounter. Even experienced crewmen are never comfortable with this aerial fireworks show.

Suddenly, the air was smooth and the clouds were gone. The moon brightened the dark mountains below. The lights of Myitkyina were far off to the left, and a plane below could be seen heading toward India. Myitkyina was in northern Burma, over the first great ridge of the Hump. Since there were no more Japanese planes over the Hump, it was good to see the lights of a large city, sparkling in the blackness of the jungle.

Jensen was on the radio, talking to a plane returning from China. I heard the weather message: "Clear from Myitkyina to Paoshan . . . ice and rain to Kunming . . . stacking at Kunming."

The turbulence had loosened one of the gas drums, but the flight engineer lashed it back down. Turbulence often broke cargo loose, and sometimes, in severe icing, cargo had to be kicked out the door to lighten the plane.

Here, at twenty thousand feet over China, in the midst of great danger, the amenities were not completely lost. The flight engineer made soup in the plane's small galley, before going into the messy weather near Kunming. Terrell served the soup with crackers and cheese from a rations kit — and danger gives gourmet status to the most lowly of foods.

Flying the Hump in bad weather was the most hazardous assignment a flight crew could draw — more dangerous than combat. More cargo planes were lost over the Hump than combat planes fighting against the Japanese. During the Hump operation, over six hundred planes and a thousand crewmen were lost. One route was called the "aluminum trail."

As we entered the clouds near Paoshan, turbulence began increasing. The moonlit darkness turned to pitch blackness, clouds closed in, and heavy rain began. And thunder!

As we approached Kunming, ice began to form on the wings and on the windshield in front of the pilots. I could still see through the side windows to watch the glaze build up on the wings. I had seen worse icing, but the bumpy turbulence was a new experience. It was like a washboard—a rhythmic, high-frequency bumping that shook the plane and instruments without letup. We decreased airspeed to 170 and the turbulence was easier.

This was a dangerous part of the flight—the crew was tired and there were still many miles of bad weather before China. The cargo on this flight was heavier than most and, thank God, Terrell, the flight engineer, had talked the ground crew into full tanks.

The last 220 miles from Poashan to Kunming was just tough, rough-ass flying; Jensen and I were fighting to control the plane. The gyro instruments tumbled, and the compass was spinning back and forth. We flew basic needle and ball. Icing slowed the flight to 150 miles per hour, and we were having trouble holding twenty thousand feet.

Good news and bad. Kunming radio (RQ) advised us to let down at Tsuyung and enter its control at sixteen thousand feet into a pattern and hold while other planes were letting down. Kunming was six thousand feet above sea level. The approach pattern starts at twelve thousand feet, six thousand feet above the field. Ceiling had lifted to one thousand feet with light rain. We would be number four to land.

Traffic across the Hump was heavy to Kunming, this ancient city, a thirteenth-century Chinese trading center. Kunming, along the Old Silk Road, was the destination of most of the planes from India, and traffic was always stacked in bad weather. Pilots circled in figure-eight patterns over the radio beacon and let down five hundred feet at a time as planes below landed. It was a torturous part of the flight.

The letdown to Kunming was hazardous. Cross the beacon at 12,000, head north, descend to 10,500 feet, one-needle descending turn to 180 degrees, cross beacon at 8,500 feet, hit glide path at 8,000 feet and approach to land. The flight pattern comes in over huge Lake Tali with a long, low approach between razorback mountains. At night, even in good weather, pilots use the instrument landing system to avoid the peaks and to keep in practice. As I followed the glide path to the runway, I could see (in my mind) the mountains on either side of the approach. As we broke out of the overcast, there was the field, sparkling in the rainy night. At the last minute, I looked outside to make a visual approach and bumped in for a sorry landing. Jensen could have done better.

On the ground, the "FOLLOW ME" jeep led us to the parking ramp. As quickly as we could shut down the engines and get out of the cockpit, the unloading crew was rolling the gas drums down the ramps. Armed guards made sure the drums didn't just keep rolling into the Chinese black market. The plane would be ready to return to India by 0800—we would have six hours of sleep. Usually, we had a one-hour turnaround, but since the Japanese had been driven back, we had more time on the ground. The cold sharpness of China was a welcome relief from the hot, muggy Indian weather.

The end of a Hump flight was a relief from the stress in the air. We always kept a closely guarded happy secret from new crewmen. In the Kunming twenty-four-hour operations mess, the first stop after checking in, were the down-home delights of fresh eggs, ham, bacon, real milk, and country fried chicken. No crew was tired enough and no flight had been hard enough for the men to pass up this meal.

As we drove away from old 702, I marveled that wars are won one shot at a time. We made one flight at a time, bringing another small addition to China's war supply. Four men and a plane, in five hours of terrible weather, had crossed the great Himalayas and delivered three Chinese soldiers and enough gasoline for one bombing mission for one plane. The war against the Japanese was won by thousands of flights such as the one we made on that night in June, 1945, in Old Dumbo, C-46-702.

Now for eggs and bacon—real eggs. Forget the Hump and the weather for six hours. Back to India would be a good flight—the omens were good.

1

China's Struggle for Air Power— 1931–42

As clouds of red and black smoke rose over Pearl Harbor on 7 December 1941, the deadly sound of exploding bombs, antiaircraft gunfire, and air warning sirens cut through the cool, early-morning silence of the huge Hawaiian naval base. The Japanese had bombed Pearl Harbor. On that quiet Sunday morning, World War II had come to the United States with savage fury. There was no warning—America had slept in on that fateful day.

Only China had known that war was certain. The Chinese people had been dying from Japanese air raids from Manchuria for ten years, and China had been fighting for nearly five years. The Sino-Japanese war was real, and the world had hardly noticed. While it had been easy to ignore China when there was no Western threat, the Japanese attack forced the United States immediately to go to the defense of China.

After Pearl Harbor, Japan quickly closed the entire Chinese seacoast, captured Burma, and in March 1942 shut off the Burma Road, isolating China from the outside world. So vital was China to the Allied war against Japan that plans were immediately made to establish an air bridge over the Himalayas.

In April 1942 the First Ferrying Group under the U.S. Tenth Air Force began flying supplies from India over the mountains to China to support Chiang Kai-shek's armies—a trickle at first, and a torrent later. Between Assam (in northern India) and China are the eastern

Himalayas, with great spurs of parallel mountain ranges extending north and south at altitudes of up to twenty-two thousand feet. To cross these mountains was popularly known as "Crossing the Hump"—a distance of about five hundred miles. The Hump route, over these towering, snow-covered mountains, was often in range of Japanese airfields with their deadly Zeros.

Young, inexperienced flight crews were flying heavy planes through constant bad weather, day-after-day bad weather—weather never before encountered in any flight operations in the world. In Sanskrit, Himalaya means "House of Snow." Over the terrifying mountains, high above the jungles of Burma, the pilots were being defeated by the Himalayan weather. For the first six months, for some pilots, the weather was so bad that many never saw the mountains they were flying over. When they did get a good crossing, they were mightily shocked by their first sight of the Hump. I made many flights over the Hump and never saw the mountains for the entire trip. It was a takeoff into the clouds, crossing the Hump on instruments, and letting down to Kunming—six hours of instrument flying.

The inexperienced Allied Hump pilots, flying untested aircraft, with uncertain leadership, paid a heavy toll. Japanese Zeros shot them out of the sky, the violent weather brought them down, or their planes crashed for unknown reasons, and they parachuted into headhunter country. Still the planes kept flying from India to China and back to India for another load of vital war supplies.

In December 1942, with thirty-five overworked C-47s and nine C-87s, the ATC was charged with the responsibility for the Hump airlift. That first month, ATC carried 1,226 tons of supplies into China. In December 1943, the Hump crews delivered 12,641 tons, and crews were still dying. In July 1945, a peak total reached 71,045 tons. From December 1942 until V-J Day 1945, 167,285 trips over the Himalayas carried 721,700 tons of supplies. On 1 August 1945, in one twenty-four-hour day, 1,118 trips and 5,327 tons went into China. Indeed, China stayed in the war.[1]

While ATC was the main carrier, it was not the only outfit flying supplies. It is impossible to determine how much tonnage was carried by the ATC and how much by others. Troop Carrier squadrons, the First, Third, and Fourth Combat Cargo Groups, the Air Commandos, and other units were desperately trying to get supplies to the beleaguered Chinese and to support fighting ground troops. Their totals were often credited to the ATC.[2] Noting this should not take anything away from the ATC pilots, who did an almost impossible job, regardless of the figures.

By the end of the war, ten ATC bases in India and twelve in China were in operation. In the three and one-half years of flying the Hump, over four hundred cargo planes, with 3,026 pilots, were flying a day-and-night, all-weather schedule. More than six hundred aircraft were lost, and more than one thousand crewmen died in the steaming jungles and over the icy mountains.

This is the statistical story of the Hump flights. The human story —the sheer heroism of those in the China-Burma-India (CBI) theater— is a greater story.

Before the bombing of Pearl Harbor, it was well known that Japan had ambitions to conquer the Orient. Several people had predicted the war with Japan, including an unusual prophecy by Gen. William "Billy" Mitchell, assistant chief of the United States Air Service, in 1924. This was seven years before Japan moved into Manchuria. General Mitchell specifically predicted a "surprise aerial attack on Pearl Harbor." His report, buried in official files for thirty-four years, said in part, "The Japanese have specialized on their air force since 1918 . . . probably the second air power in the world . . . I am convinced that the growing air power of Japan will be the decisive element in the mastery of the Pacific."[3]

General Mitchell's prophecy had its beginning in a 1922 treaty signed by the United States, Great Britain, and Japan that fixed the naval tonnage of the three countries and required Japan to reduce its navy. As the Japanese sank two of their own warships, the *Satsuma* and the *Aki*, on 8 July 1924, Commander Kanji Kato was heard to say, "From this day on, we are at war with the United States."[4]

On the other hand, the United States had always been a friend to China. Pearl Buck won the hearts of Americans for the Chinese peasant on a people-to-people level. Henry Luce, publisher of *Time* and *Life*, born in China of Presbyterian missionary parents, built respect for China through the pages of his magazines. President Franklin D. Roosevelt's grandfather, Warren Delano, a trader in China for years, and FDR's mother had lived from time to time in a family house in Hong Kong. President Roosevelt once wrote to Secretary of the Treasury Henry Morgenthau: "Please remember that I have a background of a little over a century in Chinese affairs."[5]

These and other influences over the years had strengthened the friendship of the American people, and no other country had such a record of passive friendship toward China as the United States. But not until Pearl Harbor did the United States become a military ally of its longtime friend. The reason for action then was simple: If China fell, Japan would quickly conquer all of Indochina and continue its conquest beyond the Pacific.

Global war came quickly. Japan attacked Pearl Harbor on Sunday, 7 December 1941; on Monday, 8 December, the United States and Britain declared war against Japan. On 9 December, China and India declared war against Germany, Italy, and Japan.

It is said that all Americans remember where they were and what they were doing on 7 December 1941. On that day thousands of young men in the United States began preparing for war. I was flying a Piper Cub that Sunday afternoon—getting in the last few hours of flight time before completing the Civilian Pilot Training program (CPT) at East Texas State Teachers College in Commerce, Texas. War had seemed certain, and a flying course might help me get into the Army Air Corps. I saw a red light blinking from the ground, signaling me to land. There was no radio. After a bumpy landing, the instructor waved me to the hangar. I learned we were at war.

During the next few days, the nation was in torment. "Japanese fleet of thirty-four ships between San Francisco and Los Angeles" (false) . . . "Britain's newest battleship *Prince of Wales* and British battle cruiser *Repulse* sunk" (true) . . . "Japanese attack on Los Angeles imminent" (false). War was new and people were in near panic.

Two weeks after Pearl Harbor, I was a cadet in the Army Air Corps at Kelly Field, San Antonio, Texas, with thousands of other young men —Class of 42-H. Education and jobs were forgotten. We marched in civilian clothes and carried sticks for rifles—there were no uniforms and no guns for us.

War was our new teacher and the enemy we would live with for the next five years. Compared to the Great Depression we had just been through, war might bring a better standard of life. We were young —we didn't know.

To understand the value of the American effort in China and the need for the Hump airlift, one must recall that although China had been fighting the Japanese for ten years, the country still was not prepared for a modern war. Chinese soldiers were poorly trained and equipped and had little will to fight. Chiang Kai-shek's armies were rotten with graft, politics, and greed. Chinese generals, selected on the basis of political influence, often refused to lead their armies into combat. Chinese pilots who "washed out" in flight training were certified as proficient so their families would not "lose face." These pilots more often killed themselves than the enemy. At one time, in 1941,

China had fewer than seventy-five planes that were operational, and Japan was able to march with almost no resistance.

China is 300,000 square miles larger than the United States. Weather-torn mountains and an undeveloped rail and highway system made ground defense almost impossible. The only way to defend China was through air power, which, in 1941, did not exist. Japan controlled the sky and bombed at will.

As the Japanese threatened to engulf China, political and military leaders began a dogged campaign to build a strong ground and air force. Five international champions of intrigue, persuasion, and coercion, notable for their superb leadership, their quest for personal power, and their undying love for China, dedicated themselves to building Chinese military strength. The role of these leaders, as they fought a political and military war, explains how the Hump airlift came into being and why it was continued despite extraordinary losses.

Perhaps the most influential non-military figure was China's Dragon Lady, Madame Chiang Kai-shek, the demanding third wife of Generalissimo Chiang Kai-shek, China's military and political leader. Born May-Ling Soong, daughter of Bible publisher, missionary and revolutionist Charlie Soong, Madame Chiang was one of three daughters in China's influential and wealthy Soong family. She was an iron woman, exquisite but tough, and ready to lay down anyone's life for her beloved China. A graduate of Wellesley College who spoke perfect English, she never accepted the possibility that Japan would overrun China. She was of the old China, but knew China's salvation was with the new world. Madame Chiang always identified her husband with China's destiny and as the indispensable leader toward China's national salvation.[6]

In 1933, on a cold winter day in Hangchow, Madame Chiang attended the first graduating class of Chinese pilots from a new American-supervised flight school. Madame watched silently, her black eyes taking in everything. Suddenly, she turned to Olga Greenlaw, wife of one of the American instructors, and said, "This is what China needs—what China must have! Thousands more like these boys—and thousands of airplanes for them to fly and fight with!"[7] She was the first to conceive and promote the idea of the American Volunteer Group—the famous "Flying Tigers."[8]

Another important force on the political front was Madame Chiang's brother, China's banker–foreign minister, Soong Tze-ven, who was determined that the United States would provide an air force for China. Dr. Soong was China's minister of finance from 1925 to 1933 and chairman of the Bank of China in 1935, and he became foreign minister to the United States in 1941. He was educated at Harvard, Columbia, and Vanderbilt. At one time, Dr. Soong was thought to be the world's richest man. In November 1939, he asked President Roosevelt for help in developing a four-hundred-plane air force, with eight hundred pilots.[9] The request was impossible to grant.

Soong later convinced President Roosevelt of the feasibility of the Hump airlift into China. It has been said that Dr. Soong won the battle for China in the corridors of Washington.

On the military front was China's Methodist Buddha, Generalissimo Chiang Kai-shek. He had become head of the Nationalist party (the Kuomintang) in 1925 after its founder, Sun Yat-sen, died. Chiang had worked with Mao Tse-tung and Chou En-lai in the beginnings of the Communist party in China, but had broken with them in 1927 and had been fighting the Communists since that time. When Chiang married May-Ling Soong in 1927, he was baptized into the Methodist church. To Chiang, Japan was a threat, but his real war was with the Communists, a battle he lost in 1949.

Chiang was a frustrating ally. He was never understood and sorely tried the patience of Western leaders. He used biblical language and Chinese logic to communicate with the United States. A speech made on Good Friday in 1937 in Nanking compared his kidnapping and detention by Chinese rebels in 1936 as "forty days and nights in the wilderness." The demands of his captors were "the temptations of the devil," and because of his threatened execution by the rebels, he compared himself to "Christ at Gethsemane."[10] He was the strength and spirit of China. As Ambassador Gauss wrote to President Roosevelt, "Without his leadership, unity in China would vanish and there would be no resistance to Japan."[11]

An American advocate for airpower in China was Texas-born Claire Lee Chennault, military advisor to the generalissimo.[12] Chennault was a retired U.S. Army pilot who had fallen from favor in the United States military when he annoyed his superiors with unorthodox ideas about aerial warfare.[13] Chennault's career had been routine as an instructor and stunt pilot. He came to China to help build an air force, and, by default, became commander of the Chinese Air Force.

A writer for *Life* magazine described Chennault as being "obsessed with one consuming passion, to beat the Japanese . . . [this] has established this wrinkled, scar-faced, half-deaf, fifty-one-year-old, ex-barnstorming pilot as the one genius that war on the Asiatic mainland has produced."[14]

Another major American influence in the drama of the Hump was a caustic military genius known as "Vinegar Joe" Stilwell. Speaking fluent Chinese, with a deep respect for the Chinese soldier, U.S. Lt. Gen. Joseph Warren Stilwell believed that wars were won on the ground. He was one of the American military's all-time outstanding field commanders.[15]

Stilwell had no use for diplomatic amenities—he called Generalissimo Chiang Kai-shek "Peanut," President Roosevelt was "Old Softie," and he referred to Chennault's air tactics as "medieval jousting." Once, in his diary, he wrote, "Black Friday. Peanut says he won't fight . . . what a break for the Limeys . . . they will quit and the Chinese will quit and the goddamned Americans will go ahead and fight. Chennault's blatting has put us on the spot; he's talked so much about what he can do that now they're going to let him do it."[16] Stilwell had great contempt for Chiang and this was matched by Chiang's hatred and distrust of Stilwell.[17]

General Stilwell had the impossible job of trying to coordinate the armies of four countries, each suspicious of the others. He had the responsibility to distribute supplies flown over the Hump and was constantly in confrontation with Chennault and the Generalissimo. His caustic personality and bitter outlook earned the name of "Vinegar Joe." When Stilwell's "burr under the saddle" personality resulted in his recall from China, he wrote in his diary, "Get me out of this odorous sewer . . . and I'll never more shovel manure."[18]

During the thirties, there was keen competition for airline routes through China. The U.S. State Department was asked to help Pan American Airways gain permission for an air route from Shanghai to Canton to be the last leg of their trans-Pacific flights. British and German airlines were also trying to establish routes in China.[19] In March 1933, Pan American Airways bought a 45 percent interest in the China National Aviation Corporation (CNAC), which later became a major influence in establishing the Hump airlift. The first plan for the Hump airlift was to build up CNAC to twenty-five C-47s to maintain "essential communications" between Kunming and Calcutta.[20]

The most significant American help to the Chinese toward building an air force came in August 1932, when Col. John H. Jouett, with eleven other U.S. Air Corps reserve officer pilots, established a program for training Chinese Air Force pilots. The instructors were on a three-year contract with the Central Aviation School in Hangchow. Jouett and his staff trained 335 new Chinese pilots and certified 50 previously trained pilots.

The first official review of the embryonic Chinese Air Force was on 12 November 1933 in Nanking, to honor the birthday of Dr. Sun

Yat-sen. Willis R. Peck, the U.S. consul general at Nanking, described
the air show in an official memo to the U.S. secretary of state:

> The show was a Chinese triumph. Pilots were Chinese cadets,
> of the military aviation school at Hangchow. They . . . flew like
> seasoned birdmen. There were slips, to be sure—one element of
> the pursuit squadron missed its signals and passed the reviewing
> stand ten minutes late; the star aerobat locked his brakes on land-
> ing and came within a hair's breadth of somersaulting; the para-
> chute jumper miscalculated the wind, overflew the field by two
> miles, but . . . in view of its pioneer character, it was indeed re-
> markable. . . .
>
> Every participating ship was American made and practically
> every pilot was American trained. . . . the program was a genuine
> success.[21]

After Colonel Jouett and his instructors left, China had pilots, but
few planes.[22] The U.S. Congress was afraid to offer help to China for
fear of antagonizing the Japanese.

Sensing the danger that China faced, Madame Chiang continued
to be concerned about the sorry state of the Chinese Air Force. Without foreign help, China lacked the technology and the skill to keep
her fighters and bombers in the air. Madame Chiang naturally looked
to the United States, the country of her youth and her education, for
help. She understood the American mind and knew how to manipu-
late the United States to her advantage.

How Madame Chiang came to be in charge of the Chinese Air Force
is a unique story of nepotism. In late 1936, Generalissimo Chiang Kai-
shek was taken hostage by Chinese rebels in Sian, in northern China,
and was about to be executed. Madame Chiang went to Sian, "ready
to die with her husband," according to the ambassador in China. Complex diplomatic maneuvering by China's top civilian leaders and Chinese Communist leaders saved Chiang. He was released, although he
suffered for months from injuries received during his imprisonment.[23]

Chiang's confidence in his wife was demonstrated while he was
still in prison, when he publicly quoted from the thirty-first chapter
of Jeremiah: "Jehovah hath created a new thing in the earth: A woman
shall encompass [protect] a man."[24]

Because of his poor health, the generalissimo put his wife in charge
of the Chinese Air Force. She promised that she would build an organization capable of an effective defense against the Japanese. Although her military experience was limited, her sincerity was convincing. Thus Madame Chiang Kai-shek became the first woman in
charge of a national air force.

In apparent desperation, Madame Chiang hired former U.S. Air Force stunt fliers William C. "Billy" McDonald, John C. "Luke" Williamson, Sebie Smith, and Rolfe Watson to help train pilots. These men recommended Claire Lee Chennault as a person who could put Madame Chiang's air force into shape for war.

Chennault was well known in China. A visiting Chinese delegation had seen his air show in Miami in 1936. Peter Mow, leader of the delegation, was impressed with Chennault's skill and suggested that China could use someone of his talents. However, Chennault, still on active duty with the U.S. Army Air Corps, refused the offer. But the Army retired him for disabilities on 30 April 1937.

Chennault was then invited again to China in May 1937, on a secret mission. His assignment was to find out why the Chinese Air Force was such a failure. Chennault studied the situation and made a frank but negative assessment of the Chinese Air Force. The generalissimo was impressed with his honesty and offered him the job of creating an air force to fight the Japanese. Chennault returned to the United States before making a decision, but then returned to China in July to accept a three-month $1,000-per-month contract. He stayed for eight years and became one of the most brilliant air defense tacticians of World War II.

Call it fate, coincidence, or just an extreme example of bad timing, but Japanese planes struck the capital city of Peiping in late July while Chennault was there. Acting in this emergency, he rallied Madame Chiang's novice air force. Under his assumed command, the poorly prepared Chinese pilots flew heroic missions, but few came back alive.[25]

To build an air force, Chennault resorted to desperate measures. He advertised for volunteers to join his "Fourteenth Volunteer Bombardment Squadron." Malcolm Rosholt, author of *Flight in the China Airspace* and a newspaperman in China when these events were taking place, describes Chennault's new air squadron as a loosely organized group of volunteer pilots from all parts of the world. Most of the volunteers were misfits and drifters who left almost as quickly as they came. The Fourteenth was deactivated 22 March 1938.[26]

The Japanese were too strong and their military momentum was too great. In spite of Chennault's skill and the determination of the Chinese airmen, by October of 1937 the Chinese Air Force was almost completely destroyed. The United States had not yet committed itself to support the Chinese. In desperation, China turned to Russia.[27]

Concerned that Japan might invade Soviet territory, the Russians began sending aid to the Chinese, which lasted until the spring of 1941. Being practical, the Russians used this aid as an opportunity to train their own pilots, including limited combat against the Japanese.[28]

The significant part of the Soviet aid program was the establishment of a "Russian Hump," at least three years before the American Allies began flying their Himalayan Hump routes. Following the seventh-century T'ien-shan silk route, the Soviet pilots flew from airfields in eastern Turkestan, across Sinkiang Province, into Lanchow and Sian.[29]

Russian pilots flew over uncharted mountains with no navigation or weather aids. "Without knowledge of what lay ahead, the pilots would fly eastward . . . to Urumchi, and Hami, . . . Sinkiang to Lanchow, stopping at intervals of not more than two hundred air miles . . . the entire flight was so hazardous . . . only 50 percent of the planes arrived, the others being seriously damaged or destroyed en route."[30]

The Russians also operated an overland highway system from Alma Ata to Lanchow. From 1937 to 1941, approximately 1,350 trucks delivered over seven hundred aircraft and forty thousand tons of weapons and ammunition. Wool, tea, furs, and tung oil were carried back to Russia. This Turkestan Road had a capacity of eighteen thousand tons annually when it was discontinued in 1941. Aside from shortages of gasoline, the problems of the Turkestan Road were the same as those later on the Burma Road: corruption, political intrigue, jealousies, and incompetence.[31]

Extending its war beyond Chinese targets, on 12 December 1937, Japanese planes bombed the USS *Panay,* an American gunboat anchored in the Yangtze River. The ship was sunk and two American sailors were killed. This increased the anger of the American people. However, the Japanese were not ready for war with the United States. They apologized and paid damages.[32]

When the Japanese bombed Chungking on 4 May 1939, over five thousand Chinese were killed and other thousands injured. The conscience of the United States was troubled. Henry Luce spoke for China through *Time* magazine: "The world waits to see whether China and its Generalissimo have the moral and material stamina to go on fighting Japan. . . . Chiang's prospects are now worse than were ever those of the American Revolution's George Washington. Chiang has heretofore shown himself a man of remarkable courage."[33]

After Japan had closed all Chinese ports, China's leaders built the famous Burma Road (opened in December 1938) to maintain a flow of critical supplies and to bring in nonmilitary commercial goods. It was a 681-mile gravel road that began at Lashio, Burma, snaked through malaria-infested jungles, across the southern part of the Himalayas, over snow-laden mountain passes of China to Kunming, and on to Chanyi, Chungking, Chengtu, Nanning, and Hengyang. Hundreds of thousands of Chinese laborers had worked for two years to complete it.

Later, in 1941, when the American Volunteer Group (the Flying Tigers) came to China, the group's primary assignment was to protect the Burma Road, which was an open target for Japanese fighters. The Tigers flew air cover for the trucks on the road and tried to protect the few transport planes that were beginning a feeble airlift over the Hump. Olga Greenlaw, in her book *The Lady and the Tigers*, wrote, "[The Tigers] died keeping the Burma Road open so that the red corpuscles of war might flow into China's veins for a few extra days or weeks."[34]

In March 1941, President Roosevelt had asked Congress for a $100 million loan for China. Henry Luce supported the loan: "For $100,000,000 China promised to keep 1,250,000 Japanese troops pinned in the field; to keep Japan's formidable fleet blockading the China shore; to retard the aggressors' march in the direction of U.S. interests. The merchandise was fantastically cheap at the price."[35]

Then, eight months before Pearl Harbor, as the Nazi war machine was rolling across Europe, the United States declared itself the "arsenal of democracy," and lend-lease was born. Although it was intended primarily for Britain, for the war in Europe, Chinese military leaders began demanding their share of lend-lease. On 15 March 1941, President Roosevelt pledged assistance: "China expresses the magnificent will of millions of plain people to resist the dismemberment of their nation. China . . . asks our help. America has said, 'She shall have our help.'"[36] Besides Britain, China was the only major recipient of lend-lease aid before Pearl Harbor. To implement the United States' policy of supporting the Chinese in their battle with Japan, some $200 million worth of military hardware was given to China.[37]

To get the lend-lease aid to China, the Himalaya airlift became a top priority. In addition to truck traffic on the Burma Road, the China National Aviation Corporation (CNAC) operated a tenuous passenger and freight service between Hong Kong and the interior of China. CNAC offered one of the most positive and essential services in the struggle to keep China fighting. The planes, although small in number, maintained vital passenger service and freight movement after the Japanese blockade.

In one of the first military attacks on a commercial aircraft, on

24 August 1938, Japanese fighters forced a CNAC plane to land in a river and continued to shoot at it until the riddled plane sank. The fighters continued to machine-gun the pilot, although he was able to swim to safety.[38] After this attack, CNAC began to fly secret irregular schedules, and when the war intensified, the planes flew only at night or in bad weather; but the vital flights were not stopped.[39]

In June 1940, the war in China took a bizarre turn. The Japanese government demanded that Britain close Hong Kong and the Burma Road to all war materiel bound for China. The British said no to closing Hong Kong but did agree to close the Burma Road for three months.[40] And so, in July, China's isolation was complete.

Quickly, T. V. Soong went to the United States for help. On 15 August, Soong met with U.S. Secretary of the Treasury Henry Morgenthau, asking for a loan. "China is nearing the breaking point on the material side and [is] desperately in need of assistance." A loan of $5 million was arranged. Then, on 25 September, as the Japanese moved down the China coast, Congress agreed to lend China another $25 million, with more to come.[41]

As Dr. Soong was making his appeal in the United States, the British, in a turnabout, reopened the Burma Road on 18 October. As sixty American-made trucks moved out on the road, Japanese planes began bombing along the route. Cities were leveled, traffic was halted, and Kunming, at the China terminus, was heavily damaged.[42]

In actuality, the Burma Road delivered a minimum of supplies. In the first eighteen months of operation, only 96,808 long tons (a long ton is 2,240 pounds) had been carried into China. This included arms and ammunition, gasoline, explosives, motor vehicles, airplane parts, machinery, etc.—a minor part of the needs of China.[43] Although the road was capable of four hundred tons a day in peacetime,[44] it was delivering only about 176 tons a day when it was reopened. A more dependable method of supply had to be found, and interest in the airlift over the Hump was intensified.

In the meantime, American military leaders had not completely ignored the Japanese threat. With the help of the British and the Chinese, the United States had secretly organized a small civilian air task force to fight the Japanese when war did come.

By 7 December 1941, this small group of renegade pilots and flight crewmen was trained, standing by and ready to strike in China. The American Volunteer Group (AVG), commanded by Claire Lee Chennault, had been anxiously training in Burma but had been careful to avoid contact with the Japanese before war was declared. However,

The Burma Road was a long, dangerous, twisting gravel highway that was China's lifeline to the outside world. It provided over six hundred miles of target practice for Japanese fighters as the trucks carried supplies to starving China. This photograph shows an Allied convoy ascending the famous twenty-one curves at Annan, China. *Courtesy Army Pfc. John F. Albert from the National Archives*

when war did come, the AVG, a gung ho assortment of daredevil pilots, flying cast-off Curtiss P-40B fighters, was ready to tangle with the Japanese. High in the clouds over China, anxious AVG pilots watched with anticipation as Japanese bombers made milk-run daylight raids on Kunming. The AVG had 74 pilots and twenty planes ready to attack the entire air force of Japan. Another 150 men and more P-40s were moving up from Burma to bring the total to one hundred planes.

Chennault's Flying Tigers shot down the first Japanese planes on 20 December, just twelve days after Pearl Harbor. Because they were young and fearless and fought the unorthodox warfare of Claire Chennault, the Flying Tigers quickly became the heroes of the dark early days of the war. How this famous flying group came to be is a most interesting and dramatic chapter of the history of World War II.

When Madame Chiang had first proposed a group of volunteer American pilots equipped with fighters to fly protection over the Burma Road, Generalissimo Chiang had sent Chennault to Washington to find the necessary planes. Chennault learned that the British had refused a shipment of one hundred Curtiss P-40B Tomahawk fighters because they were too slow and were obsolete for modern war. The British wanted newer and faster fighters. Chennault asked for the rejected planes, and with the promise of better fighters from the United States, the British relinquished the Tomahawks to Chennault to be shipped in crates to Burma.[45]

Next was the need for pilots and ground crewmen. Concerned that the Chinese might surrender to the Japanese, President Roosevelt signed a secret order allowing U.S. officers and enlisted men to resign their positions in the U.S. armed services and join the AVG, without endangering their military status. With this order, Chennault was allowed to recruit pilots and air crewmen from the three military services on a one-year contract to "manufacture, repair and operate aircraft for the Central Aircraft Manufacturing Company (CAMCO)."

Unofficially, it was hinted that the pilots would fly combat missions against the Japanese and would earn $500 to $750 a month and a bonus of $500 for each enemy plane shot down.[46]

More than three hundred men volunteered; 110 were pilots with an experience range from just out of flying school to one pilot with more flying time than Chennault. There were also mechanics, cooks, clerks, weathermen, a physician, and four women—two nurses, the wife of the group's executive officer, and one clerk already in the Orient. There was also one part-time mortician.[47] Because it was illegal for American military personnel to fight in the service of a foreign country, and the United States was not at war with Japan, these airmen would fight as civilians.

Recruits for the newly-formed American Volunteer Group sailed from San Francisco on 10 June, 11 July, and 24 September 1941 in unmarked Dutch ships, carrying passports as clerks, musicians, undertakers, artists, teachers, etc. None were identified as pilots. The first American airmen to see combat in China were on their way. The United States, without official declaration, had entered China's war.

First official recognition of the AVG was contained in a brief message, on 14 July 1941, from the consul at Rangoon, Burma, to the U.S. Secretary of State: "I have the honor to report that . . . thirty American volunteer airmen will reach here in the next few days . . . to become identified with China's air force. . . .

"The Americans will take charge of the Curtiss P-40 pursuit planes, 68 of which are now in Rangoon, and ten of which have been assembled."[48]

The AVG pilots arrived in Rangoon in September 1941. After a short train ride to Toungoo, the airmen, with golf clubs and tennis rackets in hand, saw Kyedaw airdrome, their training field, as a place of "moldering troop barracks, oppressive heat, an incredible proliferation of insect life, giant rats and poor food . . . The runway was surrounded by quagmire and pestilential jungle. Matted masses of rotting vegetation carpeted the jungle and filled the air with a sour, sickening smell." The shock was more than some could take. Five pilots immediately resigned.[49]

Olga Greenlaw, wife of the AVG executive officer, adds her description of the Burmese training base: "[A] main street, rumbling day and night with trucks bound for the [Burma] Road . . . a bazaar . . . open market stalls . . . forty Europeans . . . and all the bugs God created . . . on the ground, floors, walls, ceilings, into your food, down your back, up your legs and in your hair—beetles, lice, spiders, flies and fleas, moths, mosquitos, centipedes, bedbugs, ticks. . . ."[50]

The AVG, and later the Hump crews, were repulsed by the hostility of the China-Burma-India theater (CBI). American volunteers, who had signed up for a glamorous mission, found themselves at the anus of the war. No one knew they were there, and no one seemed to care.

Hugh Crumpler, writing in the *HPA Newsletter*, described the CBI as "the only war theater where a soldier could be felled by a Jap sniper, bitten by a poisonous snake, trampled by a rogue elephant, decapitated by a headhunter, and devoured by a man-eating tiger. And that's just on the way back from the latrine."[51] Winston Churchill once compared fighting the Japanese in Burma to going into the water to fight a shark.

Throughout the operations over the Hump, the jungles of Burma, miles below their aircraft, held a special fear for the airmen. To go down was almost certain death—to try to walk out was almost impossible. The dark, silent jungle was so thickly matted with undergrowth, it was impossible to penetrate except on trails cut by natives. And headhunters lived in these jungles.[52]

In 1941, as the American volunteer fighter squadrons were being organized, a heavy bombardment group was proposed. With the approval of the president and key cabinet members, a plan was conceived to provide the Chinese with B-17 heavy bombers to attack Japanese strongholds in China. Treasury Secretary Henry Morgenthau informed T. V. Soong, who relayed the information to Chungking. The Chinese then officially requested an additional heavy bombardment group. However, because of Chennault's enthusiasm for fighter aircraft, the heavy bombers were never provided.[53]

Even with the protection of the AVG, it soon became clear that the Burma Road, with its vulnerability to air attack, was not the answer to the China supply problem. The air bridge across the Himalaya needed to be established quickly. William L. Bond, operations manager for CNAC, decided to check on the feasibility of an air route from Kunming to India. He traveled by train to Myitkyina, Burma, and discussed the possibility of construction of an airport at Myitkyina. He was assured by the British that the airfield would be built if an air route could be established.[54]

There were two ways into China by air. One was across the high peaks from Assam to Kunming, and the other across the lower mountains of northern Burma. The Japanese, moving into Burma, made the lower routes impossible.[55]

Bond, with CNAC pilot Hugh Woods, took a DC-3 to look for a route from the air. Bond and Woods flew up the Irrawaddy Valley to Myitkyina, where Woods selected a site for the airfield the British had promised. They flew northward beyond Fort Hertz, the last British outpost in northwest Burma, climbed to fourteen thousand feet, then swung eastward over the Naga Hills to determine the height of the unexplored terrain. "Without landing," Woods recalled, "I proceeded on to Likiang and Tali mountains to establish their exact position and altitudes as our maps were unreliable . . . there had never been an airplane flown over this part of the world before."

Although he did not know it at the time, Woods had flown the first trip over what was to become known as the Hump. The flight was on 2 November 1940.[56] Bond reported: "We know the country is high and [the route] can be flown in weather similar to what we had, but if the weather should be much worse . . . it would be extremely dangerous, costly and very nearly impractical."[57]

On 8 May 1941, operations manager Bond presented a lengthy report to T. V. Soong proposing an air route over the Himalaya Mountains. Bond wrote: "The best air freight route would be from Myitkyina in North Burma to airports . . . in the vicinity of Yunnanyi. . . . There are many difficulties . . . the country between . . . is high and rugged and . . . west and north of this route . . . is even worse."[58]

Bond recognized the hazard of bad weather with winds of forty to seventy miles an hour most of the year. In clear weather, flights could be made at altitudes of twelve to fourteen thousand feet. But to the west and north are peaks more than seventeen thousand feet. However, Bond believed that with proper care and training, flights could be made. Actually, bad weather and the high peaks would become safety factors, as the Japanese planes were not likely to go very far in pursuit of Allied planes over the high peaks in bad weather.[59]

Bond recommended a fleet of thirty-five planes with about fifty-six pilots to form the first supply group. He also recommended the use of Douglas DC-3s because of their dependability, low maintenance requirements, and payload. "It would be a mistaken kindness and the height of inefficiency to send to China any varied and numerous types of planes . . . it would simply doom the entire project."[60]

Bond warned that flight operations in China would be difficult. In addition to extreme weather, uncharted mountains, primitive navigational aids, and practically no ground facilities, the operation would be about twelve thousand miles from the source of most of its supplies, in a country under complete blockade. There would be constant enemy ground raids, and Japanese fighters would attack from the air. But, Bond said with complete optimism, "CNAC has shown after nearly four years of such operations, that it can be done successfully."[61]

Much of the early exploratory work of finding routes through the Himalaya Mountains was done by Gen. P. T. Mow and Capt. Moon Chin, CNAC pilots. These determined airmen were flying in areas completely uncharted. Captain Moon tells of flying past unknown peaks that were over 33,000 feet (Mount Everest, the world's highest known mountain, is 29,029 feet): "The tops of the peaks were higher into the clouds."[62]

During the years of flying the Himalayas, many pilots reported seeing mountains higher than Mount Everest. On a flight in mid-1944, Hump pilot Milo F. Walter reported seeing two mountains that appeared to be higher than 30,000 feet. His aircraft apparently had been hit by the jet stream and blown off course far to the north. With both altimeters registering 30,200 feet, the aircraft broke out of the clouds and he and his crew saw two mountains higher than their altitude.

"Where were we? . . . I do know that the mountains were not in the Amne Machin Range—the C-46, with full tanks would not have had the ability to fly that far from our base at Chabua."[63]

In March 1944, the pilot of a four-engine ATC transport plane, lost and to the north of course, reported breaking out of the clouds at 30,000 feet, and seeing, less than a mile away, a peak towering at least 2,000 feet above his flight altitude. He was frozen with fright and could find no such mountain on his maps.[64]

In the spring of 1945, pilot Bob Riley of the Thirty-second Fighter Squadron of the Fourteenth Air Force, reported a peak so high that his P-38 reconnaissance plane could not fly over it. He got enough gas the next day to locate and photograph the peak. It could not be found.[65]

As Hump routes were being surveyed, the news of Pearl Harbor reached Burma, and the AVG pilots realized that they were in the middle of "one hell of a big war."[66] They were in the first phases of training—some were having trouble learning to fly the fast, unstable P-40s—and Chennault's unorthodox method of aerial fighting was a nightmare in their dream of glory in the skies. With only a crude warning system and no radar, the pilots kept their engines warm, scanned the eastern skies for Japanese planes, and expected to scramble any minute.

Chennault's warning system, called "Jing Bao," was an adaptation of the system developed by CNAC crews when threatened by the Japanese.[67] It was so efficient that when Japanese planes were warming up on their bases, Chennault would know about it. Thousands of Chinese civilians used telephone, telegraph, radio, and a primitive system of alarms to warn of an air raid. Air Forces Commander Gen. Henry Arnold called Chennault's Jing Bao the "most efficient aircraft warning system in existence." It was completely dependent on the friendliness of the Chinese country people and their willingness to warn of approaching enemy aircraft.[68]

Chennault worked out a plan for the P-40 to beat the Zero. He never accepted the idea that the famous Japanese fighter was invincible. The P-40 was sturdy, the pilot was protected by armor, and the plane could dive at speeds up to 550 miles per hour. The rule when fighting the Zero was, "Never get into a conventional dogfight. Make a pass, shoot and dive away. Don't fight again until you can repeat the procedure."[69]

Chennault knew that the Japanese, trained to follow orthodox methods, were predictable. They could not follow surprise, sudden strikes, or variable approaches. Chennault was a street fighter—he knew the rules but never followed them. He knew the enemy did follow the rules—he knew where they would be and he was there. When Chennault had fuel, his AVG and the Fourteenth Air Force were unbeatable. He taught one great truth in war and in life—never fight by the other fighter's rules.

General Arnold described Chennault's fighting as "aerial guerrilla warfare." Some pilots thought these tactics of hit and run bordered on cowardice. Many preferred to hold their positions and "fight it out" in the manner of World War I dogfights. But Chennault knew that the Japanese Zero could climb faster and had a higher ceiling and greater maneuverability than the slow and heavy P-40.

Chennault also said that if he had had the Zero and the Japanese had the P-40, he would change his tactics and come off even better.[70] He knew the tools his enemy had to work with. Many times he would sit in caves or in a field near an aerial battle, watching with binoculars, studying the tactics of the fighters, to learn the best way to victory.

Theodore White, *Time-Life* correspondent, wrote, "His squadrons were so mobile they seemed to be everywhere at once. . . . With, maybe, ten major centers needing fighter protection, Chennault manages to have his few fighters everywhere they are needed, whenever they are needed. Chungking and Kunming have not once been bombed since the AVG went into action."[71]

As the time for combat neared, accidents by inexperienced pilots flying hot P-40 fighters, and the lack of replacement parts for damaged planes, reduced the AVG to forty-three operational aircraft and eighty-four pilots. The AVG was divided into three squadrons, the Panda Bears, Adam and Eves, and Hell's Angels.

With the Japanese threatening Burma, Chennault closed Kyedaw air base in Burma and took most of his group to Kunming, China on 18 December. One squadron, Hell's Angels, moved to an air base near Rangoon to help the British protect the port city from Japanese air raids. Some of the other two squadrons braved the Hump in their single-engine fighter planes and others took their crippled planes, maintenance crews, and spare parts over the Burma Road to China by truck.[72] These AVG pilots made the first Allied flights over the Hump.

It must have been a weary-looking bunch who moved into Kunming, but they were happy to be away from the Burmese jungles. In Kunming, they had clean beds, showers, and good food. The weather at six thousand feet was cool and pleasant. There were no snakes, bugs, or Dhobi itch to plague the crewmen.

In China for only two days, the AVG was ready to take on the Japanese, who had been making routine daylight bombing missions against Kunming from Hanoi. On 20 December, an early 0600 alert sent the anxious Tigers into the air for a before-daylight patrol. With no enemy in sight, the disappointed pilots returned to the base. Then at 1000, another air-raid alert sent the pilots back into the air. This time a formation of ten "Sallys" (Mitsubishis) was headed lazily toward Kunming in the skies they had dominated for months.

Seventeen P-40s looked down on the unsuspecting Sallys. Following their tactics of "strike and break away," the Tigers made pass after pass as the Japanese planes frantically dropped their bombs on the mountains and turned back to Hanoi. Four bombers went down, and every aircraft still in the air had been hit and was trailing smoke. These were the first enemy losses from fighter attack and the first time Japanese bombers had been turned back from Kunming. There were no Tiger losses, although some of the planes were riddled with bullet holes.[73]

Where did the AVG get its famous name? Remembering a Chinese proverb, "Like tigers plus wings, their strength is irresistible," the Chinese called them "Fei-Hu"—"Flying Tigers"—and the name became a legend.[74] The pilots preferred to be called, simply, the "American Volunteers."[75] Following an idea used by the British on their P-40s and the Germans on their Stukas, the AVG pilots painted tiger shark faces on the noses of their planes—shark's teeth in a blood-red mouth, and an evil eye. This had a devastating effect on the Japanese pilots.

The dramatic news of the AVG victory hit newspapers around the world. This small band of nonmilitary volunteer Tigers became the Cinderella airmen of the Chinese war—a type of fighting unit from which legends are made. The AVG pilots met the Japanese head-on and fought a kind of guerrilla war in the skies: fight in groups, hit and break away—avoid the one-on-one aerial dogfight made famous by Germany's Red Baron. The Tigers created a swashbuckling mystique that added to the lore of flying the Hump.

This victory was the first good news of the Asiatic war. The legend of the Tigers in their obsolete P-40B Tomahawks became a symbol of Chinese-American tenacity in the air. They were often called Madame Chiang's "angels." In late 1941, they were badly needed heroes.

The Battle of Rangoon continued to rage, and the Hell's Angels squadron and the British Royal Air Force (RAF) fought side by side. The AVG suffered its first combat losses. Harry Gilbert was first to die and Neal Martin was second; four planes were lost. The victory in Kunming and the losses in Rangoon brought the grim realities of war to the Tigers.[76]

In late January 1942, Chennault notified the British command that he was recalling his AVG units in Burma back to China. The British, having no replacements, complained to their chiefs of staff, who contacted the Combined Chiefs of Staff in Washington, who presented the problem to Prime Minister Churchill. The prime minister, in alarm, called President Roosevelt. Quickly, through War Department channels, Chennault and the generalissimo were advised that the AVG was indispensable in Burma and were asked to delay their withdrawal; and the AVG units remained in Burma.[77]

In two engagements over Rangoon, the Hell's Angels and the British RAF brought down twenty-seven Japanese bombers against their own loss of two men and four planes. The AVG accounted for ten of the bombers and thirteen fighters.[78] The Battle of Rangoon lasted for seventy-five days, but the city could not be saved, and "the Allied defense of Asia turned from disorder to chaos."[79]

Even in defeat, the Tigers impressed the steel-nerved British. In his order of the day, British Air Vice-Marshal Stevenson, Royal Air Force (RAF) commander in Burma, wrote:

> Today, the First American Volunteer Group destroyed its one hundredth Japanese aircraft in the defense of Rangoon . . . to Colonel Chennault, their commander, . . . and to the fighter pilots and maintenance crews, [I express] the deep admiration of the Royal Air Force in Burma for this remarkable piece of fighting.
> The American Volunteer Group bore the brunt of . . . unrestricted Japanese air attacks. . . . The high courage, skillful fighting and offensive spirit displayed marks the American Volunteer Group as a first class fighting force. . . .[80]

One of the AVG pilots said, "When a Britisher admits that Americans are good, then we are good,—by damn!"[81]

While the AVG pilots were fighting in Burma and China, T. V. Soong was waging diplomatic war in Washington. Soong was in the United States trying to convince President Roosevelt that an air supply route over the Himalaya Mountains could supply China's needs.[82] In January 1942, Soong presented his proposal to the president. Soong ex-

plained that the Burma Road was in great jeopardy by Japanese successes. Rangoon was closed, and if China was able to keep fighting
it would be necessary to open the long-discussed aerial lifeline to
China. His proposal said: "That lifeline is conveniently at hand. From
Sadiya . . . to Kunming or Suifu is only 500 or 700 miles, respectively,
flying over comparatively level stretches. These alternate air routes
have been surveyed for year round operations by Pan-American Airways . . . and the project has been declared feasible by the American
military mission."[83]

In his presentation, Soong described the Hump route as "500 or 700
miles over comparatively level stretches." This was an extreme example of diplomatic persuasive language, since the route Soong described was over some of the Himalaya's highest peaks. Soong was
aware of the successes of CNAC, whose experienced pilots, veterans
of years of mountain flying, made the proposed air route seem easy.
No one had considered that the thousands of Allied pilots who would
fly these mountain routes would be untrained for the job, with no
weather and no mountain experience. The Hump proposal was desperate and daring.

On the same day that the Battle of Rangoon started, the Allied Combined Chiefs of Staff met in Washington. In the group were President
Roosevelt, Prime Minister Churchill, and various lords, admirals, and
generals of the two world powers. Just sixteen days after war was declared against Japan, global strategy was being made. From notes made
by Air Forces commander Gen. Henry Arnold, concerning China, the
chiefs agreed that: (1) China must be kept fighting; (2) we must establish air bases in China for our bombers and transports; and (3) we
must get more transports over there at once.[84]

China remained the most effective base for bombing Japan, and the
greatest challenge to the progress of the war was supplying China.[85]
President Roosevelt realized that supplies would have to be taken in
by air. This, according to General Arnold's notes, was "the real start
of the 'Hump' operations."[86]

2

The Hump Begins— 1942

World War II was now three weeks old, and the war continued to go badly for the Allies. Manila fell on 2 January; Singapore fell on 15 February; the Allies lost the Battle of the Java Sea twelve days later; Bataan surrendered on 9 March; and on 6 May, Corregidor fell and over twenty thousand prisoners died of malnutrition or mistreatment on the Bataan Death March.[1]

Islands were taken almost by appointment. The Japanese seemed invincible. To fight a war halfway around the world was more than the Allies were prepared for, but the chiefs of state quickly decided that China, in due time, would be the base for long-range bombers to take the war to Japan. Militarily, however, China would be a holding action until the war in Europe was won.

As 1942 began, Japan was trying a daring strategy—attempting to isolate one of the largest countries in the world. The plan was working. With the Burma Road closed, Chiang Kai-shek requested lend-lease aid to build a new overland route to China. This would be the Ledo Road, beginning in Assam, India, and winding through the Burmese jungles to a point joining the old Burma Road at the Chinese border.[2] But the Ledo Road would take two years to build.

The Sino-Japanese war, from 1937 through 1945, was a conflict between these two military strategies: the traditional view of war as a struggle on the ground and, now, the use of air power. In addition to fighters and bombers, the cargo plane would assume a major role

in air power as the means of victory. The isolation of China forced
this decision. General Arnold realized that the greatest single challenge to the air force was the supply of China.[3]

His opinion was not shared by others in high command. When Admiral Mountbatten arrived in Southeast Asia as supreme commander,
he was assured by the desk-bound generals that air supply was impossible; that it was impossible to fight during the monsoon; that Japanese infiltration was impossible to stop; that an offensive in Assam
was impossible—everything was impossible.[4]

At a meeting of top-level military and political advisors in May
1942, the consensus continued to be negative: "Burma is completely
gone . . . all possible routes to China are closed. . . . the air freight route
is no longer feasible as the planes must now fly in bad weather at
23,000 feet . . . even in good weather [the planes] must fly so high as
to render attempts at ferrying freight into China useless."

This gloomy assessment was agreed on by Col. Louis A. Johnson,
personal representative of President Roosevelt; Col. Arthur W. Her-
rington, American Technical Mission to India; Wallace Murray, advisor on political relations; Paul H. Alling, chief of the Division of
Near Eastern Affairs; Calvin H. Oakes and William L. Parker, also of
the Division of Near Eastern Affairs.[5] President Roosevelt, in spite
of contrary advice, seemed to have been convinced by China's foreign
minister Soong that such an aerial supply line was practical.[6] The president continued to urge chief of staff George C. Marshall to keep the
pathway to China open.[7]

In planning the early India-to-China Hump routes, American and
Chinese military leaders selected the path of the sixth-century
Yunnan-Burma "Silk Road," between Szechuan and Yunnan. Beginning
in southwestern China, the route went into Burma where it separated
into two branches, one branch leading down the valley of the Sweli
to the junction of the Irrawaddy, passing near Mandalay across the
Arakan range into India. The other westward branch went through
Tengyueh and Bhamo, across the Irrawaddy and the Chindwin rivers,
over the mountains into Assam, India. These were the trails and rivers
traveled centuries before by ancient monks and scholars. Since its
beginning in antiquity, the mountains and weather have made the
Yunnan-Burma route one of the most perilous of China's trade roads
to the West.[8]

Fourteen centuries later, Hump pilots from China, the United
States, Canada, Australia, and England were tracing, in a few hours,
what took the monks years to travel.

However, diplomats were not convinced that the Hump airlift was the answer to the supply problem. Throughout 1942, as the U.S. Army First Ferrying Command and the China National Aviation Corporation (CNAC) were cautiously beginning supply flights, military planners were desperately seeking alternate routes to the flight over the Himalayas.

A series of diplomatic documents, from 10 April to 3 December 1942, from the U.S. secretary of state, the American ambassador to China, various ambassadors of different countries and other diplomats, describe an intensive search for overland routes to get supplies into China. Routes through Iran, through the Soviet Union, from Alaska to Siberia to China, and through Tibet were proposed.

A fleet of one thousand trucks, a caravan of animal carts, camels, and a mule pack train were considered. The proposals requiring animals were turned down because many of the routes were heavily infested with rinderpest, a cattle plague, and would require extensive veterinary personnel and equipment.[9]

Secretary of State Cordell Hull proposed to President Roosevelt that supplies be carried overland from India through Tibet. This was an extremely delicate idea since Tibet was ruled by a religious rather than a political leader and, an even more sensitive issue, China considered Tibet to be a part of its country while Tibet considered itself autonomous and not a part of China. Chiang was extremely reluctant to even consider Tibet as a route. He did not feel that it was necessary for China to ask permission to cross Tibet, but he did not want to pursue the idea.

President Roosevelt wrote the Dalai Lama of Tibet, proposing a delegation to Lhasa to ask for permission to move supplies across Tibet. Although the Dalai Lama received the delegation, he replied with a firm "no" on the grounds of his desire to stay out of the war.[10] Throughout the long search, no practical alternate route to China was found.

CNAC, ever optimistic and cooperative, believed that an alternate air route from India across Sinkiang Province in northernmost China would be possible. These flights would cross the highest mountains in the Himalaya and would require a thirty-thousand-foot minimum flight altitude.[11]

On 14 January, Gen. George Marshall proposed to Chiang Kai-shek that Maj. Gen. Joseph W. Stilwell be sent to China to direct the Chinese ground forces. Chiang accepted the suggestion. Stilwell was one of the best field generals in the United States Army and had been in China, off and on, since 1911. He spoke fluent "countryside" Chinese and had a deep respect for the Chinese soldier, although he had little regard for the leadership of China or its political system. Stilwell also believed that wars are won on the ground. Sending Stilwell to China was a clear indication that the United States was seriously committed to China.

In addition to frequent good news from the AVG, another "moral victory" for the Allies was Lt. Col. Jimmy Doolittle's super-secret bombing raid on Tokyo, from "Shangri-La," the USS *Hornet*, on 18 April 1942. It was a risky venture for sixteen land-based twin-engine B-25 bombers to take off from an aircraft carrier, fly 650 miles over the ocean, bomb Tokyo and other cities, and continue another 500 miles to the Japanese-held China coast. Some damage was done to steel mills, oil refineries, and rail yards. Pilots were ordered not to bomb the emperor's palace. The great damage was psychological—Japan had never considered that the Allies could reach their mainland.[12] Doolittle's raiders paid a high price of eight lives and fifteen aircraft. No American who saw it can ever forget the photograph of the captured Doolittle pilot about to be beheaded.[13]

The Tokyo raid brought quick retaliation. Entire Chinese villages were annihilated if anyone there was suspected of aiding the Doolittle raiders. Fifty-three battalions of Japanese infantry killed 250,000 Chinese and destroyed every airfield in a twenty-thousand-square-mile area.[14]

Bombing the Japanese capital city and endangering the life of the emperor fueled the fanatic fervor of the Japanese to rid the Pacific of American aircraft carriers. This brought on the decisive Battle of Midway in early June, where Japan suffered a crushing defeat at sea. The First Fleet, Japan's best naval force, was destroyed. Four aircraft carriers, a cruiser, and 275 aircraft, plus Japan's hope of winning the war, went to the bottom of the Pacific. Their eastward movement was stopped, and their eventual defeat was inevitable. Doolittle's raid was a success.[15]

While the United States was planning the Hump, the China National Aviation Corporation (CNAC) had taken the lead in establishing operations. As early as November 1941, CNAC had flown over ten thousand refugees out of Burma into India. Yet this tiny Chinese-American company did not have the planes or crews to carry all supplies headed for China. So if there was to be an air supply route, the United States would have to do it.[16] Development was slow; there were few airfields, as well as a scarcity of aircraft and trained crews.[17]

CNAC flight crews also found the weather to be unexpectedly severe. Pioneer CNAC pilot Capt. Robert J. Raines, former Flying Tiger with Chennault, tells of one early flight over the Himalayas:

> I was trying to get around a typhoon and wound up in a strange pass . . . at about 16,000 feet in a heavily-loaded DC-3. Suddenly I was caught in an updraft that whisked me up to 28,000 feet. There wasn't a damned thing I could do but try to keep the plane steady and ride to the top. Then, just as suddenly as I started going up, I started going down. It was like being swept over Niagara Falls in a barrel. In a little more than two minutes I was dropped from 28,000 feet to 6,000 feet, and when we stopped, it was such a jar that I still can't see how the wings stayed on that plane. I just didn't think that planes could be built that would take that sort of punishment.[18]

The saga of the Flying Tigers ended quickly. Fighting as civilians in a military operation, the Tigers became the center of political controversy and victims of their own publicity. The AVG was a bastard operation, American staffed, controlled by the Chinese, supported by the British, and with constant pressure to bring the crewmen into the U.S. Army Air Corps. These civilians in a military operation were irritating to the army command.

As the spring of 1942 wore on, the Tiger pilots were tired and increasingly rebellious. Wave after wave of Japanese planes continued to bomb China—there was no way to stop them. Regardless of their successes, the Tigers were no match for the sheer numbers of Japanese planes. Chennault demanded raids that the pilots did not want to fly. Morale declined.

For example, one incident almost caused a mass resignation. The Tigers were scheduled to rendevous with British Blenheim bombers to strafe and bomb. R. T. Smith, squadron leader, explained:

> "They were to drop their bombs, and then we were to strafe! We wouldn't have had a dog's chance to get away. By the time the Blenheims got there . . . there wouldn't have been any element of surprise. . . . The Blenheims can't hit anything anyway. . . . We refused to escort them."
>
> The Colonel [Chennault] said, "If you want to show the white feather, you can all quit!"
>
> "My God; white feather!" continued Smith, "after what guys like Tex Hill, Lawlor, Keaton, Older and even I have shown what we can do in the air, with all the odds against us!"

No one resigned, but Chennault was sore as hell. Tom Jones said, "We went, but the mission fizzled—Blenheims never showed up. On the way back we strafed hell out of a Jap convoy. . . ."[19]

The Tigers were often accused of being a group of mercenaries. They were, of course, civilians hired to fight and paid a bonus for every Japanese plane shot down. Leland Stowe, an American correspondent, once noted, "Most of them are 100-percent mercenaries, over-cocky and know-it-all. They seemed to have the notion that shooting down Japanese was like hunting squirrels."[20]

The one-year contract for the AVG expired on 4 July 1942. Lt. Gen. Lewis Brereton had refused the expansion of Chennault's group in favor of having the AVG crews join the Tenth Air Force. However, because they had fought as civilians, they would not be able to transfer their AVG records to the military. When given a chance, only five pilots and a few ground crewmen transferred. General Stilwell, in his report on the CBI, stated, "Forty members of the AVG appeared before the board for induction. American authorities were disappointed that more did not volunteer, because pilots experienced in combat against the Japanese were sorely needed."[21] Some crewmen took jobs in China with CNAC.[22] Some simply left—buying tickets on commercial transportation back to the United States.[23]

Almost every account of the record of the AVG lists a different number of Japanese aircraft downed. The figure 284 was from an official Chinese publication, but even that was not the total of the month-to-month numbers listed in the same publication. When the AVG was disbanded, the Chinese government paid the pilots $146,999.87 as a bonus of $500 per Japanese plane destroyed. Divide that out and we have 279 planes downed.[24] That was the lowest reported figure, with 1,200 as the highest number of planes destroyed, and 700 probables.[25] Accounts vary.

On 3 July 1942, the Chinese newspaper *Ta Kung Pae* wrote, "The American Volunteer Group will be organized into the American Army Air Corps tomorrow. . . . As an expression of respect and admiration, the Chinese people have turned the name of the AVG into 'Always Very Good.'"[26]

Gasoline, especially 100-octane, was the most precious commodity in China, and much of the cargo of the early Hump flights carried fuel for the fighters. Hump pilot Ivan W. Eveland, Helena, Montana, was a civilian pilot on detached service from Pan-American Airways Africa, Ltd. to the Tenth Air Force. He remembers, "Flying the Hump in the pioneer days of April and May 1942, we were trying to evacuate refugees and wounded. We also carried ammunition, supplies and 100-octane gas in five-gallon cans to the AVG. We flew our C-53s and C-47s on 90-octane (except for takeoff and landing) to conserve the 100-octane for the fighting P-40s."[27] Pilots thought that some accidents were caused by the use of the low-octane fuel, especially at times when the engines were under stress.

Jim Grace from San Antonio, Texas, felt that he cheated death one night in a C-46 as he, with pilot Olin Grubb, Los Gatos, California, took off with 90-octane gasoline. He tells this story: "We climbed to approximately 200 [feet], gear up and everyone happy. At that time both engines started severe detonation with rapid loss of power."[28] Pilot Grubb switched the fuel tanks from main to auxiliary; both engines smoothed out and performed to perfection. They learned later that their plane had been refueled in the main tanks from the automotive truck. "Grubb's quick shift of tanks," says Grace, "saved some highly valuable parts of our anatomy."[29]

Large refueling trucks could not be carried into China, and most aircraft were refueled from five-gallon cans. This was a primitive, slow, and dangerous job. Throughout the war, in some remote areas of the CBI, planes continued to be filled from hand-carried cans. I still remember the shock I had when flying into a remote part of China. As we waited for the refueling truck, a long line of Chinese came down the field, each with a five-gallon can of gasoline on his head. A refueling truck would have put a lot of Chinese coolies out of work.

War numbs a fighter's sensitivity to life, but Allied crewmen could never accept the Chinese army's lack of respect for human life. There were unconfirmed stories of Chinese soldiers being thrown out of transport planes high over the mountains because they were sick. This lack of regard for human life often hardened the Allied soldier's respect for the Chinese.

On one mission, waiting for takeoff at the end of the runway, I saw the pilot of the plane immediately in front of me abort his takeoff run because a Chinese worker had darted across the runway in front of the plane. I steeled myself to see a person cut to bits by the propellers—it was that close. The pilot spared the man's life by cutting his engines. The tower operator gave the pilot hell and told him he was never to stop the takeoff run to avoid hitting a Chinese. Directives for one Allied air movement of Chinese troops stated simply, "If you have to get out of the plane, forget the Chinese."[30]

The Chinese believed many things we would call superstitions. One such superstition was the "Dragon of Bad Luck." Coolies working around air fields believed that if they would run in front of a fast-moving airplane close enough, the propellers would kill the dragon and not the coolie, thereby changing the man's luck for the better. Many were killed trying to destroy their dragon.[31]

To implement President Roosevelt's order to supply China with the Hump airlift, the Ferrying Command, on 25 February 1942, was directed to activate a group of three squadrons, each with 350 men and twenty-five C-47 aircraft.[32] This number of aircraft was based on a report by Gen. Earl L. Naiden, chief of staff of the Tenth Air Force, who had decided, in early March 1942, that no more than twenty-five aircraft could be operated over the air route. General Stilwell accepted his report and told Washington to send no more than twenty-five planes.[33]

The First Ferrying Group, called the Assam-Burma-China (ABC) Command, as part of the Tenth Air Force, began regular Hump flights. Constituted on 3 March 1942, the group cadre sailed to India by boat on 17 March. To provide aircraft for the group, President Roosevelt ordered General Arnold to commandeer twenty-five DC-3-type planes from the airlines to become a part of the first air fleet to open the supply line into China.[34] This group was to be under the command of Brig. Gen. Donald D. Olds.[35]

General Olds made the very first Ferrying Command trip over the Hump on a highly secret mission on 8 April 1942. His cargo was marked "Supersecret" and "Special Rush"—it was gasoline to refuel the Doolittle planes in China after they had bombed Tokyo.[36] The first assignment of the Ferrying Group was to haul thirty thousand gallons of gasoline and five hundred pounds of lubricants for the Doolittle raiders—supplies that were never needed. Later, the ABC Ferrying Command flew Colonel Doolittle back across the Hump to India.[37]

From 18 April to 13 May 1942, twenty-six Ferrying Group crews left Morrison Field, Florida, in their C-47s to fly the 12,225-mile trip to India. It was an awesome flight even for experienced crews—over the Caribbean Sea and the Atlantic Ocean, and across three continents. Morrison Field was the "jumping off place" for the Orient; the military more properly called it a Point of Embarkation (POE). Leaving Morrison, the airmen flew down the Caribbean to Puerto Rico and across the top of South America to either Belém or Natal in Brazil. From Brazil crews flew to Ascension Island, to French West Africa, over the top of Africa, across the great Sahara into India, and on to the Hump.

For most young American men, going overseas was a new adventure. Hump pilot Harold D. Weatherly, Tulsa, Oklahoma, on his trip to India, remembers asking a waitress in the officer's mess at Puerto Rico, "What nation does Puerto Rico belong to?" "Santa Maria, you North Americanos do not know your own possessions!"[38]

Throughout 1944, I was stationed at Morrison and watched the planes and their crews leave. Almost every pilot wanted to serve overseas, and there is no pain like that felt by a "state-side" pilot as he watches crews take off for foreign duty.

In early 1945, it was my time. My flight crew and I volunteered for a "special mission," and we began a long flight from Morrison to an "unknown destination" in a B-25 Mitchell. As a crew, we were experienced in over-water and weather flying, having spent 1944 flying weather reconnaissance across the North Atlantic and hurricane reconnaissance in the South Atlantic. As we headed down the beautiful Caribbean, we did not know what our assignment was. We flew from Morrison to Borinquen, Puerto Rico; to Waller, Trinidad; and on to Natal, Brazil—over 3,700 miles, three jumps in a heavily-loaded twin-engine B-25 medium bomber.

We were kids headed for the great adventure. In Brazil I even ran into Maj. Gene Shelton, the tough kid on the block where I grew up in Greenville, Texas, who beat me up once every day when I was just a boy. How glad I was to see him in Brazil. It was a party. We had not seen war; we had not faced death. We were young; we were not yet lonely; we were not yet homesick.

From Natal we would head out over open water for Ascension Island, a small thirty-four-square-mile speck of land 1,448 miles from Brazil in the middle of the South Atlantic Ocean. As we prepared for takeoff from Natal, we saw the end of the runway littered with radio gear, guns, boxes, and other items thrown out by crews to lighten their planes before taking off for tiny Ascension. The Air Corps seemed to load overseas flights with every gadget known to aviation.

The eight-hour flight to Ascension was pure hell for many of the crews as we kept in contact with each other across the water. Never had the airwaves been so busy with radio calls from crews who just wanted to know that they were not alone over the Atlantic. There was no radar. We simply flew east until the Natal ADF (automatic direction finder) faded and then we homed in on Ascension with the radio compass. The radio compass was called the "bird dog," the friendliest instrument a pilot had. The nearest land to Ascension was seven hundred miles and the nearest airfield was over a thousand miles. We were alone.

The landing runway at Ascension was lava rock, in a valley between two mountain peaks. Most pilots came in high and fast because of the ocean updrafts and the fear of flying into the side of the cliff if they undershot. The next morning, taking long showers, our crew used all of the water in the tank. When we learned that all water had to be hauled to the shower, we decided it would be best to take off for Africa as quickly as possible before someone else came to bathe.

Then, more open ocean to Liberia. On to Dakar, across the top of Africa, over the pyramids, across the Sinai desert into dark, beautiful, and mysterious India. India looks mysterious—I don't know why.

For young Americans in their early twenties, India was the end of a miracle that is every pilot's dream—flying halfway around the world. The airplane was truly a magic carpet. It was beyond belief that, as young boys, we were flying aircraft over routes that airline pilots took years to qualify for. This South Atlantic route was an aerial highway for crews going to and from the Orient. Some were flying their own aircraft, some were passengers in Air Transport Command planes, and some were "hitchhiking" from base to base waiting orders. Few knew where they were going. The miracle is that it all worked out.

It is easy to see why inexperienced flight crews feared this long over-water flight. Pilot John T. Foster, 425th Bomb Squadron, from Keene, New Hampshire, has had nightmares for the past forty years because of his experience flying from Natal to Ascension Island. Foster and his crew got their China orders and flew from Florida to Natal. Information in Natal was that enemy subs in the South Atlantic were sending false radio signals to divert planes flying to Ascension. "No sweat," Foster remembers. "We would fly at night; our navigator was skilled in celestial navigation."

Night over the Atlantic: "As the Natal range faded, our navigator got a pinpoint [celestial] fix, calling for a slight correction." Celestial navigation is the result of precise star readings and accurate time hacks (checking a watch against Greenwich time) to record the second, minute, and hour when readings are taken. Foster remembers: "Our navigator's fixes were great but, soon, common sense and a fading radio signal indicated we were far off course. The sun was about to rise and I suggested that he take a reading and plot our position. The navigator admitted that he had forgotten how to do that."

The clear ADF signal indicated that Ascension was far to the south. So, sub or no sub, Foster turned south and flew for thirty minutes and found Ascension. "After getting the sextant checked, we took off for Accra, on the African coast. Again the sun lines were off. With a sharp right turn and a radio beam, we found Accra. Suddenly, the navigator gave a whoop, 'I've found the problem. It's really simple. You won't believe it. All the time I was using a July instead of a June almanac.' His sightings had been precise to the second, but in the wrong month."[39]

Part of American aid to China was a program called the American Military Mission to China (AMMISCA), which offered help, both military and diplomatic, where it was most urgently needed. The first crews assigned to the Tenth Air Force were part of AMMISCA and were airline pilots on military reserve with thousands of hours of flying experience. However, few of them had over-water experience and none had flown over mountains in monsoon-type weather. These AMMISCA crews were assigned to the First Ferrying Group and would be the first Allied airmen to begin regular missions over the Himalayas.[40]

While making Hump flights as often as possible, the Allies' first major priority was to build airfields. General Naiden asked the Royal Air Force in India to provide three fields in the Assam Valley: Chabua, already built, and new fields, Sookerating and Mohanbari. Two other fields in northern Burma, Myitkyina and Bhamo, were to be built.[41]

The first plan of the Hump was to fly supplies into Burma, off-load to trucks, and complete the supply operation over the Burma Road to Kunming, China. It was not suspected that the Burma Road would be closed almost as quickly as this plan had been worked out, and the aircraft would be required to continue the trip to Kunming.

As feeble as these first flights over the Hump were, they were more practical than the Burma Road. Trucks on the road offered five hundred miles of target practice for the Japanese fighters. In addition, there were eight customs points along the way where duty had to be paid to the local governments. Military leaders continued to feel that the overland Burma and newly proposed Ledo roads were essential, although during the total period of Hump operation, March 1942 to September 1945, the planes of the ATC and CNAC carried more tons of supplies into and from China than the Burma and Ledo roads combined.[42]

In early 1942, the only airfield in the Assam valley suitable for large transports was Dinjan in the Brahmaputra flood plain. Dinjan was five hundred miles from Kunming over the ten-thousand-foot Patkai range, fourteen- to sixteen-thousand-foot ridges near the valleys of the Irrawaddy, Salween, and Mekong rivers, and, finally, over the 20,000-foot Santung range. Until the Japanese captured Burma, the Hump planes could fly at ten thousand feet to Myitkyina and then to Kunming, missing the higher mountains. Later, with Burma occupied, the Hump suffered a setback when crews had to fly the high and dangerous northern route from Assam to China.[43]

With delays in completing airfields, diversions of planes for military emergencies, pilot inexperience, awesome weather, and enemy fighter planes, the Hump airlift was bordering on disaster and had failed to gain the volume the planners had promised. Planes were constantly being commandeered for duties other than flying supplies over the Hump. For example, crews that had been assigned to fly gasoline to China for Doolittle's Tokyo raiders were diverted to evacuate General Stilwell's wounded soldiers and Chinese refugees or to drop supplies to Stilwell himself, who was trapped in Burma with a defeated, sick, and dying army.[44] These were missions of expediency and mercy, but they reduced the volume of cargo over the Hump. Supplies to China, in actual operations, had a low priority—military emergencies were first.

Because CNAC pilots and operations personnel were more experienced in mountain and weather flying, and their delivery rate was greater than that of the U.S. Army, Washington considered having CNAC provide the freight service over the Hump on a contract basis.[45] President Roosevelt's personal representative to India telegraphed Secretary of State Cordell Hull: "After observing parallel operations [by] Army and Pan American across Africa, I am convinced that . . . vital aid to China can most quickly be accomplished by Lend-Lease contract through Army to Pan American and China National Airways."[46]

General Stilwell refused to accept this idea, believing that the military should control combat operations—perhaps remembering the unhappy experiences with the American Volunteer Group.[47]

The Allies were being beaten in almost every part of the war. General Stilwell's defeat in Burma was a serious military setback and crushing to morale. The Chinese seemed to have no will to fight and Chiang Kai-shek began to try the patience of Allied leaders by refusing to commit his troops to battle.[48] Gen. Tu Yu-ming, Chinese commander in Burma, explained why his army would not fight: "The Fifth Army is our best . . . it is the only one that has any field guns, and I cannot afford to risk those guns. If I lose them, the Fifth Army will no longer be our best."[49]

One great problem of the China-Burma-India (CBI) theater was the inability of the leaders to plan strategy with any expectation of Allied cooperation. The CBI was a political jungle; each of the Allied countries had different objectives.

Britain wanted China to receive just enough supplies to stay in the war, but not enough to build a strong Chinese military force that would threaten Burma or India. The British did not want the Ledo Road built because of the possibility that it might provide the means for a closer relationship between resurgent China and rebellious India.[50] Churchill's goal was to protect India, Britain's "Jewel of the Orient," where Mohandas Gandhi was demanding Indian independence in exchange for his country's help against the Japanese. The British could not understand or accept the new Indian leader.

It was also felt that the British were prepared to sacrifice Burma rather than make concessions or be indebted to the Chinese. If China was allowed to fight for Burma, the British promised no support. The British believed that Burma would be retaken by the Americans and returned to them at the peace table. There was no need to fight.[51] Yet Burma was one important key to the success of the Hump airlift since the aircraft had to either fly over occupied Burma and risk Japanese fighters or fly to the north over extremely dangerous mountains.

Nationalist China was fighting two enemies — Japan and the Communists. It was often suspected that many of the Hump supplies were never used in the war and were kept in reserve to fight against the Communists when the Japanese were defeated.

The deep underlying fear of the Allies was that Chiang Kai-shek would sue for peace in exchange for the Japanese fighting the Communists. Chiang was realistic; he could see that the Allies were sustaining great military defeats, that China was a low priority in the war, that there were incredible problems in supplying over the Hump, and that things were moving very slowly.

If Chiang Kai-shek surrendered, China would no longer be in the war; China's soil would not be available for operations against Japan, and China's inexhaustible manpower would fight for the Japanese against Great Britain and the United States.[52] The suspicion that China might surrender to Japan placed greater emphasis on the Hump.

Throughout the war there was a fear that Chiang would surrender to the Japanese. This fear was unfounded. Evidence in diplomatic papers in 1945 showed that Chiang had turned down at least twelve Japanese peace offers. W. H. Donald, Associated Press reporter, was quoted in the *New York Times*, 28 February 1945: "I am convinced that the Generalissimo is genuinely fighting a sincere and determined war against Japan." Chiang constantly pledged his loyalty to the Allies: "There will be no peace while a single Japanese soldier remains on Chinese soil."[53]

For these reasons it was absolutely necessary that the Himalayan airlift be successful. The Hump offered the best way to keep China as a fighting member of the Allied forces. A memorandum from the State Department, 27 June, stated (in emphatic italics): "Continued Chinese resistance cannot be taken for granted; *that the best way to insure against a Chinese collapse lies in sending materials, especially planes, and establishing an effective air transport into and out of China;* . . . We therefore recommend and urge that every reasonable effort be made to establish on a substantial scale air transport between India and China."[54]

While diplomatic channels moved slowly, CNAC and the U.S. Army kept increasing the number of flights and building tonnage over the Hump. From August through December 1942, CNAC flew 873 round trips, carrying nearly two thousand tons of supplies into China. On the return trips, CNAC transports carried eighteen hundred tons and seven thousand troops back to India. Chinese troops were trained in India and flown back to China or Burma to fight.

The fall of Burma forced Hump aircraft to use a more northerly route, from Assam to Kunming, where mountain peaks rise from fifteen to twenty thousand feet. This was the real Hump, a distance of approximately five hundred miles, flown in four to six hours, depending on weather. Later, in 1944, when Burma was in Allied hands, the Hump was extended to include Southern routes from the Calcutta area to China. This was called the "Low Hump"—longer but much less hazardous.

General Tunner, who became commander of the Hump airlift in August 1944, wrote, "I still can't help but feel great admiration for those desperate Army Air Corps planners who proposed to do what had never been contemplated before."[55] The Hump was a daring proposal. Edmund Townsend, Royal Australian Air Force (RAAF) pilot, described his first experience over the mountains: "The Hump suddenly bared its teeth . . . to show us a land of desolation and terror— an airman's nightmare . . . this is the Hump, the world's most risky air transport route."[56]

While ATC pilots were fighting weather and high altitudes over the mountains, other crews were engaged in drop missions to troops behind the lines. Flying the heavily loaded C-47s at treetop, dropping supplies while dodging enemy fighters, was as hazardous as the Hump freight flights at any time.

Richard "Sahib" Foster, Venice, Florida, relates one of his experiences when the Hump was just getting started: "On 15 August 1942, we loaded my C-47 'Hells' Hangover,' for a rice-dropping mission over Burma. I was flight engineer. We took off from Chabua; the Japanese had taken Myitkyina and we were supplying British and Americans by air."

Foster's load was four hundred-pound bales of supplies that were pushed out the door. The crew could not work with parachutes on, and since they flew too low over the drop zone, parachutes would have been useless anyway. They tied ropes around their waists and to the side rails of the fuselage for safety. After the drop, they climbed back to altitude and suddenly received a call, "Go see Uncle Tom." This was the code for Japanese fighters, and they were coming in fast.

Foster continues, "Lieutenant Morton put the C-47 in a dive for the ground—past the red line of 250 miles per hour. We hugged the ground up and down over the Naga Hills and the two Jap fighters were making pass after pass. The C-47 was groaning at full power as we took evasive action. We were being hit, but continued toward Assam. The fighters suddenly left us.

"We thanked our lucky stars to be on the ground. The left elevator had been shot off, there were holes in the wings and tail section, and fuel was leaking out of the gas tanks. We were lucky to be alive."[57]

The demands on the Hump crews increased. Military cargo continued to crowd warehouses in Assam, India, and supplies were often stockpiled in open fields. Assam was a state of its own, separated from India by the mighty Brahmaputra River. Not a bridge crossed the six-hundred-mile Brahmaputra from Calcutta to Assam. Shipped by sea from the United States to Calcutta, the cargo was carried by the Assam-Bengal narrow-gauge rail. Each state had a different gauge railroad, and as the cargo moved from state to state, the freight cars had to be off-loaded and reloaded onto another train. The rail system had been created in the days of the British tea plantations, and the railroad workers handled the cargo at the leisurely pace of the plantation past. The trip took weeks.

Every drop of fuel, every weapon, every round of ammunition, and all other supplies, including carbon paper, Kotex (to strain fighters' engine oil), troops, lend-lease supplies—everything—went over the Hump. As traffic increased, so did accidents. There was an average of two accidents for every thousand hours flown, and a plane went down for every two hundred trips over the mountains. For every thousand tons flown into China, three Americans gave their lives.[58]

To think that the cargo the Hump planes carried was always directly related to war would be too limiting. Many flights carried whiskey (ten thousand pounds of Canadian whiskey zealously guarded by the British), mules (four mules per plane with four Chinese "cow-boys"), a load of catsup for the fighter squadrons in Kweilin, and money, bales and bales of Chinese paper money, printed by the American Bank Note Company. Pilot 1st Lt. W. E. Bowman, South Bend, Indiana, made one cargo run over the Hump with $79 million in Chinese money. At an exchange rate of 210-to-1 that would have been over $376,000 American. "I stroked each box lovingly as I crawled over them."[59] On one flight a CNAC plane crash-landed in a village near the airstrip and exploded, sending showers of Chinese paper money over the entire village.[60]

Flying different types of cargo had frustrations beyond the danger. Pilot Robert B. L. Taylor, now living in Columbus, Ohio, reported a strange mixture of cargo on three successive flights: "I had an old Gooney [C-47] that was ready for the depot . . . there was no doubt . . .

"First, I picked up a load of grain—oats, bran, etc . . . burlap bags leak like hell and there's no place for it to go but into the belly of the ship . . . o.k. a base layer of grain down there!

"Secondly, my next load was a bunch of goats . . . they started getting nervous and number one'd and number two'd all over the floor . . . we now have fermenting grain and a layer of goat do-do!

"Thirdly, I took a load of Chinese troops from Myitkyina to China. . . . I thought my gestures to the Chinese captain explained the use of the 'relief tube.'[61] 'Ya! Ya!' said the captain . . . [then] pappa san captain yanked the tube out of its place . . . instructed the boys how to use it . . . while standing in the middle of the compartment . . . you know what was going down—you know where—to the belly of the ship.

"OK! So, now, we have fermenting grain, goat do-do, and Chinese wee-wee, all in the belly of the ship. The old Gooney was ready for the depot, for sure."[62]

The variety of cargo over the Hump was beyond imagination. In one month, the ATC was called to fly more than one hundred five-ton trucks, two hundred smaller trucks, eleven road scrapers, each weighing over twelve tons, and fifty jeeps. Some of these vehicles were cut into sections before being flown into China.[63]

When the AVG was disbanded on 4 July 1942, the army immediately organized the China Air Task Force (CATF), a fighting unit combining Chinese and American air crews. General Chennault was named commander of the CATF and it became a part of the Tenth Air Force. Chennault had been a brigadier general in the Chinese Air Force, and when he rejoined the Army Air Force, in April 1942, he was given the rank of U.S. brigadier general.

The mission of the CATF was to continue the momentum and successes of the AVG in defending the Hump route and to provide air support for Chinese ground forces in China. The strength of the CATF was twelve bombers and fifty fighters.[64] In addition to the CATF, the defense of the Hump air routes was also given to the Indian Air Task Force (IATF) under the command of Brig. Gen. Calib Haynes. The IATF had two squadrons of P-40s, with about thirty-five planes each, stationed in Dinjan.[65]

General Chennault was not satisfied with the CATF. He wrote General Stilwell that if "he was given one hundred new P-51 fighters and thirty B-25 medium bombers, he would be responsible for the destruction of more Japanese aircraft than . . . [he would lose of] his own force, destroy enemy naval and military establishments, disrupt Japanese shipping, and the destruction of Japanese morale by destroying supply depots and production facilities." Stilwell ignored this and replied that he wanted Chennault to make the defense of the Hump ferry route his primary mission, with a secondary mission to destroy Japanese military aircraft, shipping, etc.[66] Chennault was kept in a defensive position and was rarely permitted to fight offensively, as he sorely wanted to do.

When the AVG was made a part of the Tenth Air Force, the Adam and Eves (first), Panda Bears (second) and Hell's Angels (third) fighter squadrons of the AVG became the seventy-fourth, seventy-fifth, and seventy-sixth squadrons of the CATF. With the Sixteenth Fighter Squadron, from India, the Eleventh Bomb Squadron, and the Ninth Photo Squadron, the CATF was formed—an outfit of four to five hundred people.[67] The CATF immediately went into combat against the Japanese but was greatly outnumbered and managed to stay alive only because of experience and superior fighting tactics.

Chennault was not only a skillful warrior, he knew how to work the military bureaucracy to his benefit. Milton Miller, editor of the *jing bao Journal*, publication of the Flying Tigers of the Fourteenth Air Force Association, tells the following story about Chennault "stealing" a squadron of fighters. "When the AVG was disbanded," Miller says, "Claire Chennault figured that if he was to command a viable fighting force, he would have to beg, borrow or steal men, planes and supplies." Chennault learned that the Sixteenth Fighter Squadron, of the Tenth Air Force, was grounded by the spring monsoons in Assam. The Sixteenth was equipped with new P-40Es. Chennault saw a potential fighting force languishing in Assam and the P-40s rusting in the rain.

According to Miller, "With hat in hand, Chennault flew to Delhi to Tenth Headquarters. 'How about having the 16th fly to China to gain combat experience? The squadron could then return to Assam with experience and fly devastating missions against the Japanese, sure to produce headlines in the United States.'"

Chennault's request was approved, and the squadron flew the Hump to China. With it came Johnny Allison, Ed Goss, Johnny Lombard, Harry Pike, Harry Young, and George Hazlett—pilots who became combat leaders of the CATF.

Months later, a Tenth Air Force staff captain asked, "What ever became of the 16th?" A second captain asked, "Didn't we lend it to Chennault?" They radioed to Chennault, "Do you have knowledge of 16th Fighter Squadron?"

Chennault denied any remembrance of the Sixteenth. "And that is how Chennault stole the 16th Fighter Squadron."[68] Throughout the war in China, the Sixteenth fought in all of the hottest actions with the seventy-fourth, seventy-fifth, and seventy-sixth squadrons of the Twenty-third Group of the CATF of the Tenth Air Force.

Chennault created the idea for the Fourteenth Air Force when he asked Stilwell to separate his CATF from the Tenth Air Force. Wendell Willkie, a special representative for President Roosevelt, made an inspection tour of China and, with General Stilwell's permission, talked with Chennault about his ideas for an increased air offensive against the Japanese. Willkie was shocked at the poor state of air power in China and asked Chennault to write a letter to the president which he would deliver.

Chennault was careful in his letter. Any request for increased air power was not practical, because there was not enough fuel being flown over the Hump to supply the planes that were already in China. The long and detailed letter was delivered to President Roosevelt and may have been influential in winning Washington to the Chennault strategy. He was careful to defuse any objections from Stilwell by stating that the letter was an order from Willkie.

Chennault told the president that Japan could be defeated in six months by an air force so small that other theaters would consider his request ridiculous. He asked for 105 fighters, 30 medium bombers, and, later, 12 heavy bombers, with replacements. "I can cause the collapse of Japan," he stressed, and "I can make the Chinese lasting friends with the United States for generations." Chennault recalled the successes of the AVG and how he was accepted and trusted by the generalissimo and Chinese leaders. He was also critical of the Allied leadership, the orthodox, rigid military mind, and an "unwieldly, illogical

Air Transport Command operations tents on remote Chinese base. Tents could be moved quickly if Japanese threatened.

organization by men who do not understand aerial warfare in China."

Chennault concluded the letter with a request that might have weakened his appeal: "It is essential that I be given complete freedom of fighting action [and] be able to deal directly with the Generalissimo and the Chinese forces."[69] Even in hindsight, the letter raises the haunting possibility that Chennault might have been correct. The war lasted three more years with tremendous loss of life, the horror of atomic warfare became reality, the U.S. lost the friendship of China, and the face of the globe was changed forever.

This letter placed the conflict between Chennault and Stilwell on the desk of the president of the United States. Chennault was speaking from a position of strength and success, but the fatal flaw in the proposal was that Chennault must be placed in "full authority" of all American military operations in China.[70] That was Stilwell's role.

On 20 June 1942, the U.S. Air Corps Ferrying Command was re-designated the Air Transport Command (ATC). The ATC was to be an agent of the entire War Department, not just the Army Air Forces. ATC was made responsible, on a world-wide basis, for: (1) "Ferrying all aircraft within the United States and to destinations outside the United States . . . ," (2) "Transportation by air of personnel, materiel, and mail for all War Department agencies . . . ," and (3) "Control, operation and maintenance of establishments and facilities on air routes outside of the United States."[71]

The Hump airlift, as a part of the Tenth Air Force, was not meeting military expectations or needs, and on 9 October it was proposed that the ATC take over the supply route from India to China.[72] This proposal was accepted, and on 21 October the ATC officially took over the Hump freight airlift. Col. Edward H. Alexander was named commanding officer of the India-China Wing of ATC. From that time until the end of the war, the ATC was the principal carrier for supplies over the Himalayas, although other military units flew cargo and troops over the Hump for their specific needs.

From the beginning, the ATC did not command the respect of other more combat-oriented flight units. Combat outfits looked down on noncombat units, and soon a military "pecking order" was established. Murray Weiss, Elmsford, New York, remembers his concern when ATC took over the Hump flights: "We were assigned to the Air Transport Command, a new outfit hauling freight, in old ex-airline DC-3s. Only the Training Command ranked lower in respect. We were often called 'Allergic to Combat,' or the 'Army of Terrified Copilots.'"[73] Pilots were called "aerial truck drivers," but they accepted the title.

It was difficult for crews from Combat Cargo, the Air Commandos, and other airmen who were fighting a "hot" war and faced enemy guns on every flight, to accept the ATC crews who flew so-called noncombat missions. ATC crewmen were often aloof to other outfits, and this added to their unpopularity. Airmen from other units who flew into ATC bases sensed discrimination. John Martin, Ashland, Kentucky, Combat Cargo pilot, wrote, "Hell, we had to go to the end of the chow line because we had mud on our boots."[74]

The disrespect for the ATC came out in many ways. Wallace Little, Memphis, Tennessee, Seventy-fifth Fighter Squadron, tells about one time when he and his wing mate Charlie Vest were returning from a mission. Flying at eleven thousand feet, Little spotted the Luichow runway. The radio is a good shield, and this is the conversation with the Luichow control tower:

Little: "Luichow, this is Charleston 41, flight of two, request landing instructions, over."

Lui Tower: "Roger, Charleston 41. Clear for break for 36 [altimeter]; call final gear down and locked."

ATC Pilot: "Luichow, this is ATC 1234, turning wide downwind. This is a C-47. Since we are already in the pattern, request you hold fighters until we land. Over."

Lui Tower: "No problem, ATC 1234. The 51s will be on the ground and off the runway before you turn final. Continue your pattern."

ATC Pilot: "This is Colonel (blank). Luichow is an ATC base and we are an ATC ship. I insist you let us land first."

Vest: "Nyah, nyah, nyah, Colonel. I'd rather have a sister in a whorehouse than a brother in the ATC."

ATC Pilot: "Who is the stupid pilot that made that remark? Give me your name, rank and organization."

Vest: "Colonel, don't you know the name of that stupid pilot?"

ATC: "No! Give me your name immediately. That's an order!"

Vest: "Colonel, this 'stupid pilot' ain't that stupid!"[75]

Being an ATC pilot was no easy job, regardless of how other pilots felt. From airdromes in the valley of the Brahmaputra, the heavily loaded Hump transports would take off, spiraling up to altitudes of two to four miles before setting out toward China.

Once on their way, ATC crews flew over snowcapped mountains, still within range of enemy fighter planes. But weather was a greater threat than Japanese Zeros. Flight crews were threatened with icing, fierce winds, and having to fly through weather buildups higher than Mount Everest. From May to October, there were monsoon rains and, most serious of all, there was the constant stress of instrument flying, with few navigational aids. This was "Able" route, which, because of these dangers, earned the reputation as the most hazardous regularly used air lane in any part of the world. Able, from the Assam Valley, across the northern Hump to the Chengtu area, was over nine hundred miles of icy hell. Able began at Rupsi, thence to Misamari, to Sadiya, to Fort Hertz, to Likiang, to Hsiching, and on to Loshan. Able set the character for the entire Hump.

On the long, tedious flights over the Himalayas, pilots often resorted to tricks to "initiate" new copilots or other crewmen to the rigors of flight over the mountains. There were special peak formations new crew members were asked to look for. "The Three Sisters" were popular; also "Los Dos Chisos" (the two bosoms) teased copilots. The most popular, and the best-kept secret from new pilots, was "Duncan's Tunnel," a so-called "secret pass" that planes had to fly through on instruments to get across the high Hump. Timing was important, and

the "initiation rite" only worked when the plane was in the soup.

Alerting the copilot, the pilot would ask for a ten-second time check when the beacon flashed on the instrument panel. Beacon flashes; copilot calls time; pilot turns sharply fifteen degrees. "Give me fifteen seconds." Copilot responds. Pilot turns sharply opposite, climbs one hundred feet, levels off and relaxes. "That pass sure is a bitch to get through."[76]

Chabua, in the upper Assam Valley, was a major base for Hump flights from early in 1942 until the end of the war. The Chabua airfield was built on an old British tea plantation, and late in the war, air crewmen lived in "comfortable" British-style tents. Each tent had one forty watt light globe. A cold-water shower and an eight-holer toilet were about a hundred yards from the tents. The mess hall, orderly room, and open-air movie theater had thatched roofs.

Chabua could not have been a worse choice for the flight to China—if there had been a choice. Leslie Anders, China historian, described the Hump from Chabua: "Few areas on earth posed more terrifying challenges to air transportation than [between] . . . Assam and Kunming. . . . On some days the icing level was beneath the summits of the Hump. . . . Floods could close airfields with no warning."[77]

Food in Chabua was dull but healthful—canned fruit, Spam, fresh bananas, eggplant, and water buffalo. In China there were fresh vegetables, boiled chicken, and eggs—fresh eggs. Eggs were more valuable than Chinese money. For example: There was an unused piano in the Chabua mess hall that Jim Stark (374th Bomber Squadron), from Midland, Michigan, thought his squadron needed in China. So, as a special deal, Stark and his crew tried to persuade the mess sergeant to trade the piano for "twelve dozen fresh eggs from China." "No!" "Twenty-four dozen?" "Yes!" So, on the next B-24 flight, twenty-four dozen fresh eggs were flown into Chabua, and after dark the crew carefully loaded the piano in the B-24 and took off for China. It furnished the music for a barber-shop quartet in the Chengkung recreation building—at the price of 288 fresh eggs.[78]

Chabua was surrounded by tea farms operated by the British. The war did not seem to slow the tea pickers just outside the bounds of the Chabua air base. These tea pickers were attractive Indian women who wore a type of "working sari" with only one strap over the shoulder. When bending to pick tea, the ladies, apparently unabashed, revealed one shapely breast—a considerable distraction to the airmen, who set up constant watches.

However, even in remote Assam in northern India, the Japanese had no respect for the shapely tea pickers, or the air base, and often dropped bombs.

On 25 October, Richard Foster—who narrowly escaped death in August on a rice-dropping mission over Burma—Venice, Florida, hit the slit trenches during a Japanese attack on Chabua. Foster and his maintenance crews were getting the C-47s ready for flight and were loading fifty-five-gallon drums of gasoline. All flyable aircraft had left for China in the early morning. One plane was loaded with five thousand pounds of black powder.

"We heard aircraft approaching—twin-engine bombers. . . . we thought they were the new B-25s rumored to arrive. The aircraft opened their bomb-bay doors and dropped leaflets. Leaflets, hell, those were Japanese and they were dropping bombs. Hit the trenches!"

The bombs hit the gasoline tank car near the runway, and the planes came back across the field, dropping five-hundred-pound antipersonnel bombs. Five C-47s and one gasoline truck were hit, including the plane just loaded, catching the load of black powder on fire. The heat was so intense, Foster and his men ran for another slit trench to avoid being burned alive.

The bombers left and fighters came to strafe. "Bullets kicking dirt in our face. . . . we were not hit, although five C-47s were destroyed and several natives were killed. We had no fighter protection—completely at the mercy of the Japanese, and they came back on Monday and Tuesday, and strafed and, on Wednesday, the bombers returned. We had dispersed the aircraft and there was little damage. We lost one airman, stationed at Mohan-Bari."[79]

Conditions at the Assam Valley bases were primitive. As the Hump developed, there were six bases in the Assam Valley: Sookerating, Mohanbari, Jorhat, Tezpur, Dinjan, and Chabua. Chabua was the ATC headquarters terminal.[80]

Gasoline was carried to the planes in five-gallon cans on the heads of natives. There were no hangars, and crews often worked at night because the intense heat of the day made maintenance almost impossible—the planes were too hot to touch. Enemy air raids were frequent, and aircraft were dispersed and hidden to prevent their being destroyed on the ground.

Maintenance and loading crews worked through the night, and to avoid enemy attack, planes that were in flight condition were in the air as soon as possible after daybreak. Night flights over the Hump were not scheduled because there were no navigation beacons along the flight routes. It was indeed a primitive operation.[81]

One story told throughout the early history of the airlift involved Col. Edward Alexander, commander of the India-China Wing of ATC. His headquarters was a tea bungalow, and most of his staff and pilots were from the airlines, with little army training. As they stood in the open, watching an air raid, the executive officer shouted, "Take cover you dumb bastards." From that time, the headquarters unit was known as "Dumbastapur."[82]

By nature the Assam was a wild and dangerous place. Crews were ordered to wear their guns and carry gas masks at all times. One night, returning from the mess hall in Chabua, I saw a tremendous beetle, almost as large as a Texas armadillo. I stepped on it and it held my weight and moved under me. Instinctively, I pulled my .45 and shot it. Robert T. Boody, Staten Island, New York, found a "krite," a small, deadly Indian snake, in his boot one morning. He shot it with his .45 pistol.[83]

Bliss K. Thorne, Wilder, Vermont, was walking between the air base and a small village. He was passing through a jungle trail and stepped on what felt like an automobile tire. He was thrown about twenty feet and saw a cobra moving off into the jungle.[84] Wild elephants were often seen crushing their way through the jungle.

By the end of 1942, Hump operations had increased so substantially that, when the ATC took over the cargo service, it was able to deliver 1,226 tons in December. Six months later total deliveries for June had increased to 2,300 tons. By the end of 1943, the India-China Wing delivered 12,641 tons and, in December, won a Distinguished Unit Citation for extraordinary performance. By that time, the number of aircraft (C-46s, C-47s, C-87s) had increased to 178. Although the tonnage for 1943 was still relatively small — some fifty-two thousand tons — the beginnings of a successful program were apparent.

3

The Hump Matures — January–July 1943

As 1943 dawned over the China-Burma-India (CBI) theater, the momentum of war was still with the Japanese. Gen. Joseph Stilwell and his reluctant Chinese armies were "taking a helluva beating" in the jungles of Burma, and the Allies were frantically trying to strengthen the Hump airlift. Supplying China over the Himalaya seemed to be the only hope for victory.

The year 1943, also, was one of high-level conferences: CASA-BLANCA, in January; TRIDENT, in Washington in May; QUAD-RANT, held in Quebec in August; SEXTANT, in Cairo in November; and EUREKA, held in Teheran in December. In all deliberations on the Far East, every decision, from the size of the air forces in China to the eventual outcome of the war, was based on the success of the Hump airlift.[1]

TRIDENT was the conference most concerned with the China theater and was called the "key event" in the history of the Hump airlift.[2] At this conference it was decided to coordinate all land and sea forces in Southeast Asia under one commander and to increase the tonnage over the Hump to ten thousand tons per month, with ATC having top priority. TRIDENT also created the number one Air Commando Group, under Colonels Phil Cochran and John Allison.[3] The Hump was receiving the priority that President Roosevelt had promised Chiang in China.

Still, sufficient supplies were not being flown into China. In February, the China Air Task Force (CATF) was forced to shut down all combat activities for lack of fuel. Generalissimo Chiang Kai-shek was unhappy, and on the eighteenth of February, Madame Chiang went to Washington and pleaded with President Roosevelt and Congress for "a more vigorous effort to deliver supplies to China."[4]

New air units were on the way to China. The 308th Heavy Bombardment Group, flying battle-tested B-24s, was scheduled to leave the United States on 7 February 1943. The 308th was a commitment toward a greater offensive against the Japanese and eventual long-range bombing from China.[5]

In March the 308th Bomb Group, with its B-24s, reached India and began to fly fuel to China. The 308th became a part of the Fourteenth Air Force when it was formed on 10 March. How the 308th Bomb Group got from the United States to India is a story of "I wonder how we won the war." Pilot John Sherman tells how group commander Col. Eugene H. Beebe took command of thirty-six B-24s in early January 1943 at Salina Air Base, Kansas. Their first stop was DeRidder, Louisiana. On takeoff, one B-24 crashed. The others headed for DeRidder, but the field had not been notified that thirty-six B-24s were coming, and the tower was closed. The field was covered with a rainstorm and only three or four planes were able to land. The others managed to land at Dallas, New Orleans, and other alternate fields near there. Three days later, all planes were at DeRidder.

Later, after they had flown to Morrison Field, Florida, and were ready to take off for India, group navigator Ed Ballenger went into West Palm Beach and bought a map. Ballenger now likes to tell how he led the thirty-five B-24s from Florida to Puerto Rico to Georgetown to Belém to Natal to Ascension Island to Accra to Maduguri to Khartoum to Aden to Salalah to Karachi to Chukulia to Chabua and finally over the Hump, using a drugstore *Rand-McNally World Atlas for Navigation*.[6]

There was a noticeable lack of interest in the future of the CBI at the CASABLANCA conference in January. It was apparent that little was going to be done in China in the immediate future. This was quickly noted in Chunking.[7] Perhaps President Roosevelt sensed China's concern, because after the conference he wrote Chiang Kai-shek a letter and asked that General Arnold deliver it to the generalissimo. In it he stated his determination to "increase General Chennault's Air Force at once. General Arnold will work out the ways and means with you and General Chennault."[8] This angered General Stilwell because of his belief in the foot soldier and the impossibility of the Hump airlift supplying fuel, air crews, and maintenance to support two thousand planes in China.

Immediately after General Arnold, accompanied by T. V. Soong and General Chennault, delivered the President's letter, the Chinese began to apply political pressure to the Allies for a separate air force in China.[9] The Chinese Air Task Force (CATF), as a part of Maj. Gen. Clayton L. Bissell's Tenth Air Force, was a disappointment. No one liked Bissell, and to solve this problem, General Marshall wrote General Stilwell of his plan to create the Fourteenth Air Force in China with Chennault in charge. Marshall's plan was to promote Bissell and Chennault to major general at the same time, with each in command of an air force in China.[10] Stilwell quickly replied that he "wanted Bissell promoted now, and he felt that Chennault had been sufficiently rewarded for the present."

Stilwell did not want two air forces in China because of the supply problem. General Marshall thought differently. He explained to Stilwell the "continuous pressure from practically every individual concerned with the Chinese problem, or who had traveled in China."[11] Marshall insisted that Chennault would be promoted and that his ideas of leadership of air operations in China should be accepted.

Stilwell replied, "What you say makes sense. I agree that it would be wise to promote Bissell and Chennault without lapse of time. In working on my own small manure pile, I am inclined to forget how much larger yours is, but I hope you understand my motives."[12]

Actually, Marshall had made his decision much earlier. On 4 January, 1943, he had written Fleet Admiral William D. Leahy, "Chennault . . . is the man . . . to command our all-out air effort against Japan from China when the supply of the necessary force can be assured."[13]

General Arnold, like Stilwell, did not want another air force in China and said so to General Marshall. Arnold cited great distances, lack of facilities, absence of weather stations, delay in receiving supplies, plus the complete dependence on supplies over the Hump.[14] However, General Marshall's decision prevailed.

Perhaps not aware of this decision, Chiang continued to press for a separate air force under Chennault, the only person who had the confidence of the Chinese. He also wanted five hundred additional U.S. planes in China by November and increased supplies over the Hump.[15]

To pacify Chiang, the United States created the Fourteenth Air Force in China—the smallest air unit of the war. The Fourteenth, activated on 10 March 1943, grew out of the CATF, and Brigadier General Chennault became a major general. The Fourteenth was isolated, without sufficient supplies, crews, planes or fuel—depending completely on the Hump airlift. The Fourteenth was also outnumbered five to one by the Japanese.

As his air force struggled in the destitution of China, Chennault was so conscious of nonpriority cargo coming over the Hump that he constantly checked manifests of planes coming into China. The following is a story certified to be true by Milton Miller, historian of the Fourteenth Air Force Association, although it will never be a part of official Air Force history.

Mosquitos were a problem, and all personnel were required to take Atabrine tablets to prevent malaria. In time, the mosquito problem attracted the attention of Washington with the request from Delhi that "a malarial control unit should be formed to service the China Command." Thus came the Sixteenth Malarial Control Unit under the command of Capt. Jim Fowles. His first orders were to proceed to Kweilin to serve bases in eastern China. Before getting down to his duty, Captain Fowles decided to go to Lingling, a new field, on a sightseeing trip.

Captain Fowles saw China as a land of romance—a scene out of *The Good Earth*. He caught a ride to Lingling, a Fourteenth Air Force base just being set up with only four P-40s and not enough beds for the 150 men there. Having a cup of coffee in the mess, Fowles saw General Chennault come in and decided to ask for his autograph. He noticed the adjutant frantically waving for him to tiptoe out. Chennault was on the warpath because he had just seen the list of new arrivals.

"My God, I've been begging for planes and pilots and I get mosquito chasers. Who sent him? Let me see his orders," Chennault screamed. When he was told that Captain Fowles was merely sightseeing, he exploded again. Captain Fowles took off from the mess hall and bribed a ride back to Kweilin.[16]

At meetings and conferences and in letters, everyone from the president to the ATC favored increasing the Hump supply, but promises for new planes continued to be broken. ATC had been promised ten transport planes a month for the India-China route, beginning in March 1943. However, shipment of the aircraft was postponed until June, with additional "whittling down" of the proposed schedule.[17]

The slowdown in deliveries of transport aircraft brought sharp diplomatic exchanges. The chargé d'affaires in China, John Carter Vincent, in a telegram to the secretary of state, complained, "It is easier to provide transport planes than to recover Burma and reopen highway [the Burma Road]; and responsibility for piling up of Chinese supplies in India does not lie with China or difficulty in transportation, but failure of the United States to send adequate transport planes."[18]

Actually, the main problem was not a shortage of planes but of trained crews. Col. Edward Alexander, commanding officer of the India-China Wing of ATC, was desperate. He wrote General George, asking him to "dispatch to this wing . . . 308 complete crews to keep your transports in the air. . . . I hate to see aircraft sitting on the ground. . . . An airplane doesn't need to sleep."[19]

Alexander called for more men and more planes. Pilots were then flying over a hundred hours a month—the limit of their endurance. Planes were still on the ground for lack of crews. The monsoon had closed two of the three bases in India, and Chabua was overloaded.[20]

However, there continued to be a growing optimism for the future of the Hump airlift since the ATC had taken over. General Arnold had extreme confidence in the ATC. He wrote in his autobiography, *Global Mission,* "Once it [the ATC] had established its bases around the world, and General George and Gen. C. R. Smith were operating it, I was able to forget about it."[21]

Saying that the ATC had only forty-three battered C-47s was like saying that David had only one stone when he faced Goliath. In the war over the mountains of China and the jungles of Burma, the C-47 was an unusual weapon. The lowly cargo plane, the lumbering, slow, unarmed, unheralded C-47, was more important than guns, or troops on the ground.

The C-47 was the military version of the famed Douglas DC-3 which had already established a record of mountain flying in China. It was called the "Skytrain" and "Skytrooper" by the United States and the "Dakota" by the British. Pilots called the lovable C-47 the "rocking chair of the air," or, with affection, the "Gooney Bird." The C-47 tamed the Sahara, the Atlantic, both poles of the globe, every ocean, and in World War II was crisscrossing the Himalaya.

This transport was first introduced in the summer of 1933 by the Douglas Aircraft Company. Only one DC-1 (Douglas Cargo) was built. Then came the DC-2, and 130 were built. The DC-3 followed. It was a giant of a plane, with a wingspan of ninety-five feet, a length of sixty-four feet, and a height of seventeen feet. It was designed to carry twenty-one passengers at a speed of 220 miles per hour—an unheard of performance.

The DC-3/C-47, powered by two 1,250-horsepower Pratt and Whitney radial engines, featured new ideas: the variable-pitch propeller, wing

Old "Gooney Bird," the famed Douglas C-47, was the first aircraft to cross the Hump. It continued in service as long as crews were crossing the Himalayas. *Courtesy McDonnell Douglas*

flaps, retractable landing gear, and cabin heat. The Douglas DC-3/C-47 was the world's first great working airplane and the greatest aircraft design in the history of flight.[22]

The C-47 was a plane of destiny. No other aircraft in the history of aviation was so revolutionary in its impact on flight. It is an airplane born to fly. To take it into the air is simple—the C-47 takes off on its own. To fly it in the air is not necessary—the C-47 flies by itself. You just tell it where to go and make it behave. To land the C-47 is another thing. You must force it to the ground—it wants to keep flying.

When I first checked out in the C-47, with over 1,200 hours of B-25 experience, I had trouble keeping the Gooney on the ground when landing. Airline pilots prided themselves in the "three-point" landing in which the wheels and tail-wheel touched simultaneously just as the plane stalled for a perfect, smooth landing. My three-point land-ings didn't work, so I decided that I would do a two-wheel, tails-up landing after a long powered approach. It worked. However, old-time C-47 pilots called that an "arrival" rather than a "landing" and shamed us for it.

In the CBI in mid-1942 as Allied pilots and their planes started fly-ing the Himalayan airlift, the C-47 and other DC-3s had already been in China for five years, flying the toughest missions day after day. Un-til January 1943, the C-47 was the only cargo plane to fly the Hump. As larger, faster, and more efficient planes came to the CBI, the C-47 continued its job. When the Hump closed in November 1945, the C-47 was still flying cargo across the Himalaya, a record that no other plane could match. Today, forty-five years after the Hump, the DC-3s and C-47s are still in the air and are still part of the CNAC fleet in China.

The lore surrounding the DC-3 and C-47 is almost mystical, and there is a long series of stories, legends, and old pilots' tales about the Gooney Bird. For example, there was one "DC-2½" in China. In 1941, as the Japanese were advancing, an air raid damaged the wing of a DC-3 on the ground at Suifu in the Chinese interior. The only replace-ment wing was for a DC-2, and it was in Hong Kong. With war being the unwed father of innovation, CNAC decided to try the wing. It was strapped to the underside of a DC-3, flown to Suifu by Chinese pilot Captain Chin Ho, and installed on the damaged DC-3. The hy-brid plane, with one wing five feet shorter than the other, was flown nine hundred miles back to Hong Kong and was known as the DC-2½.[23]

The C-47 carried twenty-eight troops, or a load of 5,500 pounds. But the number of passengers carried by the C-47 is a part of its leg-end. Leo Viens, South Attleboro, Massachusetts, former Hump copilot, describes evacuation flights in the last days of Myitkyina, Burma: "I personally helped load sixty to sixty-five people into our C-47. They were sitting on top of each other. I remember Capt. Ivan W. Eveland applying full power for takeoff and the plane would hardly move. It took so long to gain speed for takeoff, we picked up parts of trees at the end of the runway. How we got over the Naga Hills into the As-sam Valley was a miracle."[24]

One of the most spectacular and dangerous flights over the Hump, in a DC-3 named "Whistling Willie," was made on 11 December 1941 by CNAC pilot Charles Sharp. The plane, on the ground during a Japa-nese air raid, was hit more than five hundred times by bullets. "The

Maintenance at Chabua, in northern India, was a constant struggle to keep the aircraft in the air. Work on the aircraft was often done at night so that all flyable planes could be in the air at daybreak to avoid Japanese daylight bombing raids. *Courtesy Richard "Sahib" Foster*

engines, props, tires, instruments, gas tanks and control lines were ruined. The CNAC maintenance staff made temporary repairs, the most temporary being the use of canvas awning and home-made glue to patch the bullet holes."

Sharp decided to fly the plane to India for repairs. After takeoff, the landing gear refused to retract, and the eight-hundred-mile trip to Kunming was made with the wheels down. At Kunming, the landing gear was repaired and Sharp took off over the Hump to Calcutta. In heavy rain over the mountains, the canvas patches came off and the plane made an unearthly whistling sound. Also, the inadequately repaired exhaust manifolds allowed flame to shoot from the engines.

Over the Hump, a patrol of six Japanese planes approached the crippled DC-3. As the Japanese planes neared, and "as the wild cry of the fire-streaming transport reached them above the throb of the engines, they turned tail and streaked off."[25]

At Lashio, Captain Sharp took on seven new passengers who could not be turned down, plus mail and cargo for India. The passengers chose to continue their trip in the riddled DC-3 rather than stay in the path of the Japanese.

When the plane landed in Calcutta, operations said, "Why did you bother to radio us? We've heard you for the past fifty miles."[26] The final six hundred miles were flown without incident.[27] Following Whistling Willie's crossing, there was no Japanese interference over the Hump for the next three days. Finally a cryptic Tokyo radio broadcast said, "Enemy forces are moving into Northern Burma in force. [There wasn't a handful of soldiers within four hundred miles.] Spearheading their invasion is a new aerial weapon, designed foolishly to unnerve the Emperor's pilots. . . . This secret weapon spouts streams of flame and screeches in horrible tones as it flies. This white man's folly will be driven from the Asiatic heavens."[28]

In spite of the pilots' love for the C-47, and its dependability, the planes were too small and too slow, and a new cargo plane came to the Hump to share the burden of the overworked C-47. This new aircraft was the C-46, the Curtiss "Commando," a twin-engine transport looking somewhat like the C-47 except that it was larger, faster, and had a higher ceiling. The C-46 was designed to carry trucks, tanks, and heavy artillery too large for the C-47. Production problems kept the plane from reaching the CBI until April 1943, when thirty C-46s were flown into Karachi. But there were so many problems that all of the first thirty planes had to be flown back to the States for repairs and modification.

In January 1943, another new transport plane to see service over the Hump was the C-87, a cargo version of the twin-tailed Consolidated B-24. Three C-87s came to India in January, eleven in March, and fourteen in mid-July.

Two engines are better than one and four engines are better than two—that's an aeronautical truth most pilots believe. So the coming of the four-engine aircraft to the Hump was a boost to morale.

The four-engine C-87 was 66 feet 4 inches long, with a wingspan of 110 feet. Its use almost immediately increased the momentum of cargo movement over the Hump. The plane had a ceiling of thirty-six thousand feet and a range of thirty-three hundred miles and moved seven tons of cargo at three hundred miles an hour. It was exactly what the Hump needed. Four engines over the Hump was a safety factor for high-altitude mountain flying. However, few pilots had

Proof that life was primitive near Chabua, in northern India's Assam Valley. This giant python was killed near the crew quarters. *Courtesy Richard "Sahib" Foster*

enough four-engine experience to fly the new planes with confidence. Leaving their friendly Gooney Birds, the pilots faced the C-87 with some apprehension.

Even with the new C-87s and the B-24s of the 308th Bomb Squadron, there still remained a critical shortage of fuel to the Fourteenth and the Chinese Air Force. More planes could not be sent into China because there was no fuel. In February 1943, General Arnold announced the C-109, a new fleet of tanker airplanes — another modification of the B-24 — just to carry gasoline. General Arnold wrote, "We stripped them of everything except the barest operating essentials and, installing extra tanks, loaded them to their maximum capacity with gasoline."[29]

The pilots, with some fear, accepted the C-87s, but there was an immediate dislike for the C-109. The plane was nicknamed the "C-Dash-Crash," the "C-One-O-Boom," or, with greater animosity, the "Flying Coffin." With a cargo of highly volatile 100-octane gasoline —"more precious than gold and more touchy than nitro"—the C-109s were flying bombs. One pilot remarked, "There's always one consolation—we'll never know what hit us."[30]

The C-109s had an accident rate five times higher than other planes. Clarence Linenbach, Sanger, California, former director of operations of ATC at Jorhat, wrote describing one accident: "I remember [the] accident . . . in the traffic pattern returning from China . . . a blown tire on landing . . . wiped out three aircraft . . . all the pilots on the base wished he had wrecked the whole fleet since nobody liked the C-87/C-109 types."[31]

Flying the C-109 tanker empty was even more dangerous than flying with a full load of gasoline, if enemy aircraft were present. Milton W. Ueleke, Cape Girardeau, Missouri, remembers, "Crews carrying gasoline were more fearful on the return flight, after dispatching their cargo, than of riding the Hump into China [with full tanks]. . . . Japanese tracer bullets could ignite vapor in empty tanks, not tanks filled with gas. [Lack of oxygen in the full tanks kept the gasoline from exploding.] Being a Hump pilot was a hazardous business coming and going."[32]

However, the C-87s and C-109s moved supplies at a rate never before attained over the Hump. They could fly above much of the weather, and their B-24 prototype had been in combat long enough to have the mechanical problems eliminated. Inexperienced pilots and the dangerous cargo were the main reasons for the higher accident rate. One problem of the B-24-type aircraft was the Davies wing—a wing so efficient that any amount of ice could cause dangerous changes in its efficiency.

The estimated cost of flying gasoline into China—including losses, crews—ranged as high as $1,000 per gallon.[33] Gasoline was so precious in China that the war sometimes stopped because of the shortage of fuel for the engines of battle. Gasoline was the most difficult cargo to protect in China. There was always a constant loss, and guards could not stop it.

Although critical for military aircraft, gasoline was almost nonexistent for civilian use in China. Native ingenuity was necessary to keep the civilian trucks moving. Most motor vehicles burned charcoal gas, and it often required as many as four men to keep a charcoal-burning truck in operation. Roman Swiezy, Jensen Beach, Florida, told of a two-day trip he made by charcoal truck.

The first man was the driver. Another man would stoke the charcoal burner to keep the fire burning. The truck had a large tank, like a hot-water heater where charcoal was burned, and the gasses from

Battle-weary B-24 of the 14th Air Force. Flight crews, with their own aircraft, often painted names of their wives or girlfriends on the nose of their planes. Pilot Gene Leslie, 308th Bomb Squadron, showed confidence when he painted "Mary Jo Leslie" under his window. They were married after the war. *Courtesy Gene Leslie*

the charcoal went into the carburetor through a hose. But, there were problems. When they came to a hill, the truck refused to go over. As the truck stopped and began to roll backward, the third man jumped out and put chocks under the wheels. Looking suspiciously around, the driver turned a small valve from a gallon can to another small hose into the carburetor. The truck took off—it was a can of alcohol. They crossed the hills in this manner.

The next morning was dreary and wet. The mechanic, the fourth man, wrapped the ignition wires around the stove, quickly plugged them into the coil and tried to start the engine. No start. He jerked all the wires out and warmed them again. After three attempts, and a conference, the driver took out keys and opened a compartment and brought out a squirt can. He looked both ways and put a squirt in the carburetor. The engine roared to life. Swiezy asked what the stuff was. He whispered, "gasoline."

They completed the trip in good humor and with more knowledge and appreciation of the gasoline shortage in China.[34]

It is impossible to overestimate the value of the China National Aviation Corporation (CNAC) in pioneering and developing Hump routes from India to China and in its conscientious cooperation in helping the army learn to fly the dangerous territory. The army was constantly trying to take over the operations of this civilian carrier. Stanley K. Hornbeck, an advisor on political relations in China, wrote to the secretary of state in 1943 concerning a dispute when the army tried to take over CNAC: "CNAC pioneered . . . the practicality of flying freight between Assam and China . . . the U.S. Army has tried hard to absorb CNAC [and] finding itself unable to . . . is seeking to starve CNAC out of existence. . . .

"Man for man and plane for plane, . . . CNAC will continuously equal or top the best work of the Army (which is improving) in carrying freight between Assam and China. . . . it is good for the Army to have competition."[35]

After ATC had been flying the Hump for just a few months, operations officers discovered that their most threatening problem was weather. In summer, the Hump routes were plagued by the hot Indian monsoon winds, which lifted moisture over the mountain range and created turbulence, unprecedented rain, thunderstorms, hail, zero visibility, and icing. Mount Everest's famous "plume" is caused by hurricane-like winds blowing snow from the top of the 29,029-foot peak. At flight altitude, pilots often ran into 100-MPH winds.

The summer monsoons—evil winds that brought heavy rains— were a phenomenon that American airmen had never experienced. The Indians say that the monsoon "bursts." Moist winds pouring in from the Bay of Bengal bring more than seventy-five inches of rain each month from June to October. In Assam, from 425 to 500 inches of rain fell annually, with over 100 inches each month during June, July, and August. Throughout every day in the summer it rained— hard, driving rains that were hard to believe. The rains came quickly and stopped just as quickly—but they always came, and flight operations were curtailed. During the heavy monsoon rains, air bases in Assam were closed, with runways, taxiways, and parking hardstands under water.

Danniel S. Dennis, pilot from Roosevelt, Utah, described monsoon flying at Lal-Hat: "The monsoon created its share of challenges. For two to three months at Lal-Hat it never stopped raining, day or night, and the ceiling was fifty to one hundred feet much of the time. We used to fly a regular let-down pattern coming over the radio at four hundred feet, descending and hoping to break out in time to make a landing. If we missed the runway, we would fly a box pattern at one hundred feet, going out ninety degrees for thirty seconds, turn parallel for one minute, another ninety degrees for thirty seconds and turn onto final approach. This usually worked out all right if you didn't get too low and clip the trees on the turn. One plane with passengers did clip the trees and we lost them all."[36]

In the spring of 1943, Colonel Alexander wrote his headquarters, in a bitter understatement, "The weather has been pretty awful. The icing level starts at 12,000 feet. Today a C-87 went to 29,500 feet on instruments . . . and could not get on top of the overcast. It has rained about seven and a half inches in the past five days. All aircraft are grounded."[37]

The world's most violent weather comes into Asia because it is the meeting place of three turbulent air masses: low pressure from the west moves along the main range of the Himalaya between Tibet and India to the Hump, where warm, wet high pressure systems from the Bay of Bengal clash with frigid low pressure from Siberia. The polar vortex, and the heat rising from the jungles of Burma, intensify the weather movement.[38]

Winter brought the best weather, except for the absence of ground fog, which was always a smooth flight experience. From November to March were the best flying conditions in India and Burma, but in China there were freezing rain and typical winter conditions. In late January, one cold front after another brought snow to the mountains and ice to the clouds. Winter would give way to the thunderstorms of early spring and the start of another cycle of bad weather. The drama of the Hump was weather—a battle of men and their planes against wind, shattering turbulence, ice, and below-zero temperatures.

In 1944 Gen. William Tunner came to India to try to reduce the terrible losses of the Hump. As he personally flew the Hump, he experienced weather changes from minute to minute and mile to mile, from "the low steamy jungles of India; to the mile-high plateau of western China . . . a law unto itself . . . thunderstorms building out of nowhere . . . icing . . . turbulence greater than I have ever seen elsewhere in the world . . . winds of as much as one hundred miles an hour, piling onto the steep barren slopes, would glance off to create updrafts over the ridges and down drafts over the valleys . . . planes could drop at the rate of five thousand feet a minute, then suddenly be whisked upward, at the same speed."[39]

In the personal history of the Hump—pilot reports, letters written home—and in magazine and newspaper articles, crewmen wrote more on weather than on any other Hump experience.

Pilot report: "From India, we took off in pea-soup fog . . . monsoon rain was flooding down the windshield in torrents. At 12,000 feet the rain turned to snow. We couldn't see our wing tips. . . . Our Douglas C-47 kept climbing with her heavy load . . . I could see a thin layer of ice spreading over the windshield . . . that thin film grew into a layer six inches thick. We started to drop slowly . . . we lost the last slit of visibility . . . the windows were frozen over solid from the inside." The plane brushed along the side of a mountain, trees softening the crash. The crew miraculously suffered only one broken and one sprained ankle, walked for sixteen days through snow, were helped by Naga headhunters, and survived to fly again.[40]

Pilot report: "Flying a C-47 from Myitkyina to Kunming, at daybreak, we entered a solid cold front at 16,000 feet. Suddenly the entire plane began to vibrate . . . ice had built up on our props and we were unable to break it loose . . . I ordered the crew to prepare for bail out and I would remain and try to get rid of the ice . . . the crew elected to remain with the plane . . . we broke out of the overcast . . . we had dropped into a river valley surrounded by mountain peaks piercing the very bottom of the overcast . . . we were below 11,000 feet . . . suddenly it sounded as if the engines were coming apart. . . . We had entered the warm air and the clubbing props were letting loose large chunks of ice . . . ice began erupting from the wings in large sheets . . . we were still flying, just skimming the treetops at 9,800 feet.

"We remained in the valley for some time . . . and climbed to our originally assigned altitude . . . at Kunming the aircraft was grounded, as the entire fuselage in line with both props was literally demolished . . . our cargo had been explosives . . . another normal day."[41]

Pilot report: "Lt. Gilbert and my plane landed at Kunming, along with Lt. Hunter's plane . . . we unloaded gas . . . weather was bad for the return flight . . . Gilbert and Hunter pleaded with operations for a night's stay . . . [operations said] we had to leave. Three hours out, we were in heavy weather, ahead boomed thunderheads, up to 40–50,000 feet. Lt. Hunter was in sight until dark . . . we hit that thunderhead head on . . . God!, that was rough! There was lightning you wouldn't believe . . . I kept my eyes glued to the fuel tank gauges . . . we were running on the red line . . . we couldn't make it home, so we better try Chabua. We heard Lt. Hunter calling for a bearing. He had engine trouble and was low on fuel. His radio pleaded for a fix. . . . transmission was terrible. Lt. Hunter called that his port engine had quit. . . . Silence . . . then came the call we knew would come . . . 'We have had it, we are going in.' . . . complete silence from our crew. We landed in Chabua, gassed and went home to Misamari. Then came the shakes and tears of 'grown men crying.' We had lost another to the Hump . . . we blamed Kunming for refusing us to stay, but the field was loaded with aircraft—sitting ducks."[42]

ATC, with 146 planes, moved fifteen tons per plane to China, while CNAC moved thirty-seven tons per plane during the same month of June.[43] Neither the pilots nor ATC operations personnel had learned to handle overloads.[44] Many pilots, prior to their coming to the Hump, reported no experience with actual weather flying, and their training included little instrument instruction.

The accident rate on the Hump was high. From June to December, there were 155 accidents with 168 crew members killed. General Tunner stated, "It was safer to take a bomber deep into Germany than to fly a transport plane over the Rockpile from one friendly nation to another. Complaints and protests from wives, parents and relatives of men lost on the Hump began pouring in to the President and to Congress."[45]

Brig. Gen. Cyrus R. Smith, in a letter to General George, described the problem of inexperienced pilots and shortages of crews and planes: "We are paying for it in men and airplanes. The kids here are flying over their heads. . . . we are asking boys to do what would be most difficult for men . . . we are going to pay dearly for the tonnage moved across the Hump. . . . With the men available, there is nothing else to do."[46]

Pilots had an in-house joke about "babies flying the Hump and old men sitting around operations doing nothing."[47] With the main Allied offensive in Europe, the CBI was sent the least experienced pilots and crewmen. Of course, crews in all parts of the war, throughout the world, were young and inexperienced. In World War II, everyone was young. There were not enough experienced crews available.

On 18 July 1943, in an effort to improve the experience level of the Hump pilots, a special mission called Project 7-A was put into operation. Requested by President Roosevelt and General Arnold as a part of America's Military Mission to China (AMMISCA), Project 7-A was a group of experienced American Airlines personnel assigned, as an emergency, to a special mission to India to work with young crews over the Hump. This would be the greatest war-time assignment in the history of American Airlines.[48] Crews were told only that they would have to live in tents and would be carrying passengers in India and China. Flying from Morrison Field, Florida, they knew their actual destination only after they had landed in Natal, Brazil.[49]

Ten C-87s were diverted from a South Atlantic operation, with 180 crew members, supplies, and spare parts to operate in the CBI for ninety days. This was a "voluntary" mission since the airline personnel were under no obligation to continue the flight after they learned of their assignment. According to Tom Barnard, San Clemente, California, a member of the 7-A mission, "The crews were told . . . that a 10 percent loss was expected. Those who chose to withdraw could continue with their previous assignments with no prejudice. No one withdrew."[50]

Pilot Ted Lewis, Laguna Hills, California, in a report written on 20 November 1943, summarized the work of 7-A:

> On 1 August, the first Project 7-A plane landed in Tezpur, in Northern India, and, on 2 August, the same plane, with Captain "Toby" Hunt, made the first Hump trip for 7-A. There was no training, no indoctrination, no briefing. As other planes arrived, they were put into service just as quickly. Even though the American Airlines pilots had thousands of hours of flying time, mountain flying under extreme weather conditions was a new experience to which they quickly adapted.
>
> When the planes arrived at Tezpur, the field was nearly flooded with monsoon rains. The crews were tired, rain-soaked and some suffered from dysentery. . . .
>
> Getting from the camp to the latrine . . . had to be well timed and made fast. For civilian pilots, accustomed to first class living conditions on the airline runs, Tezpur was a shock. Barracks had been occupied by goats and cows. The heat and the rain, combined, were hard to take. Everything was mildewed. Food spoiled while you watched it, and ants did everything but open the canned goods. Men slept naked under mosquito netting, waking up as tired as when they went to sleep. Call the crews at 5 a.m. . . . to a truck . . . it's raining . . . it's dark . . . it's hot . . . through mud to breakfast, then to the airport where the mechanics are getting the engines warmed up.

Lewis described his first flight:

> The plane manifest shows a load of 1,000 gallons of aviation gasoline, six 500-pound bombs, several cases of fuses—takeoff at the maximum gross weight of 65,000 pounds—a big bomb.
>
> In the early months we carried nearly 1,000,000 pounds of gasoline and bombs for Chennault's gang to use on the Japs. That was a large part of the total delivered. In the latter months, the army

(ATC) got geared up and, while we carried 1,500,000 pounds a month, our efforts did not represent such a big part of the whole.

A war is not fought with planes and guns, alone. We saw that our personnel were suffering from lack of eggs, green vegetables and fruits. Arrangements were made to buy these in China and bring them to Tezpur. This improved the meals, as did an arrival of baking soda and peanut butter.

On their regular days off [the 7-A crews] flew as Captains, on army-crewed planes to give the young pilots the benefit of their experience — how to handle engines — how to take off and climb with heavy loads — how to fly instruments and get to the destination. As a side issue, they sold a little confidence to each man and bought a lot of friendship.

Our mechanics did the same thing on the ground and the army feels that our stay in Assam lifted the experience level of the men to a point that the real value of Project 7-A was the example set — more than 5,000,000 pounds delivered on 1,075 Hump crossings.[51]

Five crewmen of the 7-A project were killed in the CBI in line of duty on their flights. On 23 August, three weeks after 7-A began operations, Capt. Harry Charleton and his crew of five crashed on takeoff from Tezpun — an engine had failed. First officer Robert H. Dietz, flight engineer Joseph Smith, navigator John Keating, and radio operator Robert E. Davis died with Captain Charleton. The reality of war had come quickly to the civilian pilots. Since the American Airlines crews were civilians, there were no military citations for their work.

As other pilots had done, Capt. John Jones flew for a month before he saw the mountains he was flying over. "When I did get a good look at those mountains, they didn't look like any featherbed to pilots flying a load of gasoline and bombs." The airline pilots, accustomed to flying radio beams, had to learn to fly instruments because the radio beams would hit the mountains and glance back.[52]

On one flight, Capt. "Toby" Hunt, the pilot who had made the first trip over the Hump for Project 7-A, and his crew were at twenty thousand feet with so much ice that the plane was not able to hold altitude. To bail out was death, to be taken captive by the Japanese or a long walk out of the jungles. So, without oxygen, crew members opened the cargo door and rolled out fourteen drums of gasoline to lighten the plane so that Hunt could get back to Tezpur.

Tragedy struck again near the end of Project 7-A. On what would have been his sixty-sixth crossing, Captain Hunt was to make a 7-A record for the greatest number of Hump flights. His load was small-arms ammunition that could not be jettisoned. Over China, one engine failed and another was not putting out full power. Pilot Hunt ordered his crew to bail out and he would try to make an airport. Two attempts to land in Kunming failed. He died in the crash—his sixty-sixth crossing never completed. His crew came home with one broken leg, two sprained ankles, and a lot of bruises. The Chinese carried Hunt's body out of the mountains in a huge hand-hewn coffin that required ten people to carry. He was flown to India and buried in the shadow of a small Buddhist temple near the burial place of Captain Charleton, his crew, and many of Chennault's Flying Tigers.[53]

Project 7-A made a difference. The 7-A crews taught the young crewmen of the ATC how to fly as professionals. They also moved a lot of cargo at a time when it was critically needed. They struggled and died like any of the other flight crews, whether they were civilians or in the army. In four months, 1,075 crossings were made—six round trips a day. Almost five million pounds of cargo were carried into China, mostly bombs, ammunition, and gasoline, and hundreds of Chinese were brought back to India for training.[54]

The last group of the American Airlines crewmen left India on 1 December. Captain Jones's summation was, "There's one thing all of us agreed on—the U.S. Army Air Transport Command, for whom we were flying, was a remarkable group of men, whether they were stationed in South America, Africa or India."[55]

4

Working Out the Problems —
July–December 1943

Flying weather on instruments continued to be the most threatening ordeal for Hump pilots. Piloting a plane through the angry limbo of clouds was strange and frightening — flying twenty-five tons of metal, gasoline, high explosives, and humanity at 250 miles per hour through an unknown sky. "Flying instruments" sounded simple — so precise and scientific. In actual flight, instrument flying in bad weather was the most stressful and agonizing part of a mission.

Weather was a blessing in the early months of Hump flight because the unarmed cargo planes could hide in the clouds from the Japanese fighters. Later, when the Zeros were gone, weather became the Hump's great challenge. Pilot Phil Sunderman, Pittsburgh, Pennsylvania: "I completed my time in the CBI with 706 hours and 5 minutes flying time . . . 75 percent of that was instruments, or night, or both."[1]

On many flights, within seconds after a heavy, sluggish takeoff in India, the plane disappeared into a world of visual nothingness. Climbing, flying, navigating, fighting turbulence, winds, and ice — all completely by instruments — with no reference to the ground. Long hours later, at the end of the flight, a tiny pointer on the instrument panel spins from zero to 180 degrees and tells the pilot, if he is lucky, that he has crossed the beacon. His landing field is somewhere below. Nosing down through the clouds to the landing approach; down, down, down, the plane suddenly breaks into the clear and the pilot sees the runway in China less than a minute before touch down.

As one pilot said, "It's enough to purge the sphincter of the Sphinx."

Flying by instruments in bad weather means that a pilot puts his complete trust in his instruments and ignores his senses. All pilots, when on instruments, experience vertigo from time to time. This is when their mind, their sensations, and every cell in their body tells them the aircraft is in a crazy turn, climbing, or in a dive. The instruments say "no." Pilots trust their instruments or they die.

As student pilots, we learned to fly, but we never really left the ground in spirit. We learned to keep the plane level with the horizon. We flew from here to there by looking for landmarks. Even in the air, we were still creatures of earth. Later, we learned to fly blind by following and putting our faith in simple instruments. The instructor repeated constantly, "Needle, ball and airspeed"—flight instruments responding to gravity, pressure, and centrifugal force, the basic energies of the earth. The needle tells us if we are flying straight or making a turn. The ball says, "You are making a good turn"—obeying the laws of centrifugal force. The airspeed tells us if we are flying level—going down, speed increases; going up, speed decreases. We call it flying blind.

In the air, on instruments or in the clear, I know that I am not flying the aircraft—I *am* the aircraft. The controls, the instruments, the engines, the crew, are as much a part of my being as my eyes, heart, and bowels. I am the servomechanism of my plane as we feel our way through the clouds at incredible speed.

In training, we were safe. Our flight instructor was always there. If we got into trouble, he took over and kept us from smashing one of Uncle Sam's training planes. Yet it was rare in flight school to get actual experience in real weather. We flew when the weather was good and stayed on the ground when it was bad. Many pilots came to the Hump with no actual instrument time. But in the CBI, over the Hump, we flew when the birds were walking.

Making a blind approach to a landing field was a completely new extension of instrument flying. In 1943–44, the instrument approach and letdown system was just being installed in the CBI and only a few pilots were trained to use it. The procedure was simple in theory and agonizing in practice. When the pilot arrived over the field, on instruments, other planes were also coming in to land. Planes were then "stacked." Pilots were ordered to fly at certain altitudes, usually five hundred feet apart, in a figure-eight pattern over the "cone of silence," a point directly over the radio tower where no signal is received. The "cone" is an accurate position indicator. As pilots on the bottom of the stack landed, all other aircraft were allowed to descend another

The Hump needed the speed, dependability, and freight load of the four-engined aircraft. This is the Convair B-24 bomber. The C-87 freight model and the C-109 tanker were reluctantly welcomed over the Himalayas. Pilots lacked the skill to fly them and were afraid of them, but they soon became workhorses of the Hump. *Courtesy U.S. Air Force*

five hundred feet. By holding, pilots could land, one at a time, to prevent a midair collision. But sometimes the system didn't work.

Edison B. Vail, Jr., Halliford, Virginia, tells of his memorable experience. After taking off and heading north for about two hours on top at nineteen thousand feet, Vail tuned the automatic direction finder (ADF) to the beacon and homed on in. He remembered seeing mountain peaks coming up through the clouds—peaks above nineteen thousand feet. The tower gave instructions to let down at five hundred feet a minute, north and south, over the beacon. A thousand feet down, another ship asked for let-down instructions. Their instructions were the same. That seemed odd, but they continued to let down through the overcast.

In his own words,

> About that time all hell broke loose. Another pilot below us was calling . . . the controller told him to let down at 500 feet per minute. . . . every airplane in the area was letting down over that beacon. 'My god, they're going to let down on top of us, and we're going to let down on top of somebody.' We were totally on instruments—the tension began to build . . .
>
> All of a sudden I remembered that we had seen those peaks sticking up through the clouds at 19,000 feet. Then it became a matter of real concern. We were still on instruments . . . we continued to let down. We broke out 300 or 400 feet above the ground. It was raining . . . the visibility was poor. . . . we didn't know where we were . . . called the tower . . . saw the lights of the field. . . . called for landing instructions. The tower advised that the field was closed.
>
> I'll never forget my dismay, consternation, anger, tension, excitement, or whatever . . . I asked the guy, 'Just what in the hell do you think we are going to do?'
>
> He came back, cool and calm and said another field within a few miles was taking traffic and gave us a heading. We took up that heading. . . .
>
> We were in and out of the clouds, not daring to get lower because we didn't know if we would hit a hill or mountain. We saw the lights of the field, but immediately lost sight of it in the clouds, and we were back on instruments again.
>
> We made a timed turn . . . dropped down just a bit more and came in lined up perfectly with the runway. The lights were on. You have never seen a more beautiful sight—that white line down a black macadam strip stretching for two miles greeted us.
>
> We put the flaps down and flew right into the runway and let her roll, and roll and roll, down the 10,000-foot runway. It was raining just as hard as you can imagine . . . we parked and a truck took us to operations. Another officer pilot called, 'Hey, lieutenant, were you in No. ____?' (I forgot the number of the plane) 'Yes, why?' He said, 'I sure am glad you knew where you were going, because I was sitting right on your tail all the way down.' I said, 'Fellow, you just don't know. That was the blind leading the blind.'

Vail learned later that there were about thirty airplanes letting down that night on that field.[2]

After pilots worked their way down the holding stack they would follow the "localizer and glide path," the new landing system that allowed aircraft to land in almost zero conditions. A pilot making a blind

Death-head B-25 medium bomber from the 409th Bridge Buster Squadron, stationed at Warazup, Burma. *Courtesy Jack Corns*

approach would fly to a beacon several miles off the end of the landing runway, to establish an exact position. On the aircraft instrument panel was an indicator for the blind landing system, a small dial with vertical and horizontal pointers or "cross hairs." The vertical pointer was the "localizer," to align the aircraft with the runway, and the horizontal pointer was the "glide path," to establish the correct landing angle onto the runway.

On the field, a transmitter at the far end of the landing runway was sending out two radio beams. One beam, the localizer, was projected down the center of the runway out toward the aircraft approaching in the clouds. The other signal, the glide path, gently curved upward from the runway into the sky. Pilots could, with the cockpit instrument, visually "lock on" to these two signals several miles out from the field and fly the aircraft to the runway.

By keeping the glide path indicator perfectly horizontal—on zero —the pilot knew that he was in a proper glide and was being led down to the runway. He had to constantly adjust speed and rate of descent to keep the instrument centered. Meanwhile, "needle, ball and airspeed." It was like juggling three balls with a carton of eggs balanced on your nose. But it worked and saved many lives.

With skill, pilots could actually "fly onto the runway" for a successful blind landing, although the aircraft usually "broke out" fifty to a hundred feet above the field. The pilot never had to worry about seeing the field—the tense crew would always let out a cheer and scream in the pilot's ear. "There's the field."[3]

ATC pilot Wallace Mieras, Moxee City, Washington, credits the work of his friend M. K. "Dutch" Osterhout with saving his life on a storming night in Assam. In the middle of the monsoon season, Mieras was coming back from China empty. The right engine blew a cylinder, and for the next two hours he limped home to Chabua. Chabua radio advised that a rainstorm had dropped ceiling and visibility to zero. On a single engine there would be only one chance to land, and bailing out was almost sure death.

Dutch Osterhout was operations officer at Chabua and was in contact with Mieras. He asked if he was flying one of the new ships with a "cross-haired gizmo" in front of the pilot. Mieras quickly answered "yes." The cross-haired gizmo was a localizer and glide path. But the trouble was that the ground transmitter had not been installed, no pilots had training or practice on the new system, and security prevented Osterhout from telling Mieras how to use it on the radio. However, Osterhout offered to haul the transmitter on the back of his jeep to the end of the runway if Miereas wanted to try it.

Mieras continues, "Dutch was sticking his neck out but I told him to get out there. When I was letting down he ordered me to turn on my landing lights and call out my altitude continually because when I broke out of the storm I would be aiming right at him and he was going to leave at the last instant, fast!

"He did, and the landing I made was not one of my best by far, but landing in a foot of water is not easy. That's how I learned to use the instrument landing system and found out what a true friend Dutch Osterhout was."[4]

In learning to fly the Hump, pilots looked to the more experienced crews for survival techniques. Pilots of CNAC had a special "secret" let-down technique, although it was not recommended by ATC operations. When the field was not crowded with traffic, the pilot would come in over the beacon, put the radio compass needle to 270 degrees (off the left wingtip) and spiral down in a tight, counter-clockwise circle. When he broke out of the clouds, the field was directly below, he hoped. If not, he lost his "hat, ass and spats"—a favorite expression for Hump pilots.

In emergencies, the Hump crews often put themselves in danger to help aircraft in trouble. Lt. Don Downie, pilot from Hesperia, California, tells how he and his crew were coming in over Kunming, just skimming the top of a heavy storm, with a load of artillery shells. Downie called the tower for let-down instructions.

The tower came back: "Are you on top?" Downie: "Affirmative, just barely." Tower: "Remain on top. We have two P-51s lost (Fourteenth Air Force fighters), on top and just about out of gas. We'll have them meet you over Kunming marker. You are cleared #1 all the way down. Maintain over 160-MPH so you don't stall the fighters. Fire a red flare."

The fighters saw the flare and locked onto Downie's wing. Winds at that altitude were above one hundred miles per hour and the fighters did not have enough instruments to make a safe letdown. However, the fighter pilots were famous for flying tight formation.

Downie continues: "The letdown was rough with changing wind-drift corrections, icing, turbulence and, finally, heavy rain. When we were down to 7000 feet and the ground was 6000 feet and we were still on instruments, I had a fleeting thought, 'If I've goofed this letdown, there's going to be the damndest explosion in about twenty seconds.' Then we saw the Kunming runway through the fog. The fighters rolled belly up and headed for their strip at Chengkung. After we landed, the C.O. of the fighter squadron called to say that his boys had made it in OK on fumes."[5]

During long flights across the Hump, pilots often tuned to Tokyo Rose on the liaison radio. Edgar D. Crumpacker, Hump weather pilot from Kailua, Kona, Hawaii, remembers, "It was uncanny. . . . She gave the individual names of our crews and what our current missions were. It makes you nervous."[6]

Pilot Len Reinig, Great Falls, Montana, heard his promotion announced by Tokyo Rose before he received official orders. Crews in flight in all parts of India and China heard the sexy voice of Tokyo Rose, in perfect English, threaten that all captured Hump crewmen would be shot.[7]

Journalists looking for a story were frequent visitors to the Hump. Those who did their job right were usually in the thick of combat and often flew with the Hump crews rather than interviewing them on the gound. On 2 August 1943, CBS correspondent Eric Sevareid was a passenger on a flight to China in one of the new C-46s—the Curtiss Commando. Over northern Burma, the C-46 lost an engine. The crew and passengers, twenty in all, were forced to bail out over the jungles of the Patkai range, home of the Naga head-hunting tribesmen. The Naga were sometimes friendly and sometimes savage.

Within an hour after the twenty parachutes had settled over the jungles, the downed airmen were surrounded by half-naked natives with spears and big-blade knives. Sevareid wrote of his experience, "Some instinct, born no doubt of the wild west novels of childhood, prompted me to step forward, raise my palm and say, 'How!' However comical, it seemed to be taken as a gesture of friendship. They [the natives] stuck their spears into the ground . . . and slipped the big blades into a sheath and came up chattering, their mongoloid faces breaking into smiles."[8]

As Sevareid and the crews were making peace on the ground, planes of a search-and-rescue squadron found the men and dropped supplies and a radio transmitter. A short time later, out of the storm clouds, another plane dropped three medics who landed within yards of the downed crewmen. A slim man of thirty-five extended his hand. "I'm Don Flickinger, the wing surgeon. Saw you needed a little help."[9] This was Lt. Col. Don Flickinger and his parachuting medics. Some of the airmen had serious injuries and needed medical attention.

Eleven days later, Sevareid wrote, "Out of the mist of the jungle, a tall young man, wearing a halo of shining fair hair . . . a soft blue polo shirt . . . blue shorts . . . led the group to safety. He was Philip Adams, the Sahib of Mokokchung, king of these dark and savage hills."[10]

Adams, looking like Leslie Howard with his peppermints, chess set, and jug of rum, had walked eighty-five miles in five days because he heard from a runner that the Naga natives were planning an attack on the downed airmen. Sevareid and the crew were saved.[11]

Dropping the medics was one of the first rescue attempts of "Blackie's Gang," a specialized search-and-rescue squadron operating out of Chabua in the upper Assam Valley. Capt. John L. "Blackie" Porter led rescue teams over the jungle. Search-and-rescue was new to the Hump and was an important morale builder—the jungles didn't seem quite so forbidding if there was a chance that crews could be found if they went down. With two C-47s and a B-25, the team responded to accidents and crew bailouts. Captain Porter was killed in December 1943 when his B-25 and another plane were lost to enemy action.[12]

By then Captain Porter had become a legend of the Hump. He was what was often called a "hotshot," a pilot so skilled and daring that it seemed he would take unnecessary risks in the air. The "risks" Blackie Porter took showed his dedication to the job of rescuing Hump crews who held a losing hand on one of their missions.

On one mission, Blackie and his crew were credited with destroying a Japanese Zero, from a C-47, using only handguns. While on a mission, the crew saw a Zero downed in a meadow, with the pilot making repairs. Flying the C-47 like a fighter, Blackie circled and pulled up, the crew firing from the open doors of the plane. Blackie was also firing from the open pilot's window while flying the plane. After seven passes, the Japanese plane was riddled and the pilot killed. Porter and his gang painted a Japanese flag on the nose of their C-47. It was a cruel and dirty war.

On 10 December, it was Blackie Porter who held the short hand. Flying a B-25, with Lt. James Spain, Bayfield, Ohio, as copilot, the crew spotted three fighter planes. Thinking they were Allied fighters he had called to support the bombers, Captain Porter flew on. The planes were Japanese Zeros. They pounced on him and his plane was riddled. His copilot, following a bail-out order, got stuck in the escape hatch over the pilots' cockpit. Blackie stood up and pushed the copilot through the hatch. Lt. Spain was the lone survivor.

Small notices on operations bulletin boards often notified crews of tragedy over the Hump. The memo about Capt. Blackie Porter read,

> 10 December 1943, B-25 #0362, Chabua, Dead: 5 crew; Pilot Capt. John L. "Blackie" Porter; Copilot 2nd Lt. James F. Spain (lone survivor); Radio Operator S/Sgt. Walter R. Oswalt; Aerial Engineer Sgt. Harold Neibler; Gunner S/Sgt. Harry D. Tucker; Passenger Major Ralph L. Dewsnup.
>
> This aircraft was on a rescue mission, when it was attacked by Zeros. The right engine caught fire. They feathered the prop, and as they did that a Zero pulled up from 7 o'clock and shot out the left engine, setting the ship afire. No one except the copilot had his parachute fastened. Capt. Porter immediately gave the order to bail out. Lt. Spain's clothes got hung while trying to go out the top hatch and was freed by Capt. Porter. As he pulled his ripcord the plane crashed and exploded and burned on the side of the hill. No other crew member survived.[13]

Blackie's death brought a pall over the Hump as pilots realized they had lost a dedicated friend. Nevertheless, the search-and-rescue missions continued and the crews demonstrated to the end of the war the extreme dedication of Blackie Porter.[14]

In Burma there were many primitive tribes living in the mountains, some friendly and others not friendly. Some practiced head-hunting. Despite their reputation, the "headhunters" usually were helpful to downed crews. Pygmy headhunters who lived across the Naga Hills from Chabua returned several crews safely to Ledo. The most helpful tribe in the Burmese jungles was the Katchins, many of whom fought with the Chinese. Capt. James Fletcher, commander of a company of Katchin troops, rescued more than 140 downed fliers and located many crash sites. "The jungle was so thick you had to cut your way through; the Katchins were the only ones who knew where they were going in those mountains," Captain Fletcher said.[15]

In the Indian hills near the Assam valley lived the Abors, the Mishmis, and the Nagas. The Abors were stocky, clean, and usually pleasant. The Mishmis were dirty and unpleasant, although they were not dangerous. The Nagas were thought to be headhunters, but there was no known case of this custom being carried out against the Americans.[16]

Aboriginal tribes lived in the mountains of northwestern China. Among these were the fierce Ngoloks, the Lolos, and many others that were unknown. Terrifying stories about the savagery of the Ngoloks, Mongolian-Chinese nomads, circulated among the Hump crews. The Lolos were dirty and smelly, but kind, and returned many downed crews to Allied bases with no reward or recognition. The crews were always in good condition and well cared for. The chances of walking to safety without the help of a native tribe were poor, although some few crews did walk out on their own.

Briefing officers never told a cheerful story when they talked about rescue—crews were often made more apprehensive about the territory they were flying over. Three groups, in addition to local natives, were looking for downed crews: Chinese Nationals, the Japanese, and Chinese Communists. Crews found by the Nationals would be returned to one of the Allied bases within two weeks. Airmen captured by the Japanese would be taken prisoners and, according to rumor, they might be killed. The Chinese Communists would take the crews to one of the northern bases where they would be held for reward. The prisoners would not be harmed by the Communists, but their treatment would not be good. Negotiations for their release would take about one year, and the ransom was one hundred thousand dollars.[17]

Rescue of crewmen who bailed out or crashed over the mountains was never certain. The army had agreements with many of the native tribes in Burma and China to rescue downed flyers. A standard fee to the Chinese guerrillas was CN 40,000 (Chinese currency). Guerrillas picked up many Americans inside the Japanese lines, often taking weeks to carry them out. When the army was notified, a plane would be sent to pick up the rescued fliers. At Ledo in upper Assam, a reward of one hundred silver rupees was paid to natives for each American flyer brought in. Many air crewmen lived for days and weeks before they were found—and many were never found.[18]

There were stories of pilots who walked out of the jungles with the help of some highly secret intelligence and sabotage units operating behind the Japanese lines. Lt. Gene Jenkins, from Texas, was shot out of his P-40 late one afternoon. He bailed out. His wingmen reported his position and flew cover until dark. After walking for three days, Jenkins found a unit of Merrill's Marauders. A Chinese OSS agent, Harry "Skittles" Henshoon, walked with him for two weeks until they came to a small landing strip where Jenkins was taken out of the jungle by a small observation plane.[19] The OSS was the Office of Strategic Services, a wartime overseas equivalent of the Central Intelligence Agency. OSS agents worked behind the lines to protect Allied troops.

Flying the hazardous route from Dinjan to Kunming was classed as combat flying because of the jungle, bad weather, heavy loads, and poor maintenance. If crews went down an hour away from their base and were able, it would take a month to walk out.

Pilot Glen Norell, flying a C-46, bailed out northeast of Chabua; three days later, hot and dirty, he walked into the Chabua base. Three weeks later, radio officer Neal Dreyfuss and Pvt. Elmer Vance appeared at Shingbwiyang. The number of crewmen who were able to walk out after going down over the Hump kept the morale of other crew members at a bearable level.[20]

Although rescue was not its primary mission, Detachment 101 of the OSS probably found more downed fliers than any other unit. Detachment 101 conducted a super-secret espionage and guerrilla campaign in the jungles, and agents were able to see many planes go down. In exchange for planes and parachutes, 101 offered its services in finding and returning downed crews. Operating with over ten thousand Katchin guerrillas, 101 had a network of agents and contacts among the hill people. Units of Detachment 101 rescued more than 125 airmen, and, at one time, had so many rescued crews at their Fort Hertz detachment that extra supplies and medical help had to be flown in. Detachment 101 also offered a course in jungle survival for Hump crews.[21] Lt. Col. W. Ray Peers commanded Detachment 101 from 17 December 1943 until 12 July 1945.[22]

Douglas Cunningham from Stuart, Florida, a CNAC pilot, was picked up by the Chinese when his plane crashed in 1943. He and his copilot climbed out of the twisted wreckage and started toward Kunming. In his report, he wrote, "During the walkout, we were given food by the Chinese. At one meal it was some kind of meat which I found very tasty. 'What was the meat?' I asked my host. 'Did you like it?' he asked, 'It was monkey.'"[23]

Small, seemingly insignificant things associated with the Hump experience often left lasting impressions. After the long flight over the Atlantic, across Africa, and into India, my crew and I faced the new world of flight over the jungles and mountains with fear and foreboding. We were issued impressive battle and flight gear, which didn't promise friendly skies ahead. Each crew member was given a huge black Colt 45 pistol in a shoulder holster, a trench knife, and a soft leather A-2 jacket. Inside the jacket, sewn to the lining, was a beautiful large leather banner—red, white, and blue—with American and Chinese flags and Chinese characters that were supposed to identify us as Americans. We called it a "chit" and it became a famous symbol of the CBI. If we went down over the Hump and were found, the Chinese message offered a reward if we were taken to the nearest army installation. A rough translation of the Chinese characters was, "I am an American airman. My plane is destroyed. I cannot speak your language. I am an enemy of the Japanese. Please give me food and take me to the nearest Allied military post. You will be rewarded."

We asked the usual question, why the leather chit was sewn inside the jacket instead of on the back, like the newspaper pictures? The answer was starkly clear: the red-white-and-blue made too good a target for Japanese snipers. We decided that inside the jacket was a good place for the banner.

Lt. Robert Boody, Staten Island, New York, went down near Myitkyina. Boody thought that he received less than a friendly welcome from Chinese troops who thought the chit was in Japanese because of the similarity of the characters. Later, he was well taken care of.[24]

Our second question was why an air crewman would be given a trench knife. The answer: There was a grisly story of a pilot who bailed out and caught his parachute in the trees. He unbuckled his chest strap first and immediately fell head downward, hanging a few inches above the ground. He was not able to get out of the harness. There were huge ants in the jungle, and days later his cleaned bones, caught in the parachute straps, were found still hanging in the tree. The trench knife was to cut a tangled harness. Convincing! We were also told to always leave one bullet in our gun in case there was no other way out. The chit, the black Colt .45, the trench knife, and the story of the ants flew with us on every flight.

The chits worn by Allied airmen were not the only flags worn on the Hump. Every Japanese soldier carried a personalized flag to show faith in his country. Family members would inscribe poems and names of warriors on it before sending the soldier off to battle. A Japanese

Red, white, and blue leather "chit" sewn inside flight jackets of Hump crews. It directed Chinese to take downed fliers to the nearest U.S. army base.

soldier carried his flag the way an American GI wore a crucifix or carried a picture of his sweetheart.

John Clark Alberts from Wauconda, Illinois, a pilot with the 1532nd Army Air Forces Base Unit (AAFBU), watched his buddies go down in bursts of flame, shot down by Japanese fighters. After the war Alberts spent decades with a blood-stained Japanese flag in his dresser and bitterness in his heart. He had found the flag on a battlefield in Burma.

Years later, while playing a Rotary golf tournament with Tario Kamno, a Japanese golfer from Tokyo, Alberts spoke to a Japanese per-

son for the first time in his life. On the golf course, he finally con-
fided that he had this Japanese flag as a war memento. Kamno asked
if he would be kind enough to give up the flag and let him advertise
in the Japanese papers for the owner. Alberts reluctantly gave the flag
to Kamno.

A short time later, Alberts received a letter from Tusunesaburo
Wattenabe, graciously thanking him for returning the flag through the
help of a Tokyo physician, a Rotary International director who had
played golf in the United States. Alberts now strokes his white hair
and looks again at the black-and-white photo enclosed with the letter
from Japan. It pictures Wattenabe proudly holding the small flag with
Tokyo physician Dr. Tario Kamno standing by an eight-hundred-year-
old cherry tree.[25]

With inexperienced pilots, crippling weather and forbidding mountains, and the constant demand for more freight, the Hump became
a purgatory for military commanders. The failure of ATC to deliver
needed tonnage over the Hump brought on a series of investigations
in the summer of 1943. Maj. Gen. Harold L. George, from ATC headquarters, with Capt. Edward V. ("Eddie") Rickenbacker, an experienced
airline executive, came to the CBI. President Roosevelt sent Maj. Gen.
George Stratemeyer to review the problems. They found limited airport facilities, a shortage of maintenance personnel and spare parts,
inadequate navigation and radio aids, and other problems.[26]

ATC was working to its limits and often beyond, but no one was
satisfied. The apparent inefficiency of ATC was being compared to
the efficiency of CNAC. This was unfair, as Rickenbacker saw. CNAC
had been flying the Himalayas for years and was successful because
of the experience of its pilots.[27] ATC did not have this experience,
in its pilots or in its operations.

The solution to the problem was typically military: *order* more
efficiency—use a big whip on an overworked horse. In September, Col.
Thomas O. Hardin, an expert pilot and demanding commander, took
charge of the Hump airlift. Hardin was a hard driver and pushed his
crews to the limit. Planes were sent out in fair weather and foul. Pilots flew in whatever storms raged over the mountains—there was
no turning back.[28]

Colonel Hardin was responsible for the edict "There is no weather
over the Hump." The story, unofficially, behind the infamous "no
weather" order is that Hardin made an instrument letdown in a B-25
and found two crews with their overloaded C-46s waiting for better
weather so they could get through the icing level. Hardin "blew all

stacks," ordered the crews to take off, and sent the same "go" message to all bases. The "no weather" decree remained in effect until 8 January 1945.[29] Another order from Hardin was that planes could not stay on the ground because there were enemy planes reported over the Hump. As a result, six transports were shot down on 13 October.[30]

Another innovation was night flying over the Hump. Colonel Hardin gradually introduced around-the-clock missions. John Nelson, former Hump pilot now living in Boise, Idaho, claims the first night flight over the Hump. "I have logs of my 96 round trips which certify the first night flight from Kunming to Sookerating on October 17, 1943. We caught hell when the word came out what we had done, as night flying over the Hump at that time was a NO! NO!"[31] However, an "exploratory" night flight was made over the Hump in August 1943 to check the feasibility of such an operation.[32] Shortly after that test flight and the first unofficial operational flight, night missions became a regular part of the Hump operation.

Brigadier General Smith reported in December: "Hardin is steaming like an old fire engine . . . I have never seen a man work harder. . . . He works in the office in the morning and spends the afternoon going from one field to the other. He has broken most of the Air Force rules about operations. . . . If tech orders were enforced here, I doubt that there would be an airplane in the air."[33]

Immediately after Colonel Hardin took command, tonnage over the Hump increased—7,000 tons in October, 12,000 tons in November, and 12,590 tons in December. Accidents also began to increase. Between June and December, 1943, there were 135 accidents on the Hump, with 38 in November and 28 in December. General Smith complained, "For all it is worth, we are paying for it in men and airplanes."[34]

Pilots often charged that directives from operations, such as Hardin's "no weather" rule, were the cause of accidents. Another operations order was that aircraft returning from China were to be allowed only a certain number of gallons of fuel, depending on the type of plane. In Kunming, tanks were drained of every drop of extra fuel beyond what was needed for a direct flight back to India. The last miles of the flight were often an ordeal as fuel gauges hovered near the empty mark.[35]

Clarence Linenbach from Sanger, California, who was director of operations and head of accident investigation, argues that

> with certain weather, some trips required more fuel. I can think of accidents at Jorhat caused by running out of gas in the pattern, all resulting in fatalities.

In [one] accident I remember finding part of the body of the
tech sergeant and not finding the [rest of the] body until next day.
I remember finding the copilot, fatally injured. His 'chute didn't
open. The pilot hanging upside down [was] fatally injured . . . the
aircraft crashed into a bamboo patch. I heard a lot of moaning and
crying from a native shack fifty yards away. One of the landing
gears flew into the shack . . . killing a pregnant woman sleeping
on the floor between her husband and a son.

. . . another accident [was] on final approach. It was easy to find
at night because the plane was burning . . . one crewman . . . told
me on the way to the base hospital they had run out of gas on
the final approach. He died that night.

My board and I were pressured to pin 'pilot error' on some of
the accidents. We refused, shifting the blame to the people who
sent the orders we had to operate under. This got me in trouble
more than once . . . but where in hell could they send me that
was worse than India?[36]

Strange, unexplained accidents began to happen. Aircraft, for no
apparent reason, in good weather, would simply fly into a mountain.
Pilots coming in for a landing, "under seemingly perfect control and
excellent weather, would make a good approach—then fly right into
the ground, killing everyone on board."[37]

The accidents were puzzling in the absence of bad weather or engine failure. Perhaps pilots were overly tired. After much study, it was
determined that the problem was simple lack of oxygen, especially
on the Chinese side where the land elevations were higher. Lack of
oxygen is called "anoxemia." It affects vision and the ability to make
decisions and was suspected of being one of the "silent killers" of the
Hump. During the day pilots were required to wear oxygen masks
above ten thousand feet; at night oxygen was required from the ground
up. Missions were flown at a minimum of seventeen thousand feet
and often up to twenty-five thousand. Many pilots were careless about
oxygen, "big tough fellows who sneered at oxygen masks."[38] Aircraft
in 1943 were not pressurized, and the masks were uncomfortable and
a problem to the crewmen who smoked.

Where there is danger and death, there are superstitions—first, to
ward off the danger, and second, to explain the unexplainable. Over
the Hump, there was a superstition, rumor, old pilot's tale, or fact—
we were not sure—of the "descending isobar." An isobar is a level of
equal pressure. As weather pilots, we were conscious of isobars, iso-
therms, fronts, and other meteorological phenomena related to flying.

The story we kept hearing was that over the Himalayas, the isobars often sloped downward toward the mountains. Since the altimeter

indicates altitude by reading pressure, if the isobar descended toward the mountains, the pilot on instruments, following the altimeter, would fly into the mountain.

Unexplained accidents, perhaps caused by anoxemia, would be blamed on the "descending isobar," and pilots, while never admitting to belief in the theory, always kept close watch on their radio altimeters, which gave a true reading above the ground not related to pressure.

In 1943, Generalissimo Chiang Kei-shek asked for ten thousand tons of supplies per month over the Hump and the beginning of long-range bomber operations from China in 1944. General Marshall was growing impatient with the Chinese leader. He felt that the United States was already doing more in China than should be done while the war was being fought in Europe. Chinese political influence, the demands of Chiang and Chennault, the persuasion of Madame Chiang, and direct appeals to Congress and the president were wearing on the Allied leaders.

General Arnold told President Roosevelt that he could not satisfy the generalissimo. "Each time I said I could increase the tonnage over the Hump to 8000 tons, he would reply, 'I must have 10,000 tons.' If I said, '. . . 10,000,' the Generalissimo would say, 'Not enough. I want 12,000.'" Arnold then advised the president not to take the demands too seriously because "I was going to get more tonnage into China by air than the Chinese would be able to haul away."[39] General Marshall reminded the generalissimo that "these were American planes, personnel and materiel, [and] that China must fight to reopen the [Burma] Road if he wanted more materiel; there would be no further increase in transports."[40]

Chiang balked. In November, General Stilwell reported that the generalissimo was unwilling to fulfill commitments agreed to at Cairo.[41] On 15 September 1943, T. V. Soong asked Washington to recall General Stilwell. Soong's aim was to overthrow Chiang Kai-shek, gain control of China, and modernize the country according to the pattern of the Western world, much the same as Japan had done. Chiang still followed the old Chinese ideas of Confucius. His philosophy was an ancient Taoist principle: "Through not doing, all things are done."[42] Washington took no action.

Soong wanted all air activity, including flights over the Hump, under control of a Chinese general. Soong also wanted all lend-lease. However, almost like characters in a mystery thriller, Soong's two sisters, Al-Ling (Mrs. H. H. Kung) and May-Ling (Mme. Chiang Kai-shek), warned Stilwell of the plot, and he was able to confront Chiang in a conciliatory meeting and defuse Soong's requests.[43] Such political infighting in China and in India made it difficult for the army to fight a war.

The Hump was at the end of a ten-thousand-mile supply line, longest in the world. Many planes were grounded for lack of spare parts, and it took weeks or months to get the parts from the States. General George decided that there should be a high-priority air freight service from the United States to India to fly in critical supplies.

From this decision came the CRESCENT and FIREBALL runs, making regular around-the-clock freight flights. CRESCENT flew from Wilmington, Delaware, through Newfoundland and the Azores, across North Africa and the Middle East, and into India. The second service, called FIREBALL, flew from Miami, Florida, following the South Atlantic route to India and was specifically to supply the critical needs of the Hump. In some histories of the CBI airlift, the FIREBALL is erroneously called the CANNONBALL.

FIREBALL was a much publicized and glamorous freight service, much like an airborne Pony Express. Four C-87s (later C-54s) were assigned to FIREBALL, and relief crews were stationed along the route from Miami. FIREBALL planes were always in the air, day and night, and badly needed parts, engines, and personnel could be in India only two days from Miami.[44] This was important in a theater thousands of miles from the supply depot. General Stilwell reported that, for lack of parts, thirty-eight planes were grounded in November and only one in March, 1944.[45]

One of the pilots of the CRESCENT run was a young officer from Arizona by the name of Barry Goldwater.[46]

As the number and intensity of the flights increased, with night flying in all kinds of weather, morale of the crews began to sag and flying became more and more dangerous. Living conditions were not good. Theodore White, a *Life* magazine reporter who lived with troops and shared their hardships throughout the CBI, complained that the food in India was wholesome but dull beyond imagination. "There can be little fresh meat," he explained, "because local cows are sacred, local pigs are infected . . . there are no refrigerator cars."

The food in China was better. One of the rewards of flying into China was the good Chinese restaurants in Kunming and other cities. Air crews could get real eggs, real milk, bacon with Stateside biscuits, fried chicken, and steaks. Chinese restaurants specializing in American "cuisine" were always crowded.

In the CBI experience, Kunming was the special place that everyone remembered. This ancient city was the main Hump terminus in China. Pilots were forever impressed with the long, low approach to Kunming over Lake Tali between needle-like mountains, and crews never forgot the smell rising from small Chinese villages on the approach.

To remain overnight or a few days in Kunming was almost a vacation. Six thousand feet above sea level, the air was clean and cool; Kunming was known as "The City of Eternal Spring." There were flowers, and the people regarded American airmen as their "saviors" from the Japanese. Yet Kunming was a typical Chinese city. It was dirty in parts, and the streets were lined with prostitutes. Opium sellers were everywhere—poppies were grown in fields just outside the city.

Bob Cowan, Lakewood, California, writes eloquently about Kunming; his words could be a description of any large Chinese city:

> Streets crowded and narrow, dirty and noisy like no streets in the world. Public writers with their tables, papers, inks and brushes. . . . ducks and droves of sheep holding up traffic . . . kids picking up "Megwa" cigarette butts with chopsticks and dropping them in paper bags . . . huge leaking buckets of human waste . . . leaving a line of brown stench on the cobbled streets . . . sickening greasy smells of cooking . . . little boys selling soiled rice-paper bound copies of *The Memoirs of Margo* and other "french" type stories . . . old women with doll-like bound feet attempting to walk with the aid of a stick-like cane . . . a cat on a leash with bells on its collar, tied to the counter of a meat shop.
>
> [A] hot night in July at the United Nations Club . . . Chinese band playing "White Christmas" and Chinese girl in a high strange voice . . . "anh may ah yore Chrisma sa be why."
>
> . . . unlocking the floodgates of memory of Kunming, 1943.[47]

Robert Boody, on landing at Kunming after one flight, saw hundreds of Chinese, pulling a heavy roller, run over and crush to death a Chinese worker who had gotten tangled in the yoke of the rope. They continued without stopping despite the screams.[48]

A three-story brick building on Dashea Lu (Street), called Billie's Cafe, was the popular hangout for Americans wanting good American food. A Chinese cafe was always a happy place—crowded and noisy with smiling Chinese always shouting "ding hao." It seemed the mission of every Chinese[49] to speak, with a bow, to every Allied airman. A Chinese cafe had its own special smell—strange, spicy, and powerful, with a faint wisp of a putrid odor that just hinted that the standards of cleanliness were different from our own. We weren't there to care—we came to eat.

How far back in the cafe you seated yourself determined the quality and the price of the food. At Billie's, a special place at the rear of the cafe was reserved for American airmen.

Upstairs was the noise and confusion of a poker game. The Chinese were slapping their fingers against a table with such drunken enthusiasm, the entire room seemed to shake—the room *did* shake. The Chinese laughed and slapped each other on the back. Chinese restaurants were great sources of intelligence, and the owners usually knew everything that was going on with the military.[50]

Food at Billie's Cafe was good and reasonably clean. It was an approved eating place—many were not. The "à la carte" menu was a gastronomic tour of special delights, some known and some unknown. For example, browsing through the menu, there was consommé aux vermicelli or cream of tomato soup, $80; filet mignon, porterhouse, or T-bone steaks at $280; followed by chicken—pilaf, stewed, braised, grilled, fried, à la king, $300; pork, fish, eggs, rice, bread, cake, etc. There were no cold refreshments—no ice. Drinks, milk, $60; coffee, $70; or cocoa, $100. All prices were in Chinese currency (CN), subject to the local exchange rate.[51]

The exchange rate for money in China was a great mystery. It changed from day to day, and often hour by hour. Officially, at the banks, in 1943 it was about two hundred to one, but on the street, on the black market, rates as high as one thousand to one could be had. This made prices in Kunming unbelievably low, compared to American standards, if Allied airmen used black market money. Buying black market money was illegal, but no one checked.

With the difference in official and black market exchange, it would seem easy to make a profit by buying on the street and selling to the banks. But no! Exchange was a one-way trade. It seemed that every man, woman, and child on the streets was selling Chinese yuan for United States money, but no one would buy back Chinese money. Banks would exchange American money for Chinese yuan only at the official rate. (American money was always referred to as "gold.") Once the Chinese people had American gold it would not be sold back. The exchange rate continued to rise (inflation) from two hundred to one, five hundred to one, one thousand to one, until near the end of the war, Chinese paper money was practically worthless, and only gold or Indian rupees were accepted.

An old Chinese custom of drinking ceremonial toasts was a non-sobering and devastating experience for Allied airmen. "Gham-pei" (Gom-bay) means "bottoms up," and everyone must follow the custom or "lose face." At parties or receptions, as the host proposes a toast and drinks his wine, everyone, by courtesy, must follow; someone else proposes a toast and everyone must follow. Toasts were popular in China, and they continue until, to keep from "losing face," everyone "falls on face." The small porcelain Gham-pei cups seem innocent enough, but rice wine is the most potent in the world, and many Americans quickly learned to find other things to do when toasts were proposed.

At official parties, the host, usually a governmental or military dignitary, would appoint an aide to be his "surrogate drinker." This was usually explained by the interpreter, although it was never explained how the guests could appoint their surrogates. No one dared consider what would happen to the aide if he "lost face" for the official.[52]

In India, things were different. Wine was not the popular drink of the people, and for the air crewmen who spent most of their time on base, the art of "wine" making reached a stage of questionable perfection. Richard "Sahib" Foster noted that his squadron had an old wooden vinegar barrel in which they put spirits and anything else that would ferment. Foster found a gallon of medical alcohol and poured it in, and everyone added whatever they could get their hands on— gin, other booze, raisins, potatoes, etc.—until the barrel was half full. Foster's notes continue: "In due time it fermented. We skimmed the foam and mosquitos off the top and decided to have a party. Dipping from the mixture [called 'jing bao juice'] was soon a disaster. Everyone on the flight line was stoned. Four mechanics fell off the wings of our C-47s . . . most of the pilots joined in . . . so the C.O. canceled all flights until the next day."

In the absence of abundant stateside liquor, most drank Carew's Gin and a native booze put in hollowed-out bamboo tubes about three feet long (there were no bottles). This was called "booze by the yard."[53]

In a faraway, lonely country, "wine, women and song" seem to be a part of any gathering of two or more. This was true in both India and China.

Bob Mongell from Manchester, Connecticut, Eleventh Bomb Squadron, writes an eloquent tribute to the mythical ladies of love who were in every war zone in every part of the world:

Katchin natives were used to help rescue downed flight crews. This rescue
crew was photographed at Singlen Kaphta, Burma. *Courtesy Jack Corns*

Her nickname (maybe it was her real name, who knows), "Pinwheel," was here before I came to China in early 1944. Pinwheel
was a descriptive term of her prime movements. I won't explain
this. She had a face that would make Jing Bao juice taste like a
Beefeater martini. Her knowledge of the "American" language (not
English, as she used to say), was horrendous, but in a pleasing way.
She was a friend (and lover) of everyone; enlisted men, officers,
Chinese, Japanese, perhaps even the water buffalo. . . . Even back
in the States, her name was invariably brought up . . . about her
circular behavior and big heart . . . everything about Pinwheel was
big.[54]

In 1942 when the Japanese took Luichow, AVG fighter pilots flew
their P-40s to Kunming while other crewmen drove trucks and jeeps

up the Burma Road with heavy equipment. Some pilots had pretty Burmese girl friends and refused to leave them behind. With the pilot in the cockpit and the lady on his lap, both flew to Kunming in a single-seat P-40.

In Kunming, all of the men who had brought girls from Burma, and others who found girls in Kunming, were housed in Hostel No. 4, especially rented for the men by Colonel Chennault. Each morning the trucks would pick up the men and take them to the airfield, leaving the ladies at the hostel.[55]

Paul Brock, Fourteenth Air Force, remembers a shortage of American cigarettes that was so critical in parts of China that airmen of the Fourteenth Air Force squadrons were reduced to smoking Chinese cigarettes which came in a green package made to resemble Lucky Strikes. American cigarettes were selling for around $17, gold, a carton. The Chinese cigarette was called the "Green Death."[56]

As 1943 closed on the Hump, the airlift was getting into serious operation and problems were being worked out; food and living conditions were being improved, and the long-awaited C-46s began to arrive.

5

A New Challenge to the Hump—
1944

In the war-torn China-Burma-India theater, 1944 dawned over the Himalaya with a new determination and a new aircraft. The new plane that had come to the Hump was the Curtiss-Wright C-46. The pressure of war had brought the C-46 to the Hump without adequate testing, and the aircraft was full of mechanical and electrical problems that were blamed for many accidents and deaths.

In December 1943, thirty C-46s arrived in India, loaded with engines and spare parts. These were the same planes that had been sent to the CBI in April and were returned to the factory for modification and correction of mechanical problems. The C-46 was a strange giant of an airplane—a new, untried "flying freight car" designed to match its ruggedness against the ruthless Himalaya.

The C-46 was truly the transport that "conquered the Hump," in spite of pilots' anguish, operations' skepticism, and early problems. Seldom has a military aircraft been so completely compatible with its mission. The C-46 was nicknamed "Old Dumbo," after Walt Disney's flying elephant. The army, however, with proper military dignity, called it the Curtiss "Commando." Some pilots called it the "Flying Coffin," a name traditionally given to any new, untried aircraft, in any theater, in any war. It was also known as the "Pregnant Whale." Whatever the name, with history as witness, the C-46 tamed the Hump, flew through almost any weather the Rockpile offered, and kept China in the war against Japan. Many C-46s went down and many crews died, and its path across the Hump was called the "aluminum trail," but Old Dumbo prevailed. The C-46 and the Hump were Moses and the Red Sea.

Until the C-46 came, the dependable C-47 "Gooney Bird" had served the Air Transport Command and CNAC well. But a bigger transport was needed. One year before the war, Curtiss-Wright had built the CW-20, a prototype for the C-46. This was an aircraft the army hoped would compete with the four-engine Douglas DC-4 and the Boeing Stratoliner and be a plane to replace the aging C-47 fleet.[1]

The C-46 was 76 feet 4 inches long, over 21 feet high, and had a wingspan of 108 feet. It cruised at two hundred miles per hour, carried fifteen thousand pounds of cargo at over twenty-four thousand feet, and consumed only 135 gallons of fuel an hour—excellent performance.[2] The plane had two Pratt and Whitney R-2800 2,000-HP engines, the most dependable engines made, with four-blade Curtiss electric propellers. Later models were equipped with Hamilton-Standard three-blade props, which were more dependable in colder temperatures.

A two-stage supercharger with "low" and "high" blowers made the C-46 efficient in the thin air above twenty thousand feet. When shifting to high blower, there was a solid "thunk" that caused everyone in the aircraft to snap to attention. Any strange noise in a new plane can cause anxiety, and crews were skittish about the new C-46.

The army ordered 200 C-46s in September 1940 and another 256 in May 1941. Since there was no war at that time, acceptance was slow; two planes were accepted on 18 July 1942, and another three by the end of July.

Pushing the C-46 into combat before it was thoroughly tested could be blamed on Madame Chiang Kai-shek. According to Barbara Tuchman, "She importuned all of them [top men in Washington] for more planes . . . with such insistence that Roosevelt ordered the immediate delivery of Curtiss Wright's new C-46s before their performance was tested. . . . their structural flaws brought out by the rough flight over the Hump proved lethal for many fliers."[3]

Actually, some testing on the C-46 had been done. When the army accepted the new C-46s on 18 July 1942, they were turned over to the civil airlines for shakedown flights on contract carrier duty. The new planes were flown over easy routes by the airlines' experienced pilots, and only minor problems were reported.[4]

One of the best friends the C-46 had was Capt. Eddie Rickenbacker. He accepted twenty C-46A models for his Eastern Airline Military Transport Division. Rickenbacker sent the planes to his shops where

The C-46 conquered the Hump. Rugged, fast, and with twice the carrying load of the C-47, the C-46 made the airlift possible. *Courtesy Edgar Crumpacker*

they were thoroughly checked. He recommended 517 changes and had to go to General Arnold for approval. The changes were made.[5] However, over the Hump, with inexperienced pilots and punishing missions, the C-46 began to reveal mechanical and electrical flaws.

The new planes leaked badly in the heavy monsoon rains, and crews were drenched. There were so many malfunctions of the fuel and hydraulic systems that the C-46 was called a "plumber's nightmare." Carburetor ice would shut down the engines on takeoff, and many crews were killed that way. Craven and Cate, in their exhaustive history of the Army Air Forces in World War II, wrote, "From May 1943 to March 1945, the Air Transport Command received reports of thirty-one instances in which C-46s caught fire or exploded in the air. Still others were listed merely as 'missing in flight,' and it is a safe assumption that many of these exploded, went down in flames, or crashed as the result of vapor lock, carburetor icing or other defects."[6]

Many accidents were blamed on engine fires. A fire in an engine, fed by gasoline from a ruptured fuel line, fanned by two-hundred-mile-an-hour winds through the enclosed nacelle, quickly became a blast furnace. If the fire couldn't be put out, the pilot had less than one minute before the wing burned off.

General Stilwell was concerned about the C-46. He noted in late 1943, after an inspection tour, "The C-46 is full of bugs. . . . We have lost six over the Hump and the boys' morale is lower and lower." Crews were rebellious and often bailed out if the engine missed once, or refused to fly if there was a cloud in the sky.[7] They said you could find your way over the Hump by following the smoke of burning wrecks.[8] In an effort to cut casualties, General Alexander ordered that the C-46 at first would be used for cargo only, with no passengers.

The inexperienced pilots were not ready for the new, complex, and heavy C-46. The plane had a tendency to ground loop, and a flight school to qualify pilots in Assam was closed because of the excessive damage to the new planes during training flights. Mechanics were so inexperienced that wing engineering officers, manufacturing technical representatives, and the representatives' assistants were often required to personally perform maintenance.[9]

There were seemingly insignificant problems that the pilots did not know about. For example, in the older, pilot-friendly C-47 aircraft, engines could be operated at 800–1,000 RPM for long periods of time —throttles fully closed. However, if the C-46 engines were allowed to run at idle RPM for just a few minutes, the spark plugs would be fouled, and a new set would have to be installed before takeoff.[10]

As the crews gained more experience, they learned to control some of the problems of the C-46. Pilot Irving J. Wagner from McFarland, California, 315th Troop Carrier Squadron, learned that a kick here and a tap there would often correct ugly mechanical traits of the plane. For example, electrically controlled props would often run away on takeoff. To prevent the props from tearing the engine from the wing was simply a matter of switching to manual control and retarding the speed until the proper RPM was obtained.

Pilots also learned that occasionally when landing, the main gear would drop but the tail wheel would stay in the "up" position. The flight engineer would then work his way back through the cargo to the tail. In the rear bulkhead was a hole that could be opened to the tail wheel. A good shove with the foot and the tail wheel would drop into landing position.[11] Perceptive and ingenious air crews often solved the problems as they arose.

Len Reinig describes what seems to be a cavalier attitude toward the most life-threatening problem in flight: loss of both engines. Returning from China, Reinig hit a violent updraft at twenty thousand feet and the aircraft was spit out at the top of a cloud at twenty-nine thousand feet. Both engines were dead and windmilling. "I hit the primer switches, both engines started, and we happily continued at twenty-eight thousand until we cleared the ridge and went on in safely."

Reinig learned later that this violent thunderstorm was two hundred miles wide, had cut a C-46 in half, and had twisted the body and warped the wings of a C-54.[12]

Ed Crumpacker described a mysterious mechanical problem on his new C-46's first trip over the Hump with a full load. For some unknown reason it would not climb to the minimum altitude of fourteen thousand feet even with high blower. In his memoirs, Crumpacker writes, "I staggered across between mountain peaks and barely made it. We checked the engines at Kunming, but could not find the trouble . . . on the return flight to Calcutta, the poor performance persisted. . . .

"At Barrackpore, we decided to change sparkplugs. They had been known to check out on the ground, but [at high altitudes] to leak current through the porcelain housing. New plugs corrected the situation."

But Crumpacker was still not satisfied with the performance. It was a troop carrier model with a lot of "garbage" on it that made it slower than the transport model. So he removed the bubble of the astrodome (for celestial navigation), the para-racks on the belly, and the glider bar. "We hired about fifty Indian laborers to remove the camouflage paint down to the bare alloy, and give it a coat of wax. When we were finished, we had increased its cruising speed by twenty-five to thirty miles per hour."[13]

Pilots were constantly complaining about the extra equipment that was loaded on new planes, making them heavy, slow, and hard to fly. When an aircraft came off the assembly line, the army did not usually know where it would be sent. So planes were equipped with the latest military gadgetry: carburetor sand screens for operation in North Africa; deicing equipment for the North Atlantic; celestial navigation domes for who knows what, since navigation by the stars was obsolete in most aircraft military operations. There was new sophisticated radio and electronic equipment which many crewmen did not know how to operate — always the latest technology.

This was the benevolent U.S. policy: give military personnel the best equipment and the most protection possible. Often it was too much for safety. In the combat zones, millions of dollars worth of excess equipment were stripped out of the planes to make them lighter, faster, and safer in the air.[14]

After a few months and many modifications at the factory and repairs in the field, the C-46 began to earn its place as the packhorse of the Hump—literally a flying coolie. "Coolie" is taken from two Chinese words, "ku lih," meaning "bitter strength."[15]

The C-46 was more temperamental than the C-47. Ideally, cargo had to be loaded by a weights-and-balance officer with slide-rule precision to keep it stable. The ideal was rarely achieved. In flight, balance was critical for best performance. The pilot could feel the plane's center of gravity shift when a passenger walked fore and aft. The automatic pilot constantly made corrections as fuel was burned and load conditions changed. Fully loaded, the C-46 was not able to hold altitude on one engine and was not suited for air-drop missions because of instability at slow speeds.

Slowly, however, pilots learned to like the C-46. They complained but soon developed a respect for the plane. The cockpit was built for comfort and good visibility with solarium-like windows. There were plush, throne-like seats with adjustable headrests to fit any pilot; the rudder pedals and control column could be adjusted for comfort. Power-assisted controls made the heavy C-46 easy to fly, and there was a small galley with a hot plate for warming C-rations—it was an aircraft designed for the comfort of its crews.

As the C-46 brought maturity to the Hump, a new system of navigation called Long-Range Navigation (LORAN) was installed. LORAN was a new navigation aid with two radio range stations (a master and a slave station) constantly sending radio signals. A receiver in the aircraft would allow the radio operator to vector the two stations and immediately fix the plane's precise location. Accuracy was within half a mile, within a range of eight hundred miles during the day and twelve hundred miles at night. LORAN stations could also take a bearing on an aircraft and locate its position. The first LORAN system was installed in the United States in 1942. The system was quickly adopted for military use and installed on the Hump at major air terminals such as Chabua, Kunming, and others. New C-46 aircraft coming to the Hump were equipped with LORAN, although few crews knew how to use it.

Pilots were afraid to completely trust any radio navigation system because radio beams could be deflected by the mountains. Also, the

Japanese would often transmit false beams to lure fliers off course to fly into mountains or run out of gas over unknown territory. The radio operator or navigator had to constantly monitor several systems of navigation to be certain that the pilot was not following a false beam.

Richard "Dick" Walton from Salem, Ohio, former radio operator navigator, remembers how he almost bailed out when he found his plane off course. Walton and his crew were returning to Chabua from China one afternoon and he was using the LORAN for position reports in the log. He found they were far north of course and headed for Mt. Everest at only 18,000 feet—Mt. Everest is 29,029 feet high. Walton knew they were over the upper Assam Valley and ninety miles off course. He called the pilot and told him where they were.

"Being a captain and I a tech-sergeant, he didn't believe LORAN was that accurate. I told him to retune his radio compass or I was going to bail out. He did retune and Chabua was 270 degrees [south] of where we were. He immediately turned left and aligned the compass to zero—I stayed aboard and we got home."

Later Walton was summoned to see the major in operations, and he expected to get a chewing. "There was my captain, the copilot and the major. 'Sergeant Walton,' the captain said, 'I apologize for not believing that a radio operator knew anything about navigation or that LORAN could be that accurate.'"[16]

There was still another persistent, invisible enemy on the Hump—a lack of confidence, at the command level, in the ability of the airlift to solve the supply problem. The army did not seem to notice that the Hump supply was improving. There was constant discussion of reopening the Burma Road. The long, twisting, vulnerable road, closed since March 1942, was always on the minds of theater commanders. Air transport, despite its worldwide record, had still not been accepted as a major effort of war. Bombers and fighters were the heroes.

General Tunner, who would become commander of the Hump in late 1944 and was the person who brought businesslike stability to the airlift, complained bitterly after the Burma Road was reopened. He felt that the age of air transportation was born on the Hump, and the superiority of air transport over surface transportation was being demonstrated every day the ATC planes flew. For three years there had been no surface transportation between India and China, and the war had continued.

When the Japanese were driven out of Burma, the Burma Road was again put into operation, and fantastic sums were spent, with as many as twenty engineering battalions working at one time. Tunner wrote,

We on the Hump generally had no more than two engineering battalions to build and maintain our bases. China bases were entirely
coolie built, with only one strip, and no binding material but the
good earth.

The maximum amount of supplies carried over the Burma Road
at its very peak of operation was six thousand tons a month. Many
of our thirteen ATC bases in India were topping that figure, constantly. President Roosevelt called our efforts "an amazing
performance."

Yet the work to open the Burma road continued at the expense
of the airlift and a terrific cost in dollars. We all know how hard
it is to stop a large government project once it is begun.[17]

This was a continuation of the air-ground controversy. It is interesting, futile, and perhaps unfair to speculate how the war might have
been different if the Hump airlift had been given priority during the
first months of the war instead of late in 1944. General Arnold, commanding general of the Army Air Force, was often discouraged at the
inability of his top commanders to understand the use of air power
in combat and at the cramped thinking of the military.[18]

World leaders often disagreed and were able to see only their own
needs. For example, on 14 January 1944, President Roosevelt warned
Generalissimo Chiang to commit Chinese forces to Burma or face
lend-lease curtailment. On 16 January Chiang replied that he would
quit feeding U.S. troops in China unless he got a billion-dollar loan.[19]
ATC and its transport planes controlled the pace of the war. Every
Allied plan to take the war closer to Japan depended on the Hump
airlift's ability to get supplies into China. Even when the Burma Road
was reopened, the war continued to depend on the Hump supply line.

In late 1943, as victory in Europe seemed near, a new offensive for
China was proposed, with a name suggesting Allied confidence of
Japan's eventual defeat. The offensive was called SETTING SUN—a
plan to bring the B-29 "Superfortress" to the CBI and bomb the Japanese home islands from China. General Stilwell favored the idea in
principle, but he felt that the planners of SETTING SUN did not know
enough about the CBI and wanted too much too quickly. He was also
concerned about the ability of the Hump airlift to get enough supplies into China.

As plans continued to bring B-29s to China, ATC could immediately begin to feel the increased tempo and urgency. A new bomber
command, the Twentieth, was created to deploy the B-29s against
Japan. Men and equipment were carried from New York to Casablanca

by ship and then brought by air to India. The first movement involved 1,237 officers and enlisted men, 250 B-29 spare engines, 121,000 pounds of radar, gun heaters, and other equipment. This involved 155 flights of C-54s and C-46s from Africa to India. More than 250 B-29s with their crews were ferried across North Africa, under the code name WOLFE.[20]

Not completely happy with the plan for SETTING SUN, General Stilwell proposed an alternative operation, optimistically coded TWI-LIGHT. This plan would have the B-29s stationed near Calcutta, with staging bases in China. The planes would have greater security in India and could fly their own supplies into China. Stilwell, remembering the vengeance with which Japan attacked Chinese airfields after Colonel Doolittle's Tokyo raid, wanted the B-29s in India. He feared extreme Japanese retaliatory raids against the B-29s and their airfields if they were stationed in China.[21] Eventually Stilwell's TWILIGHT plan was adopted, but only after it was clear that the Hump airlift would be unable to support the tremendous fuel and ordnance demands of the B-29s in China.

The B-29 Superfortress was the largest aircraft of World War II and was called "the greatest U.S. gamble of the war." The B-29 development cost $3 billion, against $2 billion for the atom bomb.[22] Like the C-46, under pressure of war the B-29 was ordered into production as a top priority. General Arnold, in his military autobiography *Global Mission*, writes, "The Boeing Company's engineers informed me that the Superfortress would be able to reach all points in Germany from any place in the United Kingdom—if they were based there. Needless to say, we went ahead with that project."[23]

This statement has often been thought to mean that the B-29 was designed to bomb Germany. That was not true. The phrase "to reach all points in Germany" was a statement of range and did not apply to any one theater. Design work for the Superfortress was started in April 1940, and the first prototype, the XB-29, was completed in July 1942. The first test flight was made on 21 September 1942, and the first plane was delivered to the Army Air Corps on 29 July 1943, at a cost of $600,000.

It is true that the B-29 was built before it was designed. Construction was at such a pace that many sections were being built before others were designed. Skilled labor was so scarce that the design had to be simple so that workers could learn to build it quickly. The Superfortress was one of the easiest planes to build that the army had.[24]

It is a tribute to American manufacturing skill that an aircraft of this complexity could be completed in little more than two years from the drawing board to the sky. Yet in wartime, the two years to build the B-29 seemed to move at an agonizing pace. One of the designers said, "Innocence built the B-29. We could not have done it if we had known what we were getting into."[25]

The Superfortress was 99 feet long, with a wingspan of 141 feet 3 inches, and a height of 27 feet 9 inches. Four 2,200-HP, 18-cylinder Wright Cyclone 3350 engines pulled the seventy-ton plane with eleven crew members through the sky at three hundred miles per hour at a ceiling of over thirty-five thousand feet. The B-29 had a range of five thousand miles. It was the largest aircraft used by any nation during World War II, and it was used only against Japan.

General Arnold's philosophy was, "The heavy bomber ... is the most important of all air force weapons. . . . Our heavy bombers will be larger, many times larger than any airplane . . . in the world . . . capable of spreading death and destruction 5,000 miles or more from its base."[26]

On 7 February 1944, President Roosevelt allocated $500 million to build five B-29 staging airfields near Chengtu, in far northern China, 1,300 miles from Calcutta.[27] This was according to Stilwell's TWI-LIGHT plan, with the B-29s to be based in India and staged in China.

Building the B-29 staging base in China was one of the most fantastic engineering feats of World War II, equal, as an engineering project, to the Great Wall of China. In a country where there were no graders, bulldozers, steamrollers, or trucks, the huge base was built by hand. To provide workers, Chiang ordered the greatest levy of manpower in the history of China.

James Stewart, CBS correspondent in Chungking, told the story: "The roads for miles around were jammed with men, simple farmers in blue cotton trousers and jumpers and straw sandals, each with two long poles over his shoulder and enough rice to last until he arrived at one of the sites. When they got there, they set their poles in the ground, tepee fashion, and covered them with rough sheaves of straw — that was each man's shelter for months. . . . some 200,000 farmers had assembled. The number swelled day by day until there were 430,000; on one field at one time we saw 67,000 men working. They worked from sunup to sundown seven days a week."

The land had been flooded rice paddies, and in some cases, to get to solid ground, seven feet of earth had to be excavated — dug and hauled away by the men, each with a bamboo pole over his shoulder with baskets on the ends. Rock was brought from the river beds and spread over the fields. On top of that they put a layer of cobblestones, and then a layer of smaller stones. Thousands of men sat on the ground hammering big rocks until they had stones small enough to go through a little rope loop.

Stewart's description continued: "Somewhere an old broken steam-roller was found. They filled the roller with five tons of rock and iron. Day after day, with 150 Chinese hitched to the roller, the field was smoothed. . . . While we watched these thousands toiling as their an-cestors had toiled, giant U.S. Army transports from India swooped down over their heads to land cargos of gasoline, bombs and all the freight of modern war. The Chinese didn't even look up."[28]

The first B-29 ground support teams landed in India in January 1944, and the following April, as American, Indian, and Burmese service-men and workers lined the runways, the first Superfortress landed. As the huge plane touched down, a shout went up from the crowd. There would be seventeen more months of war, but when the first B-29 landed in India, the end for Japan seemed near. No one believed the Japanese could stand up to such an awesome weapon as the B-29. Two years and two months after Colonel Doolittle's raid against Tokyo, on 15 June 1944, the B-29s flew from India over the Hump and bombed Japan.

Following Stilwell's TWILIGHT plan, the B-29s were based at Charra and Dudhkundi, two huge airfields north of Calcutta. This greatly simplified the supply problem. Fuel and bombs for the B-29s could come to Calcutta by ships that were able to dock near the bases, eliminating further shipping.

B-29s were assigned to the Twentieth Bomber Command, with Brig. Gen. LaVerne Saunders as commander until 7 July 1944. Then came Maj. Gen. Curtis LeMay, who served until 29 August 1944 when he was ordered to lead the air war against Japan from the Mariana Islands.[29]

From their bases in India, B-29 crews would fly supplies and fuel to China to be stockpiled. Seven flights were required to move enough supplies to the Chinese staging bases for one B-29 mission against Japan. This was expensive, time-consuming, and a great risk of men and airplanes. The B-29s burned twelve gallons of gasoline to fly one gallon into China. For the first two raids, 700,000 gallons of fuel were flown across the Hump.

The 444th Bombardment Group was the first operational B-29 out-fit. It was stationed at Dudhkundi, a little village about forty miles northwest of Calcutta. A typical long-range mission against Japan took four days, with one day from India to China, one day in China to get organized, one day to fly the mission over Japan and back to the China base, and one day to return to India. A graphic description of such

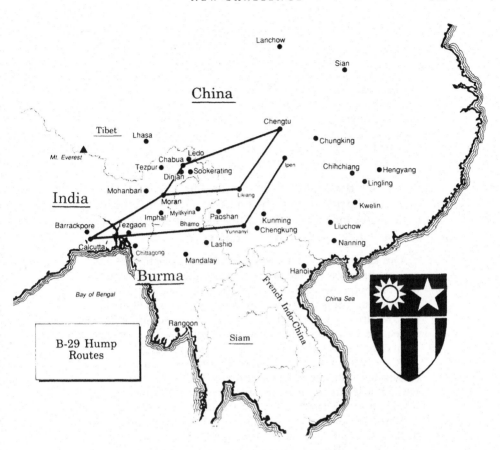

B-29 Hump Routes

a mission was written by retired Maj. Gen. Winton R. Close, a B-29 pilot:

> The first problem was the takeoff . . . Wright 3350s caught fire a lot . . . tending to make us nervous and fretful. . . . Once off the ground, we set a straight course for China . . . directly up the Assam Valley. At the end of the valley, over the Himalaya mountains, the Hump started.
>
> The second problem was the weather. The first time we approached the Hump, the weather didn't look too tough. . . . like a tremendous mass of stratus clouds . . . we innocently sailed right in. . . . visibility was reduced to about the number two engine. We hit our first thunderhead. . . .
>
> We were constantly on the verge of losing control of the aircraft. . . . The airspeed fluctuated between 140 . . . stalling . . . to 250, the red line . . . we could never get the aircraft completely

under control . . . we received upward acceleration of such sever-
ity that four bombs and their shackles were torn loose . . . and
disappeared through the closed bomb bay doors.

We could not get below the weather because the minimum instrument altitude over the Hump was 24,000 feet . . . we just bore
in blind, kept our fingers crossed. . . .

The third problem was to . . . get this thing on the ground. . . .
Over our valley in China, the ceiling would range between 150
and 1500 feet. Our main concern in letting down was to make
sure we cleared the mountain range to the west.

Approaching their China base, sometimes there would be ice on
the wings and the pilots would be forced to circle until the ice melted.
Ice on the wings increased the stalling speed and required a faster approach and touchdown. General Close continued:

Our takeoff from China was much like the one from India . . .
rate of climb was about 500 feet per minute . . . if too much ice
didn't form on the leading edges of the wing. The aircraft did not
have de-icing boots . . . as ice started to form, our weight increased,
and the efficiency of the airfoil decreased. . . . We would then be
forced to exceed maximum allowable climb power. . . . struggling
to maintain a rate of climb of 100 feet per minute. . . .

Across the East China Sea for a target on the Japanese island
of Kyushu . . . too often the target would be obscured by clouds . . .
we had little chance of hitting a pinpoint target by radar. . . . our
whole effort the last few days would be of no avail. . . .

[Then we would] turn around and start the return trip. . . . About
ten hours after we had taken off, we would land at our China base,
dog-tired, dehydrated and usually frustrated. . . . the flight surgeon
would give us our allotted shot of whiskey . . . Old Overholt . . .
100 proof.

Day four was routine. Those of us in commission would fly
back to India . . . icing and thunderheads were still there, but this
time we were not loaded with bombs or full gas tanks. . . .

Once back in India, we would fly supply missions to our Chinese base . . . with fuel and bombs. . . . seven supply sorties over
the Hump for one bombing sortie against Japan. . . . Eventually,
we would have enough fuel in China . . . and we would start again
the four-day cycle.[30]

Not all missions were bombing; nor were all missions successful.
Aerial photographer Enrico M. "Hank" Carnicelli, Ridgefield Park, New
Jersey, described the last flight of "Brooklyn Bessie," a B-29 photo re-
connaissance plane, early in 1944:

The pilot and copilot began to preflight the engines . . . the huge plane shuddered and shook from the surging power . . . gunners inspected their ammunition cans . . . photographers checked their cameras . . . takeoff. . . .

Brooklyn Bessie, heavily laden with surplus gas, struggled laboriously to lift its massive weight above the clouds . . . just before target three we were greeted by a shudder and crackling in engine number two. . . .

The flight engineer tried to feather the prop . . . the mechanism wouldn't work. Pilot and copilot trimmed the ship . . . navigators were trying to calculate if the ship could make it home with the fuel left . . . rapidly losing altitude . . . we headed back hopeful that Brooklyn Bessie could make it . . . the prop hub on engine number two was already a cherry red from the propeller spinning out of control. . . .

Number one engine began to vibrate from overwork . . . we could not hope to reach our home base . . . suddenly the propeller from engine number two loosened and struck number one engine a fatal blow, the left wing ablaze.

The order "to jump" was given by the pilot, who struggled to hold the ship level in order that his crew might be saved. The pilot made it, but Brooklyn Bessie did not return.[31]

The problem of supplying gasoline and armament to their base at Chengtu was more than anyone had anticipated. Pilots and crewmen had not had enough experience to operate the Superfortress. Unimaginable distances over China and the bitter weather were difficulties no other theater of war had experienced, and the B-29s had not been designed for the extremes of weather and high-level operations required over the Himalayas. Crews flew heroically, and many died unnecessary deaths.

On one raid aimed at an aircraft factory at Omura on 11 November, clouds obscured the target and five B-29s were lost because of weather. They were listed as "missing because of operational causes." The raid caused no damage at Omura.[32] A second strike was scheduled for Omura for 21 November, and 109 planes took to the air—one crashed and burned after takeoff. Again, weather caused the mission to fail, with only sixty-one planes bombing Omura by radar, and no damage to the factory. Five of the B-29s were diverted when the radar operator mistook Omuta for Omura. Six aircraft were lost—five to enemy action and one on takeoff—with fifty-one crewmen dead.[33]

The longest bombing raid in the history of aerial warfare was made by B-29s from Chengtu on 10 August 1944. Superfortresses bombed.

Nagasaki on the Japanese home island, and Palembang on the island of Sumatra, four degrees south of the equator, the outermost tip of the Japanese empire. The targets were more than three thousand miles apart. The total mission was over five thousand miles.[34]

Over Rangoon, Burma, on 15 December, four B-29s were destroyed by their own bombs. Before the mission, the flight crews protested when they discovered one-thousand-pound bombs loaded above five-hundred-pound, instantaneously-fused bombs. If the bombs hit each other when dropped they would destroy their own plane. Threatened with court-martial, the crews took off. Keith Wheeler in *Bombers over Japan* describes the terrible explosion in the sky: "Lieutenant Marion Burke was navigating the lead aircraft of an eleven-plane formation that came over Rangoon . . . and unloaded its bombs. . . . the gunner screamed, 'My God! The sky has turned red!'"

What Lieutenant Burke had feared had happened. Bombs released by a nearby plane had collided, blowing up the plane and showering the rest of the formation with meteorites of debris. Three other planes were ravaged and the interior of Burke's plane was destroyed. Radio operator Richard Montgomery's left hand was nearly blown off, left hanging only by a thread of tendon. The No. 3 engine was completely out of the wing and now the wing was crumbling. The crew was ordered to bail out.

Wheeler continues, "Burke's crew landed in the middle of a Japanese Army training camp and all the airmen were captured. . . . two of the stricken B-29s crashed in the city . . . one falling on a troop train, killing 700 Japanese soldiers."[35]

On 18 November 1944, the B-29 Superfortresses, in one of the last missions from their China base at Chengtu, made the first firebombing assault against Hankow, a major Japanese supply base. History records that the atomic bombs dropped on Hiroshima and Nagasaki ended the war. If this is true, the "beginning of the end" started with the Hankow incendiary bombing.

General Chennault, commanding the Fourteenth Air Force, had been fighting the war since 1937 and could not forget how the Japanese had dropped incendiary bombs on Chinese cities, with horrible results. Chennault suggested a firebomb attack on Japanese installations—fighting the Japanese with their own tactics. He had first made the suggestion in early 1944.

The plan had been turned down by General Arnold because the use of incendiary bombs was contrary to U.S. policy. Firebombing was a low-level attack and the B-29s were committed to high-altitude strategic demolition bombing. However, the Japanese firebombing of the Chinese was still in Chennault's mind.

In November, the Japanese started a drive toward Kunming—a major threat to all that the Allies had worked for in China, specifically Chennault's Fourteenth Air Force. Anticipating this offensive, in June General Chennault again urged the Twentieth Bomber Command to use one hundred B-29s to destroy Hankow's port facilities with low-level incendiary bombing. Again, the idea was turned down.

However, the Joint Chiefs of Staff had given theater commanders the right to divert the B-29s from strategic to tactical missions in an emergency. When Kunming was threatened, General Wedemeyer declared an emergency and approved Chennault's idea for the firebombing of Hankow. Chennault urged LeMay to use only incendiaries dropped below twenty thousand feet for accuracy. The general agreed.

On 18 November the Twentieth Air Force sent ninety-four B-29s from Chengtu with 511 tons of incendiary bombs to destroy dock and warehouse areas at Hankow. The Fourteenth Air Force sent thirteen B-25 medium bombers escorted by thirty-two P-51 fighters from the Twenty-third Fighter Group and forty-two P-51 fighters from the 311th Fighter Group. Chennault said that the raid "destroyed Hankow as a major Japanese base."[36]

The December 18 attack was the first firebombing raid the Superfortresses had attempted. LeMay was impressed, and when he moved the B-29 command to the Marianas, the B-29s switched from high-altitude daylight attacks to the firebombing night raids that, according to Chennault, "burned the guts out of Japan."[37]

But in spite of heroic flying, the B-29 was the wrong weapon for India and China. The CBI theater was a "different war," where unorthodox methods were more successful than "conventional" warfare, both in the air and on the ground. General Chennault had demonstrated the value of knowing how to fight the Japanese in a different way. The B-29 was a massive weapon, but too conventional for the CBI theater.

The B-29s were finding it impossible to fight an effective war against the Japanese, and their days in the CBI were coming to an end. Flying supplies over the Hump for the B-29s was crippling the Fourteenth Air Force and the defense of southwestern China. General Arnold's prewar dream of a super long-range bomber was turning into a military nightmare.

In January 1945, the B-29s called it quits in China. Less than a month after the Hankow raid, General LeMay moved the B-29s to the

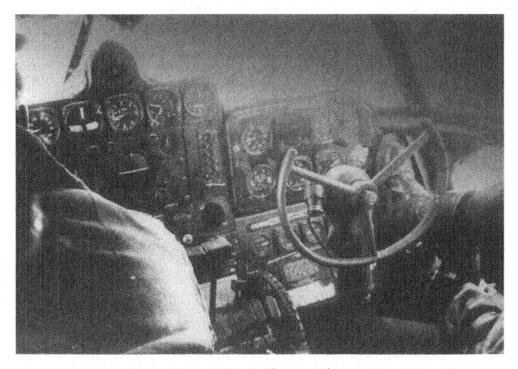

Cockpit of C-46 at fifty-eight hundred feet over China, on instruments. Note relaxed attitude of pilot with foot on dash. Natal mosquito boots were popular but non-regulation. Crews were required to wear flight boots in case of bailout. *Courtesy Jack Corns*

Mariana Islands where fuel and ammunition could be brought in by ship. The decision to move the Superfortresses had actually been made in late 1944, when Ambassador Hurley had recommended "that we remove the B-29 strategic bombers from the [China] area . . . relieving Hump tonnage which could be used to supply tactical air and ground forces."[38]

Removal of the B-29s from the CBI left the east Bengal airfields open for Hump operations and provided additional transports for the airlift.[39]

In late December 1943, ATC's tonnage over the Hump exceeded promises. There was great joy in Washington, and General Stratemeyer recommended that the India-China Wing of ATC be given a War Department citation. President Roosevelt, who felt that the Hump airlift was his operation, was proud, and approved a Presidential Unit Citation. But the adjutant general's office refused since it was policy to award such citations only to combat units. The objection was overruled, and ATC became the first noncombat unit to receive such an award. The president sent personal thanks to every officer and enlisted man involved in flights over the Hump.[40] Eleven thousand ribbons were sent to the CBI.

To receive the award, Colonel Hardin was called back to Washington, given a month's leave, and promoted to brigadier general. On 29 January 1944, he accepted the citation for the ATC. Colonel Hardin had done an excellent job, and under his leadership ATC had performed exceptionally well.

Citation or not, the Hump was a military "dead end," and three commanders before Hardin had failed to bring the airlift up to Washington's expectations. Colonel Hardin was the first commander to make the Hump work. He flew the Hump himself and knew what pilots and planes could do. His successes cost men and aircraft and lowered morale, but the airlift came into its own under Hardin. He created an efficient, around-the-clock operation that was beginning to change the direction of the war in that region. Day and night, ignoring the weather, the C-46s averaged two round trips a day over the Himalayas.[41]

A sardonic footnote in the history of the Hump: The latrines of the India-China Division of ATC will be remembered longest for the shortage of toilet paper. General Hardin sent an urgent message to the quartermaster asking for some relief. A reassuring note was returned in a radio message to Hardin, "Quartermaster aware of toilet paper shortage. A large quantity coming by water."[42]

The Hump, and the war materiel that it delivered, was a constant source of bitterness and infighting in China. Theodore White and Annalee Jacoby, in *Thunder Out of China*, wrote, "The three contenders for Hump tonnage — Stilwell, Chennault, and the Chinese government — were like men trapped and starved in a besieged city. . . . quarrels over tonnage distribution reached even to the White House . . . the airmen of the Hump could never meet the insatiable voracity of the beleaguered garrisons beyond the mountains."[43] China was a bottomless pit.

Chiang's intransigence had an adverse effect on the supply effort. For example, the Joint Chiefs of Staff had increased the allocation of transport planes for use by the ATC for the Hump to 188 C-47s or 126 C-46s for March. When Chiang refused to fight in Burma, the allocation was cut to seventy-six planes.[44] Whether Chiang's attitudes about combat were based on his Chinese philosophy or his fear of

C-46, after a belly landing, at Yunnanyi, China. Frequent hydraulic failure
caused wheels to collapse on landing. After replacing engines and propellers,
the planes were usually able to fly again. *Courtesy Jack Corns*

the Communists, President Roosevelt did not know, but he was concerned.[45]

The Chinese Communists were being held in the northern prov-
inces by Chiang's best armies—armies that the Allies thought Chiang
should be using against the Japanese. There was also the persistent
belief among Allied flight crews that the Communists, through the
Chinese black market, were getting large amounts of the supplies
flown over the Hump. Almost every Hump crew with flights into
the interior of China had a story about an experience with the Communists.

The Communists did not interfere with Allied aircraft flying in
China. In northwestern China, the Communists were a misty, un-

seen presence we heard about but were never able to see—like a shadow that, when you looked, wasn't there. We flew in and out of so-called Communist airfields in northern China, landing and taking off into the face of gun emplacements. They could have easily shot us down, in our most vulnerable positions. They did not do it. I was too young and naive to understand about the threat.

One strange experience will always be remembered. We were on a flight to Sian and Lanchow, and one engine starter motor on our C-47 burned out. At the Lanchow airfield, controlled by the Communists, we were grounded when the engine could not be started. Operations, manned by civilians, told us that there was no starter available and we would have to wait until the next CNAC flight could bring in a starter motor, one week later.

That night, we were getting ready to sleep on our plane with a member of the crew on guard duty. As darkness came, an English-speaking Chinese, driving a jeep-like vehicle, came to our plane. He said he could get us a starter motor if we would come with him. Who the man was and how he knew our problem, we never knew. He seemed not to understand when we asked questions. Our flight engineer, John Terrell, from Oklahoma, and I decided to go with the man. Terrell had taken the old starter motor off of the engine and we took it with us. We rode in the jeep for probably an hour, until we came to a typical Chinese compound—a walled enclosure, around an open court, with small rooms inside.

As we stepped through the door, I automatically unsnapped the holster of my .45. Terrell whispered, "I saw you do that." I noticed that he had done the same. Yet I felt no fear. There was little we could do to protect ourselves. We were at the mercy of the Chinese. Somehow there was a feeling of trust as the man led us to a small back room. Several Chinese were there, but they seemed to ignore us.

In the room, from under a bed, our Chinese friend brought out a starter motor and exchanged it for the one we had brought. After forty-five years, I still find this story incredible. We followed the man back to the jeep and he drove us back to our aircraft. We tipped the man with a handful of Chinese yuan and Indian rupees and filled his tank with gasoline from our plane. He said, "Thank you," with a smile and bow. We said, "Thanks," and with a Chinese handshake, he drove off.

Sergeant Terrell worked through the rest of the night installing the new motor. Just after sunrise—none of us had slept—we started the engine and checked it out. We filed a flight plan and told operations that our engineer had "fixed the motor during the night." We were cleared for takeoff with no questions.

We knew we had come in contact with the Chinese underground, or was it the OSS? We never knew if we were "allowed" to leave or "helped" to leave. It was a mysterious, a strange, experience.

Still concerned about the inexperience of the Hump pilots, Admiral Mountbatten asked Washington, in early April, for air crewmen with more experience. ATC pilots, with their regular Hump missions, were becoming seasoned to the problems of the Hump and were doing an exceptional job with their day-and-night missions. However, combat flight units lacked experience and Mountbatten was reluctant to keep calling on ATC for help.

After Mountbatten's appeal, the "Bond Project" was put into operation. This was a group of one hundred experienced multiengine pilots and copilots and seventy-five reserve officer pilots recruited for a "short-term overseas tour involving a cargo-type operation."[46]

The "Bond" crews gathered at Morrison Field, Florida, in May 1944. They were joined by ATC navigators to guide them over the long overwater flights, although their destination was not known. One hundred new C-47A aircraft were delivered to Morrison, and after intense training and briefing, the crews took off on 22 May across the South Atlantic to India and the Hump.

Crews of the Bond Project became members of the Third Combat Cargo Group, an air unit to support fighting troops on the ground. Four Combat Cargo Groups were created, of which the First, Third, and Fourth were assigned to the CBI, and the Second served in the Pacific theater. Combat Cargo crews flew some of the meanest missions of the war, flying into short fields, bringing out the dead and dying, flying under enemy fire, or dropping supplies to a starving unit cut off behind enemy lines.

The Third Combat Cargo Group was the first to come to the CBI. It was activated in Sylhet, India, on 5 June 1944, moved to Dinjan, India, on 2 August, to Myitkyina, Burma on 3 June 1945, and to Shanghai, China, after the war. The Third flew C-47s and supported ground forces during the Battle of Northern Burma. The first commander was Col. Charles D. Farr. The Third Combat Cargo Group was activated to support Admiral Mountbatten in the Battle of Imphal, in Burma. After Imphal, the group was to have been sent back to the States for more training, but, of course, it never happened.[47]

The First Combat Cargo Group was activated in Sylhet on 21 August 1944 and began operations in September. The first missions were transporting supplies to Allied ground operations in Burma and bringing back casualties from Imphal. The First brought in men and supplies to build Allied air strips, dropped dummy cargoes to lead the enemy away from troops, and dropped paratroops for the assault on Rangoon. Part of the group was in China helping evacuate Chinese units trapped by the Japanese. Other planes flew gasoline, food, arms, and supplies over the Hump until the end of the war. The first commander in India was Maj. Samuel B. Ward.

The Fourth Combat Cargo Group began operations in India with C-47 and C-46 aircraft in December 1944. Operations included moving equipment and material for construction of the Ledo Road and transporting men, mules, and boats when the Allies crossed the Irrawaddy River. The Fourth also dropped Gurkha paratroops on Rangoon in 1945. The first base in India was Sylhet, and in December the group moved to Agartala, India. The commander was Col. Stuart D. Baird.[48]

Dr. John G. Martin from Ashland, Kentucky, historian for the Hump Pilots Association and one of the original members of the Tenth Combat Cargo Squadron, Third Combat Cargo Group, explained the work of his group: "We flew through the storms over the mountains, the heat of the jungle, the rains of the monsoon. . . . mists in the mountain passes, mildew on our clothes that wouldn't go away . . . the bamboo bashas . . . the noise and smells of India and China. . . . flying into muddy bomb-torn airfields delivering mail, ammunition, food, medical supplies, bulldozers, toilet paper . . . the memory of a dead soldier floating in a rain-filled bomb crater at Myitkyina still haunts me."

Combat Cargo planes flew day and night. Night was better because it offered protection from Japanese fighters. When they couldn't land, the cargo was dropped by parachute to isolated forward posts whose sole existence depended on the supplies dropped. Many of the crews stuffed old magazines and newspapers from back home inside the bundles — cargo that was just as important as food. Combat Cargo fought a different war than the Hump pilots. Martin writes, "Never will I forget the faces of the wounded . . . American, Chinese, British, Gurkha or Indian . . . riding back to a base hospital. . . . Some died and are buried in strange places on the other side of the world. . . . They were good soldiers. They went where they were told to go and hoped they would come back."[49]

In addition to flights over the Hump, ATC planes continued to be on constant call for other missions. On 13 March 1944, Admiral Mountbatten ordered the diversion of thirty Hump aircraft to fly soldiers of the Indian Seventh Division from Arakan to Imphal, in Burma. He received permission from Washington to keep the planes and crews for one month.[50] The mountain and jungle areas of Burma were so forbidding that the only way to move troops in an emergency was by air transport, and the army commanders were always quick to call on ATC for help. In addition to moving troops, ATC planes, with British soldiers as kickers, dropped 446 tons of food, ammunition, and medical supplies to the Indian troops.[51]

It would be unfair to leave the impression that the air wars over the Hump were fought by the Americans only. In early 1942, the British Royal Air Force (RAF) teamed with Chennault's AVG in the battle for Burma and, when Rangoon was lost, the RAF continued to fight and support troops in Burma. There was no greater fighting team in the air than British pilots and their spirited Spitfire fighters.

Squadrons of the Royal Australian Air Force (RAAF) hauled over seventy-five hundred tons of supplies over the Hump in November 1943—more than the ATC tonnage for the same month.[52] On 5 April 1944, the 216th RAF Transport Squadron arrived in the CBI to support ground operations in Burma. This squadron was composed of fifteen crews with battle experience in North Africa, Sicily, Italy, and southern Europe. They were flying the C-47 Dakotas and joined the RAF 177th Transport Wing to haul troops from the Bengal area to the Imphal Valley.[53] The experience that the RAF pilots had gained in other war theaters was a great benefit to the Americans "not yet bloodied by the war."[54]

Flight units of the British Royal Air Force, the Royal Canadian Air Force, the Royal Australian Air Force, and the Royal New Zealand Air Force flew side by side with the American ATC and Combat Cargo crews over the Hump and on supply missions to the fighting ground troops.

Fight as they did and cooperate as they had to, the American pilots and airmen who fought with the Royal Air Forces never learned to like the British. The "Limeys" were arrogant, always looking for a brawl with "the bloody Yanks," and had a military life style that was the envy of other Allied troops. The British were at home in India and Burma—the Americans were visitors. Occasionally the British received reluctant respect from the Americans because they always did their best against the enemy even though it was "to hell with the other Allies."

Eric Sevareid, during his visit to the CBI, observed that, "The British walked the earth as if they owned it—the Americans acted as if they didn't give a damn who owned it."[55]

The British drank expensive Haig and Haig Scotch, fine Canadian Club blend, and Old Beefeater gin—the best. The Americans drank beer and had a reward of a two-ounce ration of medicinal bourbon whiskey, with battery acid (grapefruit juice), for each Hump mission.

The British were happy to drink with little or no ice, but the Americans liked their beer cold. To cool beer in a land of no ice required American creativity. Crews would put the cans of beer along the inside skins of the aircraft behind the doors. After a round trip at twenty-thousand feet, they would have the coldest beer in India, and the party that followed would last until the next Hump flight.

Edgar D. Crumpacker, pilot for the Fourth Combat Cargo, made many flights for the British, carrying what he considered to be "non-combat cargo." One mission was to haul frozen New Zealand lamb to the British hospital in Chittagong. The flights required close scheduling to have the meat delivered while it was still frozen, especially in the heat of India.

"Because we were Combat Cargo," Crumpacker recalls, "we were supposed to be self-sustaining, and we never had good living conditions. We lived off the local economy, sleeping in Indian grass huts on rope bunks, and all we got in the way of army supplies were C-Rations which were pretty bad."

On one operation out of Sylhet, Crumpacker and his crew had a load which included a fifty-five-gallon drum. They discovered it contained rum, the traditional 151-proof rum ration. Thrown on the bonfire, it flamed like gasoline. That evening one of the crew tapped the keg and drew off a couple of gallons for a Christmas party. After all, they reasoned, the British would not miss a few out of fifty-five gallons.

Much of the British food supply came from New Zealand, including canned fruit, cheeses, bacon, and Tom Piper's vegetable stew—far better than the C-rations Crumpacker and his crew were eating. They carefully loaded fifty-pound baskets of fresh eggs "without cracking one egg." There were also canned bacon, canned cheese, and fresh chopped onions—delicious.

"The British became aware of our pilfering," Crumpacker writes in his CBI memoirs, ". . . said to be of crisis proportions. We felt we should be allowed to eat as well as they did since we were hauling the food for them.

"The problem was particularly acute when it came to hauling fancy foods, wines and liquors which they claimed were for hospital patients . . . we suspected they were actually going to privileged officers. . . . Soon they began putting Indian soldiers as custodians . . . the guards were very conscientious, and we were not able to share their luxuries in food."

On one flight Crumpacker and his crew had a full ten-thousand-pound load of Haig and Haig "pinch-bottle" Scotch. "All we wanted was one case, but the Indians kept an accurate count. When the plane was being unloaded, the crew snuck a case off the truck and stowed it in the belly compartment . . . as we taxied out for takeoff they called on the radio to return to the ramp . . . we dumped the case on the ground and took off without a single bottle!"[56]

In late April, General Stilwell started his offensive in Burma against the Japanese and asked for Hump planes to fly eighteen thousand Chinese troops from Yunnan to Sookerating. The troops were carried as reverse-tonnage—that is, on the return flight from China.

Flying Chinese troops was an assignment ATC crews tried to avoid. On one troop-moving mission, the pilot carefully explained to the Chinese commander that, in case of sickness, the soldiers were to vomit through the open door of the plane. He pointed to the door. Later in the flight, as the engineer was watching the troops, he saw a Chinese soldier become sick. The soldier was immediately seized by his commander and thrown out through the open door to his death ten thousand feet below.[57]

Frank Kovach, Sixteenth Combat Cargo Squadron, described his experiences flying Chinese troops:

> Then came the unruly Chinese soldiers . . . with full gear including guns and hand grenades. The weather was calm, so they began to play "catch" with the grenades. I told the pilot to give them "the treatment" . . . raise the nose and drop it sharply so they are suspended in mid air. This quieted them for the rest of the flight.
>
> On the next flight we insisted that they stow their gear in the belly compartment. The first four on board grabbed our parachutes and sat on them. . . . It was a rough flight and I spread four pails down the cabin and tried to explain in sign language what they were for. When we reached Chengkung, the pails were clean and there was puke all over the place.[58]

Ted Lewis, a Project 7-A pilot from Laguna Hills, California, felt compassion for young Chinese troops on his flights. He watched as forty small, thinly-clad conscript Chinese were herded aboard with no seats, no warm clothes, and no oxygen. Each carried his "baggage" —a couple of cups of rice and chopsticks. During the flight, he still remembers, "They sit huddled on the cold metal floor; they lie back and seem to pass out because of the altitude; they look dead." On arrival in India, "they are awake, half frozen, saying a word or two. They get out, look around and realize that they are back on earth. Their talk speeds up to a rattling chatter as they are again herded into a truck which will take them to the training camp where they will learn to fight."[59]

Hump pilots learned that one easy way to control Chinese troops was to take the plane to high altitude where the air was thin. With the aircrew on oxygen, the troops, with no oxygen, quietly went to sleep and did not wake up until the plane was ready to land. Pilots learned to lock the door to the crew compartment, and often, in extreme cases, had crewmen standing guard with machine guns to keep the Chinese from storming the pilot's compartment.[60]

General Tunner tells some of his experiences: "One morning I was watching a C-46 take off from Chanyi with a load of [Chinese] recruits. . . . something happened . . . the pilot had to put the plane down in a rice paddy. The plane opened like a rose, and sixty Chinese swarmed out and took off in every direction." On another occasion, Tunner watched as a plane seemed to be shedding Chinese as it roared down the runway. At the end of the runway, "the plane flew straight up in the air, flipped over on its back and crashed, killing everyone. It was obvious what had happened. The Chinese had gone into a panic. Several had jumped out to their deaths as the plane picked up speed. The rest dashed to the rear of the plane just as it became airborne, overweighing the tail."[61]

Hump pilots were not always blameless when flying troops or passengers who were afraid to fly. Some pilots liked to taunt jittery passengers. Favorite victims were returning American truck drivers who had brought cargo over the Burma Road and were "deadheading" back to India. Many stories have been told, but there are three stories I know to be true.

During a long flight, with the aircraft on automatic pilot, the crew would leave the cockpit and stand with heads bowed in the passenger compartment. Soberly, one crew member would explain, "Last year over this spot, a crew was lost, and we always leave our stations and let the lost pilot fly the plane." Through the open door, the passengers could see the controls moving with no one near. When the automatic pilot is flying the plane, the controls move back and forth as if some unseen hand is in control.

On some flights, crews had been known to bring on a store of empty beer and booze bottles. As the plane bounced, the crew compartment door would open and an empty bottle would be thrown back into the passenger compartment. In time, with the empties piling up and the weather getting rougher, the passengers would begin to wonder, "Is anyone up front sober?"

The "map routine" worked best after the aircraft had been flying on top of the clouds for several hours. The flight engineer would rush back and spread a large map on the floor. He would be joined by the pilot and copilot, and the three, on their knees, would begin arguing about where they were. Meanwhile, looking through the open door, it seemed that no one was flying the plane.

The success of the Hump was based on one fact—the pilots kept flying. Why did they keep flying? The answer is not purely patriotic. Look back to 1942. Remember that the pilots who flew the planes over the Hump were young men, some just out of college—many air crewmen were just out of high school—with the poverty of the Great Depression still burning in their memories.

To air-minded young men, the Hump represented an opportunity to fly commercial aircraft. If they lived and built up a lot of flying time, there might be a chance to qualify for one of the best jobs in the world—airline pilot. There was no other way to get training and experience in the C-47, C-46, and C-54. This was possible only through the army at war. It is terrible to admit that war was the silver lining to the dark days of the depression. Most of the Hump pilots' ambition was to fly commercial airliners after the war, and they were willing to fly any air route the army dictated. The Hump offered experience that could not be bought. Live or die—we took our chances.

Pilots who finished flight school were graduated as commissioned officers. Two years of college were required to qualify as an aviation cadet. However, after the passage of Public Law 99 in June 1941, and for a short time, enlisted men were graduated from flying school and rated as "staff-sergeant pilots." The first staff-sergeant pilots to fly the Hump were members of the First Ferrying Group, stationed in Chabua and flying C-47s. The First Ferrying Group began regular Hump flights, and many of the pilots were not commissioned officers.

Later, staff sergeant pilots were promoted to flight-officer pilots, a military limbo rank somewhere between enlisted and commissioned officer. Flight officers wore a single striped multicolored bar and had the same uncertain status as the army warrant officer. There was one important exception: flight-officer and enlisted pilots received ten percent overseas pay compared to five percent for officers.

Why some pilots were graduated as second lieutenants and some as flight officers was an unsolved mystery. The theory of having commissioned officers as pilots was based on the idea that the pilot was the commander of the aircraft, like a ship's captain, ranking all others on the flight. However, there were many instances where enlisted or flight-officer pilots flew in the left seat with second- or first-lieutenant copilots, usually because the enlisted pilots had more experience over the Hump—they knew the way to China.

This often caused confusion. Charles Bates from Dallas, flight-officer pilot for the ATC and Ferrying Command, was flying a C-54 from China to India with a presidential representative from Washington as a passenger. As a courtesy, Bates brought the man to the front and let him fly in the copilot's seat. The man looked over and saw Bates's "Kodachrome Bar" (flight-officer's insignia of rank). The Washington VIP told Bates that flight officers could not fly four-engine aircraft—only captains could do that. "The hell I can't," Charlie said, "I've been flying these things for over a year." The VIP said he was going to straighten that out when he got back to Washington. Nothing happened.[62]

Many Army Air Corps pilots were poorly trained in the rush to graduate classes from flight school—there was just not enough time to train them properly. General Stilwell once wrote a memorandum on training, referring to Fourteenth Air Force combat crews: "Replacement crews are going overseas who haven't fired a gun at altitudes over 16,000 feet. This is a hell of a way to send these boys overseas."[63] Many of the Hump pilots had never had flight training above 15,000 feet.

Pay for second-lieutenant pilots was $166.67 per month base, $83.33 for flight pay, $75 for the family back home, and $42 for subsistence— a total of $367 per month. Higher ranks received higher pay, but it was still less than civilians, working side by side with the pilots. Yet many young pilots and air crewmen were able to save enough money to buy homes and go to college when the war was over.

6

Wingate to Tunner—
1944

The "Chindits," "Cochran's Circus," and Orde Wingate were dramatic and important new developments in the air war over the Himalayas in 1944. To protect the Hump routes and to intensify the offensive against the Japanese, the U.S. and British began a new approach to the ground war—air support for the soldiers in the jungles of Burma. Two colorful U.S. Army pilots, hand-picked by no less than Air Force commander Gen. Henry Arnold himself, were teamed with an equally colorful and brilliant British military genius. The American pilots were colonels Phillip G. Cochran and John R. Allison, both already military heroes as fighter pilots. The British military genius was Brig. Gen. Orde Charles Wingate.

Born in the Burmese hills of the Himalayas, Wingate was the son of deeply religious parents dedicated to the Bible and the strict religious precepts of the Plymouth Brethren. Wingate received a classical academic and military education in England, but he was unpopular, dreamy, sullen, and silent. He loved Burma and would fight to his death, as he did, to get the Japanese out of his country.[1] Wingate carried his Bible with him and often read Plato and Aristotle in the midst of battle. His God was the warring God of the Old Testament. His wrath was aimed at the Japanese, and his directives on the battlefields were often biblical; for example, from Ecclesiastes 9:10, "Whatsoever thy hand findeth to do, do it with all thy might."[2]

At the QUADRANT Conference at Quebec, in August 1943, General Wingate dramatically presented his ideas to President Roosevelt and Prime Minister Churchill on how the Japanese could be defeated in Burma. Fighting the Japanese in the jungles had been a disaster for Stilwell and the British. Wingate had new ideas for jungle warfare. His plan was simple and, in Wingate fashion, it was unorthodox. He proposed a guerrilla operation deep behind the enemy lines, with a fast-moving strike force, supplied by air drop and directed by radio communications from spotter planes in the air.

His troops were called "Chindits," named after a mythical beast — half lion and half eagle — the Chinthe. Their griffin-like statues were guardians of the Burmese temples.[3] Wingate saw his Chindits fighting with the ferocity of lions while having the swiftness and striking power of eagles. The Chindits were mostly Burmese and Indian troops trained to live and fight in the jungles. To move his troops, evacuate the wounded, and drop supplies, Wingate needed air power. At QUADRANT, appearing almost as a prophet of biblical times, he stood before two of the most powerful military commanders of the world and promised that he would lead his battle-tough Chindits into Burma against the Japanese, and he would win. His promise was simple and he was sincere.

After the presentation, Churchill remarked, "Brigadier Wingate, we owe you our thanks. You have expounded a large and complex subject with exemplary lucidity." Typically British, Wingate replied, "Such is my invariable practice, sir."[4]

General Arnold was impressed. "Hell, this man is serious," he thought.[5] Wingate was typically unkempt, dirty, and smelly, but impressive in his sincerity. His military success before he came to Burma had been clearing Palestine of terrorists.

To furnish the air power for Wingate's jungle fighters, Arnold, Allison, and Cochran supplied everything they wanted including fighters, bombers, gliders, puddle-jumping light planes, and helicopters. The helicopters would be the first to be used in combat.

Military leaders at QUADRANT were searching for innovative ways to defeat the enemy. Previous successes in the CBI had been through unorthodox approaches, whereas traditional methods of war had failed against the Japanese, so much so that many military leaders were beginning to believe that victory was impossible. Admiral Mountbatten, when he came to India as supreme commander, had been told by his generals that "Japanese infiltration was impossible to stop . . . an offensive from Assam was impossible . . . Wingate was — well, impossible." Mountbatten refused to listen.[6] He was impressed with this innovative British brigadier general who wanted to fight the Japanese, not man-to-man, face-to-face, as Stilwell had done, but by the use of ground troops moved, supplied, and directed from the air.

Allison and Cochran were given their own "air force": thirty P-51 fighters, twenty B-25 medium bombers, thirty-two C-47s, one hundred Waco CG-4A and TG-5 gliders, one hundred L-1 and L-5 Piper Cubs, and six R-4 Sikorsky helicopters — nearly three hundred planes and six hundred men, all under British command.[7] This was often called "Cochran's Circus."

The No. 1 Air Commando Group was activated at Hailakandi, India, on 29 March 1944 and moved to Asansol, India on 20 May. Commanders Allison and Cochran were eager to fight, and the group went into combat immediately.

"Flip Corkin," the hero of Milton Caniff's popular cartoon strip "Terry and the Pirates," was named after Philip Cochran, the commando group's leader. When Wingate and Cochran first met, Wingate complained that Churchill and Roosevelt had sent him a "comic strip hero" to be his air force commander. Cochran's first impression of Wingate was equally strange. When Cochran asked about flying in Burma, he got a lecture on Buddhism.[8] Wingate quoted Plato and the Bible. However, as the men talked, they gained respect for each other and soon were convinced that they could work military miracles in Burma.[9] Suddenly a new military team was formed with new fighting tactics based on daring, new ideas, and innovative use of aircraft.

Wingate wanted to use his troops on the ground in the same way fighter pilots fight in the air — strike deep in enemy territory, break away, and strike again at an unexpected place. The raids would be directed by radio from an observer in a plane. Wingate was convinced by Cochran that gliders could carry troops as well as artillery, and soldiers could be moved into new areas quickly. Gliders for the movement of troops and helicopters to rescue the wounded were new tactics, used for the first time in Burma by the Air Commando Group.

Cochran's No. 1 Air Commando Group carried out one of the most dramatic air operations of the year in March and April. Over ten thousand men, thirteen hundred animals, and close to a million pounds of supplies were carried 150 miles by air behind Japanese lines. In the late afternoon, 5 March, a fleet of C-47 planes took off, each towing two gliders. They crossed the eight-thousand-foot Chin hills and released the gliders 250 miles from their base. In the one operation, fifty-four gliders were sent out; seventeen were recalled, but thirty-seven were released, putting 539 men, three mules, and twenty-nine thousand pounds of stores into a small airstrip. This operation was called BROADWAY, named after the landing strip used.

In twenty-four hours engineers completed a longer landing strip, and in the next weeks, wave after wave of cargo aircraft brought additional troops, including 9,052 of Wingate's Chindits, in support of the Battle of Imphal.[10]

Pilot Stamford Robertson, Plainville, Connecticut, tells about the first rescue by a helicopter in combat. It took place on 25 April 1944 and was staged by the No. 1 Air Commando Group in Wingate's second invasion of Burma. In the first invasion, wounded soldiers had to be left behind. Morale went sky-high when it was known that they had a chance of being flown out if they were wounded. Some light planes, such as the L-5s or L-1s, were able to rescue soldiers by landing on roads, in rice paddies, or in jungle clearings, but they could not go into the heavy jungle as the helicopter could.

The R-4 helicopter was a success, although it was so underpowered that all pilots had to weigh 150 pounds or less. It didn't have much of a range or ceiling and not too fast a cruise.[11] The Sikorsky helicopter had a 180-horsepower engine with three fifteen-foot blades, and a range of one hundred miles at a speed of ninety miles per hour. This was a primitive beginning, but the helicopter changed ideas about war; it brought new life to behind-the-lines operations and new hope to casualties.

Tragically, General Wingate was killed on 24 March when his B-25 crashed into a mountain west of Imphal. His grieving Chindits, under the new leadership of Maj. Gen. W. D. A. Lentaigne, and the Allison-Cochran Air Commando Group continued his plans.

General Stilwell continued to press his man-to-man war tactics against the Japanese in the jungles of Burma. His troops recaptured the city of Myitkyina, an important midpoint on the Hump route. This was a major success for the Allies. During the spring and summer of 1944, it was never known who really controlled the town or airfield. Air force combat pilots reported, at one time, that they were taking off from one end of the air strip and bombing the other end.[12] Myitkyina was a major Japanese base, and its loss was a crushing defeat.

Everyone cooperated in the Battle of Myitkyina. General Stilwell had tremendous help from the air force. ATC Hump planes and the Combat Cargo crews brought in twenty-five hundred combat troops, airborne engineers, and equipment such as bulldozers, tractors, graders, and rollers to the Myitkyina area.[13]

Heroics in the air were common. In March 1944, troop carrier pilots Ralph Ilmanen, Riverside, California, and George Laben, Albuquerque, New Mexico, dropped two OSS agents into a rice paddy south of

Bhamo. As a "postscript" to their mission, they flew to the Japanese-held Myitkyina airfield, and, from their C-47 cargo plane, kicked out six one-hundred-pound bombs over the field. They flew so low over the field that all were direct hits. Lt. Col. Ray Peers, commander of OSS Detachment 101, was "bombardier" for the flight and did the bomb kicking.[14]

A Herculean feat for the Second Troop Carrier Squadron, late in the Myitkyina campaign, was hauling in a five-ton 105-mm howitzer, equivalent to a six-inch naval gun and the largest weapon in the Burma campaign. The heavy gun was dismantled and carried in two planes. One C-47, carrying the huge barrel, was forced down because of engine trouble. A new plane and a new crew completed the mission. Capt. Benjamin F. Beauman, Tunnel Hill, Illinois; 1st. Lt. Max L. Fisher, Chapel Hill, Texas; 2nd Lt. Robert G. Lime, Gardens, California; and 1st Lt. Robert W. Diehman, Rosenburg, Oregon, were pilots on the mission.[15]

There were no more tenacious fighters than the Japanese. Maj. Gen. Genzu Mizukami, with 2,757 troops, had stubbornly defended Myitkyina. Toward the end of July, with 790 killed and 1,180 wounded, he decided that further sacrifice was useless.

On 1 August, just before General Stilwell's troops entered Myitkyina, Colonel Maruyama, second in command, slipped out of the city with six hundred men. Major General Mizukami remained with 187 wounded. He had held out for seventy-six days against Stilwell's army and the power of the Allied Air Force. His duty as a soldier done with honor, Mizukami, following the Bushido code, apologized to the emperor for his failure and committed ritual suicide.[16]

After the Japanese were driven out of Burma, Myitkyina gave the Hump airlift a halfway station from India to China, and the field became one of the busiest in the ATC chain. In late 1944, a record of 284 transports were loaded and unloaded in one day, in addition to fighter and liaison planes coming and going around the clock. In one thirteen-hour period in October, there were 556 landings and takeoffs, including 195 transports. The Myitkyina airfield was a cooperative effort of the Americans and the British. Indian troops, paid by the British and fed by the Americans, loaded and unloaded the aircraft. Chinese armies were clothed by the British and armed by the Americans—a very cooperative and efficient arrangement.[17]

General Chennault, however, bitterly criticized Stilwell's use of Hump crews for the Myitkyina campaign because it reduced the amount of supplies his Fourteenth Air Force received. Stilwell continued to be critical of Chennault and asked that he admit failure in stopping the Japanese by air alone. Chennault refused to admit any such failure. Yet Stilwell's victory at Myitkyina made possible the future of the Fourteenth Air Force because it opened the lower southern Hump route from Calcutta to Kunming. With Myitkyina free of Japanese fighters, supplies could then be flown to Chennault across an easier route.

While Chennault and Stilwell argued over their part of the Hump supply, the feud between Stilwell and Chiang Kai-shek continued to smolder. Throughout the Burma campaign, Chiang's Chinese soldiers had been unable to coordinate a sustained attack. "Their response to orders to attack was to sit in their trenches and pour volleys of small arms fire into the air."[18] Stilwell wanted the Chinese to fight their own battles. Chiang was chafing under Stilwell's constant badgering and seemed to be increasingly troubled by a caustic American general commanding his Chinese troops. Chiang was not pleased that Stilwell controlled the allocation of supplies over the Hump, and in his distribution of the supplies, Stilwell had found it impossible to please Chiang.

A State Department memorandum admitted that the Stilwell-Chiang bitterness was affecting U.S.-Chinese relations and could have an adverse affect on the Hump airlift and the outcome of the war. The memo, in part, read, "United States Army personnel in general adopts an unsympathetic, even antagonistic, attitude toward China. Relations between Chiang Kai-shek and General Stilwell are most unfortunate."[19] Chiang Kai-shek continued to call on the seemingly inexhaustible American wealth and determined to do nothing in return in the way of attacking the Japanese.[20]

The Chinese people also believed that the individual soldiers were made of pure gold. In addition to being a land of intrigue and strange customs, China had many economic traps that were constantly plaguing Allied airmen caught in the dilemma of business as opposed to emotion. Joe Fault, an armorer for the Eighth Airdrome Squadron at Tanchuk, had to go to a machine shop three miles upstream from Wuchow to supervise manufacturing of machine-gun mounts. He decided to go by sampan. After being almost mobbed by dozens of sampan operators clawing each other for the privilege of transporting his exalted person, Joe selected the cleanest sampan, belonging to a woman with two children.

Fault made a fatal mistake — he did not set the price before he left. When he returned to dockside, he handed the woman the usual price of twenty CN (er shih). She refused and began to cry. "Er pai! Er pai!" The children began to cry. Er pai was two hundred CN, ten times the usual price. As Joe held out, the situation was getting nasty, with other sampan operators becoming indignant.

Fault gave her two hundred CN. He thought, maybe, the price in Wuchow was two hundred for a ride that was twenty in Tanchuk.

Next morning Fault was back for his second ride up the river. He tried to ignore the lady. She must have been a member of the sampan longshoreman's union because no other operator would have anything to do with him—he had to ride with the lady. "To shao chien? (How much?)" he asked. With innocent eyes, she replied, "Er shih (twenty)."

As on the previous day, twenty CN was rejected with loud wails, screams, cries, and gestures. Her oar had been split on the trip and it would cost two hundred CN to replace it. Without the oar she was out of business—she would starve. Her two children would starve. Fault paid two hundred.

This became a daily game. Always, before leaving, twenty CN was agreed on, and on the return there was always a reason for demanding two hundred—a broken tea pot, a boat leak, boils on the kids' heads, no papa, no clothes. This continued for six weeks until the gun mounts were finished.

Joe Fault found later that the woman was required to share the two hundred CN with the other sampan operators and, because of the success of "the game," the rate immediately was doubled—forty CN—for locals and increased ten times—two hundred CN—for foreign devils.[21]

Vice-President Henry Wallace was sent from Washington to try to work out the increasing antagonism between Stilwell and the generalissimo. Wallace's recommendation was that Stilwell should either be replaced or be given a special presidential representative. Everyone seemed to agree that Stilwell was the best general for China, and the U.S. wanted him to be in charge. But Vinegar Joe had a problem getting along with leadership, both American and Chinese. Nevertheless, President Roosevelt "requested Generalissimo Chiang Kai-shek to accept American Lieutenant General Stilwell as commander of all China's armed forces. This was an unprecedented proposal: no American had ever before directly commanded the national forces of an ally."[22] This increased the tension between Chiang and Stilwell.

Chiang appeared to agree with President Roosevelt that Stilwell should be permitted to command Chinese troops, but he delayed a final decision. Roosevelt continued to press for complete control of Chinese troops by Stilwell. Experience in Burma and a long-held lack of confidence in Chiang had convinced Roosevelt that the generalissimo was not capable of leading his own troops.

Chiang kept delaying a decision until 19 September when he received a letter from President Roosevelt, carried personally by General Stilwell, demanding action. The letter, in part, read, "My Chiefs of Staff and I are convinced that you are faced with a disaster . . . if you do not provide manpower for your divisions in North Burma, . . . we will lose all chance of opening land communications with China and immediately jeopardize the air route over the Hump."

Roosevelt charged Chiang with full personal responsibility for putting the war in jeopardy and urged that he take drastic action to resist the disaster which was moving closer to China. The letter ended, "I trust that your farsighted vision will realize the necessity for immediate action. . . . I have expressed my thoughts with complete frankness because it appears that all your and our efforts to save China are to be lost by further delays."[23]

Chiang became very angry because Stilwell had delivered the letter in person. This was a serious "loss of face." On 25 September, the generalissimo officially refused to accept Stilwell. On 2 October, presiding over a meeting of the Standing Committee of the Central Executive Committee of the Kuomintang, Chiang informed the group, as he spoke heatedly and banged the table, that "General Stilwell must go" and all lend-lease material must come to him (the generalissimo).

Chiang further stated, "China was better off before the Pacific War [for] then the Chinese were able to hold the Japanese; now, since the Pacific War began, China is suffering losses and reverses. This is a new form of imperialism."[24]

President Roosevelt accepted Chiang Kai-shek's decision. In a telegram to the Chinese leader on 5 October, the President wrote, "I must state my surprise and regret at the reversal of your agreement of August 12th to accept Stilwell . . . I am now inclined to feel that the United States Government should not assume the responsibility involved in placing an American officer in charge of your ground forces."

Roosevelt further stated that he would relieve Stilwell as Chaing's chief of staff and was willing to continue General Chennault as commander of the Fourteenth Air Force. However, the president restated his belief that the Hump tonnage was of such tremendous importance to the stability of the Chinese government that Stilwell should be in charge of the forces in Burma under Chiang. Otherwise, he felt that the Hump tonnage would be interrupted by Japanese action. If this was not acceptable, tonnage over the Hump would be under the direction of Lt. Gen. Daniel Sultan in Burma.[25]

On 11 October, Chiang requested that President Roosevelt recall Stilwell, and seven days later the general was ordered to return to Washington. The Stilwell days in China were over. Officially, Stilwell's recall ended the China-Burma-India theater. However, in spite of this official action, the identity of "CBI" was never changed in the minds of the thousands of airmen who served until the end of the war. Today, there are over seven thousand members of various "CBI" veterans' organizations, and with no question in their minds, they are all CBI veterans.

With the departure of Stilwell, the China-Burma-India theater (CBI) was split into two theaters: an India-Burma theater (IBT) with General Sultan as commander, and a China theater (CT) to be commanded by Gen. Albert C. Wedemeyer. General Wedemeyer would be Generalissimo Chiang Kai-shek's chief of staff and would command all U.S. forces in China. General Sultan was placed in charge of Hump tonnage allocation. Admiral Mountbatten was commander of all Southeast Asia forces.

There was a question as to whether the Chinese would accept the British Mountbatten, who immediately flew to Chungking to pay his respects to Chiang Kai-shek. Chiang was apprehensive.

Mountbatten faced China's ruler. "Sir, I have come directly to see you. I have not paused in Delhi to collect my staff. I realize you have been fighting the enemy much longer than any of us, and I know how heavily I shall have to rely upon your counsel."[26] Chiang could not believe what he heard—never had anyone from Britain spoken a kind word to him, nor recognized his position. The war immediately seemed headed for a new direction.

The drama of the Hump continued. As world leaders argued and as generals were assigned and recalled, aircraft kept flying and crews kept dying. Small dramatic incidents, in the totality of the war, were enacted over and over. For example, consider this story of flying single-engine P-51s over the Hump.

Pilots of the 118th Tactical Reconnaissance Squadron (TRS) were grounded in Chabua because of rain. With new P-51Ns, pilots were waiting in humid, hot, mosquito-ridden Chabua, only a short hop across the Hump to combat in China. The pilots were ready to go. Their personal gear had been stowed in the fuselage, tanks had been topped off, and oxygen was up to pressure. On 12 June, with a letup in the rain, clearance was given. Pilots raced to their planes. The clouds were heavy and visibility was poor, but the youthful pilots were optimistic—there had to be sunshine up there somewhere, and there was a war to be fought.

In the race to take off, two planes ran into each other on the runway and had to drop out; twenty-three got into the air and immediately went into the clouds. Suddenly reality dawned on the young pilots—how can you fly if you can't see? However, the clouds were not too thick, and soon, on top, twenty-four planes broke into the clear. The twenty-fourth plane was flown by an experienced weather pilot who had been sent to lead the eager young pilots across the Hump in weather they had never experienced.

George Kutscher, one of the P-51 pilots, believes, with certainty, that "without the weather pilot's guidance and expert flying, there would have been twenty-three corpses and shattered airplanes dotting the Himalayas. At twenty-four thousand feet the P-51s were using full power, had reached their ceiling and were stretching to keep air speed just above stalling. To stall out was to spin down more than four miles into the mountains."

Kutscher recalls that "two pilots ran out of oxygen and went down into the clouds, set their course for China and prayed. Only one made it! The other pilot said he was returning to Chabua, but he never made it and joined the hundreds of others who crashed and were never found.

"A minute is normally sixty seconds, but not when you are barely maintaining altitude. When your engine is screaming to stay alive, and you are running out of oxygen—a minute can be forever. Imagine 120 such minutes. Two hours later, the lead pilot saw a hole in the clouds and peeled into a screaming dive—the others followed."

At the bottom of the hole was Yunnanyi. The P-51s made a brief stop in Yunnanyi to recover from the harrowing flight and to meet their unknown leader, Rod McKinnon of the Sixteenth Fighter Squadron. They continued to Kunming and joined Tex Hill's fighter group of Chennault's Fourteenth Air Force.

General Chennault wrote, "Truly, they were eager. In three months, the 74th Fighter Squadron and the 118th Tactical Reconnaissance Squadron hit a quarter of a million tons of shipping, knocked out 512 enemy planes without the loss of a single pilot. They flew 6 percent of the missions and accounted for 60 percent of damage to enemy planes in that period."[27]

In August 1944, the age of "big business" came to the Hump when Brig. Gen. William H. Tunner took command of the airlift. General Tunner had been commander of the Ferrying Division of the Air Transport Command for three years—a command of over fifty thousand men, including eight thousand pilots. His ferry crews had delivered ten thousand planes per month in the United States and over a thousand per month overseas. His command was equivalent to two global airlines.[28]

Brig. Gen. Thomas Hardin was leaving the Hump to become commander of the India-China division of the Air Transport Command. In less than one year, General Hardin had brought order to the loose operations of the airlift, pushed Hump crews to their limits, and dramatically increased the flow of supplies to China.

Hardin had been so successful in increasing Hump tonnage that there was a growing confidence in the War Department that any amount of war materiel could be flown into China if aircraft and men could be provided.[29] But the price for increased tonnage was paid in men and planes. Washington was concerned.

Despite his tough demands on the Hump crews, General Hardin was liked by his airmen. As a parting tribute to their former commander, men of the ATC celebrated "Tom Hardin Day" on 22 August with an all-out effort to set a record for Hump flights in one twenty-four-hour period. A record was set. On that one day 308 sorties and thirteen hundred tons were flown into China.[30] This was more in one day than in the first whole month of Hump flying.

General Tunner felt that his being sent to the CBI was equivalent to military exile, and he was troubled about the assignment. In his book Over the Hump, Tunner explains, "Hardin had been there only a few months. It seemed strange that he would be replaced so soon. . . . if I had to go anywhere, why did it have to be to the Hump? It was the graveyard for commanders. . . . It was a place to which you exiled officers you wanted to get rid of. . . . [However], if my overseas assignment was to be the graveyard of the Hump, well, so be it."[31]

General Tunner's first official act was to personally pilot a commandeered C-46 over the Hump, with passengers and freight, to Kunming and return. He realized later that this was a foolhardy thing to have done because he had never flown the Hump and had not even flown the new C-46 aircraft. Yet he wanted to know what his pilots were going through. As he took off from Chabua, he saw black blotches on the runway—each blotch was a grim memorial to a plane that had crashed and burned. It was at this point that he realized that the reason he had been sent to the Hump was to reduce the accident rate. Men were dying at the expense of increased cargo demands.

Morale was a big factor in the accident rate. Food was bad, mostly Spam and dehydrated potatoes, and the PX rarely had candy, magazines, books, or razor blades. When off duty the men had nothing to do. Their uniforms showed lack of laundry and were badly worn, and the men wore beards and handlebar mustaches.[32]

One of Tunner's aides, who had been in India several weeks before the general came, reported, "I have never seen or heard of people living—existing—as they do here. . . . This is grim. Nothing counts but the tonnage that goes over the Hump. Morale is at the shoelaces. Everyone wants to go home—getting out of here is all they think about."[33]

General Tunner moved quickly. The pilots' number one complaint was that they could not turn back when weather was too bad to fly because of General Hardin's "no weather" rule. One of Tunner's first orders was, "Weather is a factor which every operations officer will consider in dispatching aircraft."

There *was* weather on the Hump—General Tunner knew that. When a pilot flew into a severe storm, found his plane being buffeted around and icing up to the extent that he might not make it, Tunner said that the pilot had his orders to turn around and come back. Many flights were delayed, but fewer pilots flew into mountains.[34] Nevertheless, some pilots, in writing of their experiences on the Hump, felt that although General Tunner may have formally rescinded the order, Hardin's order was still in the minds of operations officers in their desire to keep the flights going.

Crews fought a tropical fungus called "Dhobi itch," a hellish rash that persisted until they left the tropical climate of India. Malaria was a constant threat, and all personnel were required to take a daily dose of Atabrine—a yellow pill that kept malaria down. Atabrine was on every mess hall table, like salt and pepper. Soon the skin became yellow, and it was easy to identify newcomers to the Hump—their skin was still a normal color. But malaria was controlled.

Tunner was concerned about crew rotation. To qualify to go home, pilots had to fly 650 hours. Some flew as many as 165 hours a month to get time as quickly as possible. Many crew members were nearing operational exhaustion and had a greater risk of accident. So General Tunner increased the rotation time to 750 hours with a one-year minimum. This was an average of about 65 hours a month. The pilots complained, but they no longer tried to fly day and night, they were not as tired, and accidents went down.

As rotation time neared, anxiety began to mount. To pilots and crewmen almost ready to go home, the most dreaded assignment was the "last flight"—the one flight needed to complete the number of hours, or the "one more flight" operations sometimes talked pilots into as they waited to be sent home.

ATC pilot Phil Sunderman remembers his "last flight." "I had completed my tour and was sweating rotation . . . I was asked to make one more trip across the Rockpile . . . a short trip . . . no big deal . . . three hours and fifty minutes . . . CFR [contact flight rules] all the way."

So Sunderman agreed to just one more flight. Operations explained

Flight crew quarters were primitive but comfortable. This was at Chabua, India, in 1945. The author, right, and navigator John Bortz, stay comfortable in India heat.

that he might want to be careful going into Paoshan—don't overshoot since there was a ditch at the end of the runway, and the last thousand feet was under water and muddy. "Just keep the landing short. O.K.?"

The cargo was percussion caps, ten thousand pounds of mortar shells, and several thousand pounds of dynamite. Sunderman thought, "If that baby blows, I will be home faster than expected.

"I made two low passes over that field . . . [and] came in with a low, very, very slow approach . . . I swear, to this day, the so-called 'ditch' at the end of the runway was the Burma Road. I dragged the bird in just a hair above stalling speed and laid those wheels down like putting varnish on a hardwood floor . . . I don't think I would have cracked an egg on that touchdown."[35]

ATC Hump crews were often criticized because they had little respect for the regular military discipline which is so important to the army. Men who faced death almost every day could not see the importance of saluting or keeping clean and closely shaved. Uniforms were sloppy, most men wore Natal mosquito boots when not flying, and the officer's dress caps were worn as a badge of individualism. I can remember a chewing we got at a base review when the general accused the pilots of looking like a "bunch of damned taxi drivers."

General Tunner ordered the filthy living conditions of the crews cleaned up and full-dress inspections daily. We were required to wear blouse and pinks for the evening meal at the officer's club. On Saturday, all base personnel not in the air or on flight alert would have a formal parade. Men shaved, cut their hair, cleaned their uniforms, marched erect . . . and complained. But morale soon improved.

Tunner defended his orders, "I had been sent to this command to direct American soldiers, and while I was their commander, by God, they were going to live like Americans and be proud they were Americans."[36]

"Quiet" signs were put up in living quarters so that crews flying at night could sleep during the day. Mobile PX trucks brought food and drinks to the flight line, and twenty-four-hour-a-day cafeterias were set up so that food was available at any hour of the day or night. Crews were brought to the flight line in jeep "taxis," and new safety programs were set up. Search-and-rescue squadrons were better organized and more efficiently operated. A first-pilot checkout school, a C-46 mobile unit, and a LORAN navigational unit were organized. Aircrews were given training in jungle survival and how to use the emergency equipment on board the aircraft.

Special correspondence schools were organized so that crew members could take courses for professional study or college credit. The men were encouraged to take short vacations around India when not on duty. "India is a strange, exotic country," General Tunner wrote, "a land of great beauty . . . a land of extremes. As long as our men were there, I considered it a command function to make it possible for them to see some of the fascinating sights."[37] It seemed like the last meal before the execution, but we were encouraged, on days off, to hop rides on "administrative flights" and take short tours of India and China.

On one such flight, we stopped at Agra to see the Taj Mahal. In the presence of the world's most beautiful building, we walked barefooted through unbelievable muck and slime—you don't wear shoes in India's religious buildings. The Taj was an Indian maharajah's tribute to his lover—a delicate jewel of workmanship. Leaving the beautiful building, we returned to the reality of India with its crude commercialism—our shoes were held for "ransom" when we came out—cleaned and shined—"ten rupees, please." We paid.

On the banks of the Jumna River, we quietly witnessed a holy ritual—a body was being burned. Few bodies are buried in India; burning on a funeral pyre spirits the dead to the next world, and the ashes are thrown in the river. Sometimes the widows of the dead would throw themselves on the burning pyre of their husbands. During the cremation, almost as a sideshow, small boys wrestled giant turtles and dived for coins.

The beauty of India was offset by the horror of poverty and lack of concern for the lowest of Indian castes. In Calcutta, tours were arranged through "off limits" areas of the ancient city. On the streets we stepped over the dead, the dying, and the poor souls horribly diseased, crippled, and hungry. We saw unbelievable horror—the stench was a fetid barrier we passed through. I can never forget the eyes of those living bones, begging for something no one could give. I suffered, knowing there was nothing I could do. Nothing we had ever been told had prepared us for this sight. We left as quickly as we could. I am sorry we went. India was a world we had never seen, and may God spare the sight again. Somehow the British had failed—the world had failed.

General Tunner continued to try to make the Hump safer. Crews were often careless in flight discipline, and traffic control was indifferent. He ordered precise flight operations; flight plans were required, altitudes were assigned, and pilots were required to check in at regular points on all missions. Oxygen was required from ten thousand feet up on day flights and from ground up at night. Before Tunner, pilots would fly on the treetops, skimming through the mountain passes, endangering their crews and other aircraft. General Tunner stopped that practice. Proper radio communication and formal take-off and landing procedures were inaugurated. This improved efficiency, and the C-46s, generally ignoring weather, averaged two round trips per day per airplane.[38]

The most controversial new idea from General Tunner changed the procedures for aircraft maintenance. The traditional method of repair and maintenance was for each plane to have a crew chief and a flight engineer whose jobs were to make minor repairs and keep the plane operational. Major repair, such as engine changes or radio or instrument repair, was done at base maintenance. General Tunner set up a procedure called Production Line Maintenance (PLM) in which each plane, on a regular schedule, would go through a production line for standardized routine inspections and maintenance.

The regular maintenance procedure required an aircraft to be out of commission for two or three days for repairs, including routine inspection. With PLM, in twenty-two hours the plane was ready to fly. A series of stations made specialized repairs, and the aircraft would move from station to station. For example, at the first station, there would be a general inspection, with engine run-up, forms check, and a plan for needed maintenance. At the second station, the airplane would be washed and polished, inside and out; the cowlings were removed, engines sprayed and cleaned, sumps drained, and so forth. Station three would check and repair carburetion, radios, propellers, and anti-icing systems. Finally, the plane was serviced and given a flight test. Twenty-two hours and it was back over the Hump again.

Although pilots and operations were skeptical about PLM, preferring to trust their own crew members, General Tunner reported that PLM was responsible for an increase in operational aircraft from 78 percent in January to 85 percent in July 1945. Inspection time was reduced 25 percent and planes were in the air 50 percent more.[39]

More new ideas followed. To free American airmen from routine jobs, native laborers were hired to perform flight-line tasks such as washing, cleaning, and painting. Soon the natives proved so adept that they began working on engines and doing clerical work. Eventually, the Hump operation was using fifty thousand Indians and Chinese for routine work—each replacing an American airman. It was quickly learned that the native's poverty or inability to speak good English was no indication of inferior intelligence or lack of desire to work.

Especially successful were Indian guards to protect airplanes while parked or during maintenance. Indian Gurkhas, Sikhs, Pathans, and Hindus, armed only with a knife, provided security. On my base, Barrackpore, north of Calcutta, Gurkhas in turbans and native military dress were used as guards. Day or night, as we approached our planes, we were required to stop, walk to the front of our jeep, put our identification on the ground, and stand back while the guard checked. The Gurkhas used long curved knives which could be thrown with a horizontal rotation that could cut a man in two. We never checked it out.

Like most American air crewmen in India, I was too young to appreciate the opportunity we had to observe other cultures in a foreign country. Two rather insignificant incidents when we were living in India taught me that there are no "primitive" people in the world.

First, at our mess halls, I noticed that the Indian kitchen workers and waiters brought their own lunches and ate on tables behind the kitchen. Curious, I asked our waiter why. "Because," he said, "if we were to get in the habit of eating your food, when you go back to America, we would not like our food."

Capt. John Jones, Project 7-A pilot, was impressed with the difficulties and complexity of the Indian caste system. "In our own barracks, there were eight castes and seven different religions. It took a dozen men to serve breakfast, for some could handle one kind of food and some another."[40]

We learned to appreciate our Indian bearers and were humbled by their attention to us. One day at our basha, my copilot was trying to solve a calculus problem for a correspondence course. He was having trouble, and our Indian housekeeper was watching over the copilot's shoulder. After a few minutes, the bearer pointed to a specific problem and said, "Your error is there." From then on, the copilot and the bearer studied calculus together, and maybe the basha was not quite so clean, or our socks were not always folded, but we were happy to meet a native friend on common ground. The British educational system in India was efficient. The Indians were intelligent, well educated, and spoke beautiful soft English.

Another utilization of "native" labor was teaching elephants to load planes. The first such elephant, "Miss Amari," was widely publicized in the U.S. newspapers. She easily learned to put her tusks under a gasoline drum, wrap her trunk around it, and lift it carefully into the cargo bay of the aircraft.

Following the success of "Tom Hardin Day" in August, and a new record of 34,914 tons in November, the Hump crews planned a Christmas gift for General Tunner, their new commander. The crews at Misamari flew an average of thirty trips a day. With no fanfare, and no pressure on crews to fly extra missions, a goal of fifty-five trips was set from this one field for a twenty-four-hour period on Christmas Eve. When the day was finished, eighty-one trips had been flown across the Hump—a new record. On 26 December, a letter to General Tunner stated, "We did it as a Christmas present . . . a forerunner of accomplishments to be attained in the future."[41]

President Roosevelt had frequently expressed his personal satisfaction with the work of the Hump crews. In a letter to General Chennault, 2 October, 1944, the President stated, "Apparently the old supply line over the Hump is working out better than you and I thought."[42]

However, General Marshall was concerned about the cost of the Hump to the total war. He wrote, "The 'Over the Hump' airline has been bleeding us white in transport planes. . . . the effort over the mountains of Burma bids fair to cost us an extra winter in the main theater of war."[43]

As the war in Europe began to wind down, supply efforts to China intensified. A new and more efficient cargo aircraft came to the Hump. In October 1944, Douglas's four-engine "Skymaster," the C-54, was put into service over the lower Hump routes from Kurmitola-Tezgaon, in East Bengal, to China.[44] Stilwell's success in driving the Japanese out of Myitkyina had eliminated the fighter threat. The new route to China across lower Burma was faster, the mountains were not so high, and the weather was better than the northern routes from Assam.

Two new routes were established. These were eastbound "Nan" and westbound "Oboe," distances of 1,012 miles east and 1,004 miles west with minimum instrument altitudes of 12,500 feet. These were longer than the northern routes but easier to fly with the new Skymaster.

The C-54 was already a battle-tested aircraft with service in other parts of the world. It had first come to the CBI as an aircraft for commanders, with, of course, every luxury. The first C-54, the commercial DC-4, was built by Douglas and delivered to the army in June 1942. The first models were tested by the commercial airlines on the Miami-Natal (Brazil) run and across the North Atlantic to Britain on contract carrier service. The C-54 had a payload of ninety-six hundred pounds with a range of twenty-five hundred miles.[45]

When the C-54 was being developed, an army general had seriously asked Donald W. Douglas, president of Douglas Aircraft, "What *possible* use could the United States Army have for a four-engine transport?" Douglas persisted, and the design and development for the C-54 was started in 1938.[46]

The Skymaster was "big brother" to the highly successful C-47 and had the same dependability. It was immediately accepted by the pilots because of the reputation of the C-47, which was made by the same company. In the CBI, the C-54 had become known as the "general's aircraft" and was popular because of this built-in prestige. The plane could carry three times the load of the C-47 with a ceiling of twenty thousand feet at 250 miles per hour. CBI Hump pilots dreamed of flying the C-54, the nearest military equivalent to commercial airline aircraft.

With eight fuel tanks, the C-54 carried 3,540 gallons. This allowed the plane to fly to China, drop off a thousand gallons of fuel from its own tanks, and return to India without refueling. It was the most successful four-engine transport plane of the war. If the Japanese had held on for another year, possibly all C-47s and C-46s would have been replaced by the C-54.

Like the C-47, the C-54 was an exceptional all-weather plane. On 6 April 1945, a C-54 enroute to Tezgaon from China encountered heavy thunderstorms. At nineteen thousand feet a violent updraft turned the plane on its back and threw it into a spiral dive. The crew could not bail out because of centrifugal force. Suddenly, with a severe jolt, the plane righted itself at four thousand feet, after dropping fifteen thousand feet. As described by the pilot, the plane did a "split-S,"[47] diving at an estimated speed of six hundred miles per hour. The crew landed successfully with buckled wings, torn rivets, and shredded deicer boots, and the pilot was admitted to the hospital with a nervous breakdown.[48]

Vincent A. Mahoney, Concord, New Hampshire, tells a sequel to the story:

> A Douglas test pilot was checking out pilots when he heard of the C-54 on the ground at Myitkyina and decided to inspect it. I went along. The fuselage was twisted three to four degrees out of line and rivets were popped out all over the fuselage and wings. His comments were, "Incredible! Incredible! Incredible!"
>
> On the way back to the base, the Douglas pilot decided to show us what the C-54 could do. He shut down two engines on one side, and then shut down the third and flew with only one outboard engine. He pulled the nose up and stalled the plane and dropped into a dive. My stomach went down to my toes and stayed there. Then starting the other engines, he pulled into level flight and went back to the base. I was in a state of shock.[49]

M. Sgt. Fred Skelton, Dallas, tells about his C-54, with a load of passengers, flying 1,500 miles on three engines:

> I was assigned to a crew to fly a C-54 back to the United States. On takeoff, we had trouble in one engine, but we were determined

Combat Cargo C-47s supporting the Battle of Rangoon. Note bombs carried under the aircraft. Machine gunners fired through open doors at enemy fighters. *Courtesy National Archives*

not to return and gamble on a change of orders, so we flew across India to Karachi with three good engines. There were no spare engines there, so we flew to Cairo, then Casablanca, Morocco where we found a replacement engine. After three days . . . we took off across the Atlantic to the Azores at sundown. . . . Our navigator had been a land-based briefing officer for two years and had forgotten how to navigate. We got lost . . . finally found the island about midnight using radio bearings.[50]

Although the Japanese were slowly losing the war, they were still dangerous in the jungles and mountains of Burma. The Allies continued to prepare for a long war, and at the insistence of Chiang Kai-shek, opened a new road to China. Brig. Gen. Lewis A. Pick and his army engineers, with thousands of native laborers, had built the road from Ledo, India over the Naga Hills, through the jungles of northern

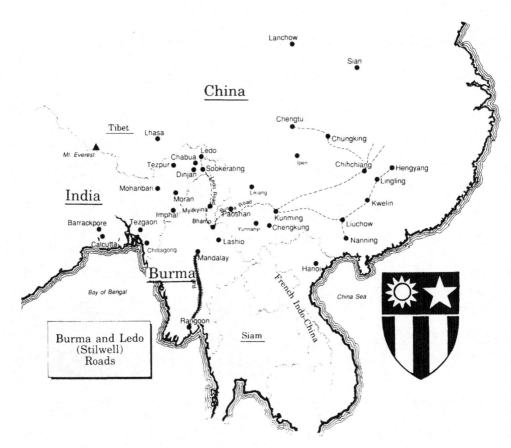

Burma and Ledo
(Stilwell)
Roads

Burma to intersect the old Burma Road. First called "Pick's Pike" and
later the Ledo Road, it was one of the great engineering feats of World
War II. One purpose of the Ledo Road was to augment the Hump
flights. There were some things that could not be carried by air, such
as large trucks and other heavy equipment.

The Ledo Road gave a tremendous psychological lift to the economy of China since commercial traffic would be permitted to supply
Chinese nonmilitary needs. While the Hump airlift was extremely
efficient, it did not allow China to fly merchandise for commercial
needs. The Ledo Road thus became a life-giving new link to the outside world, which had been closed to China since 1942.

Building the Ledo Road had been possible only because General
Stilwell had doggedly and relentlessly pushed the Japanese back into
China. The road was literally hacked out of the hot jungles of the
Hukawng Valley toward Myitkyina. As the highway was being built,

a six-inch pipeline was put down to carry gasoline and oil to Chennault's Fourteenth Air Force. General Pick predicted that the pipeline would carry thirteen thousand tons of fuel per month and that the road and the pipeline would carry from thirty to sixty thousand tons per month into China, although his estimates varied from statement to statement.[51]

As the Ledo Road was being built, General Stilwell's "X" force was pushing the Japanese back to China and Generalissimo Chiang Kai-shek was sending his "Y" Force from western China across the mountains. All of these troops had been supplied by airdrop or behind-the-lines landings by Colonel Cochran's No. 1 Air Commando Group, the Combat Cargo, the 443rd Troop Carrier Group, and the 177th Wing of the Royal Air Force. These aircraft carried troops, food, clothing, ammunition, medicine, mules, live poultry, fresh vegetables, mail, and the necessities of war. They also carried building materials and iron pipe for the new oil pipeline. Flying pipe was a difficult and dangerous job, and it was easy to overload the plane because the pipe was so heavy. Although Japanese fighter strength was gone, the supply planes were constantly harassed by Japanese ground fire, and the monsoons were raging with heavy rains and thunderstorms.[52]

Lt. Danniel Dennis, Hump pilot, remembers carrying the first load of six-inch pipe to Burma: "The runways and taxiways at Jorhat were steel matting [with] their share of lumps and swales . . . it was harder to move the plane and slower to takeoff . . . engines roared into full power . . . the end of the runway was fast approaching and we were still not airborne. At the last minute I pulled the plane into the air . . . we went mushing along about four or five feet above the ground. You could feel that wobbly sick feeling of a stall about to happen."

After the mushy takeoff, with the wheels up, the airspeed improved a little although Dennis kept full power for fifteen minutes and reached only three hundred feet. He called the tower to stop the next plane because he decided that his plane was heavily overloaded. Dennis decided to circle and burn up gasoline to reduce weight for the landing, and the loss of weight enabled the plane to climb slowly. As the tanks were getting toward empty, the plane was high enough to cross the pass at seven thousand feet. They made an uneventful landing at Swingbwiyang and demanded that the pipe be weighed. He found that his plane was carrying thirty-seven lengths plus boxed fittings. The plane was more than 3,000 pounds overweight. Depending on grade, pipe weighed 360 or 420 pounds per length—and Dennis's plane had been loaded with 420-pound pipe, but the weight had been calculated on 360-pound lengths, plus fittings.

Jack Corns beside a wrecked airplane at an emergency field in Burma. Aircraft, from Japan and the Allies, were common throughout Burma. *Courtesy Jack Corns.*

"Sometimes the margin between life and death was as thin as a split hair," Dennis says. "I kept thinking 'When that pipe slams through the front of this plane, if we crash, we're going to look like the meat coming out of a meat grinder.' That vision hovered in the back of my mind for the whole three to four months we flew the pipe."[53]

Many stories were circulated throughout the CBI — some were true. Here is one that was. Lou Minella, Seventy-Fifth Combat Squadron, stationed at Luliang, remembers the Sunday afternoon he received a call that a landing C-46 had run over a Chinese soldier. "I thought of some poor, hapless Chinese who saw the opportunity to have his dragon killed by a landing aircraft," he says.

At operations, Minella met a tearful pilot who insisted that there was a clear runway when he landed and no Chinese had run across in front the plane. Minella and the pilot went to the treatment center, and instead of a bloody, bone-broken Chinese, near death, there was a calm Chinese GI with his rifle and an injured right hand.

The interpreter told an amazing story. The plane had been in Burma, and the Chinese was guarding it. When he heard the plane was going to China, he saw a chance to visit home. He climbed into the wheel well, and the pilot, giving no thought of the missing guard, took off. How the soldier was not crushed by the tire when the wheel retracted, how he survived without oxygen, how he survived the freezing cold while the plane was flying over the mountains were unanswered questions.

The pilot and Minella decided that when the plane landed, the soldier was jolted loose and fell to the ground, and the tail-wheel injured his hand. Next day, Minella phoned the interpreter. "How's the soldier?" he asked. "Oh, they shot him," was the reply. "Why?" asked Minella, "because he left his post and went AWOL?"

"No," the interpreter answered, "because he stole his rifle."[54]

When the new Ledo Road was completed, the first convoy started to China on 12 January 1945, but it was stopped on 15 January to clear out enemy snipers. A few vehicles slipped past the Japanese and, using a secondary route, reached Kunming on 20 January. The main convoy moved out on 28 January to continue the journey and reached Kunming on 4 February.[55]

At this point Generalissimo Chiang Kai-shek renamed the road the "Stilwell Road," after Gen. Joseph Stilwell. It was a bittersweet honor for Stilwell, who had been ousted from China by the generalissimo only months before. Many pondered the motives of Chiang when he proclaimed, "We have broken the siege of China. Let me name this road after General Joseph Stilwell in memory of his distinctive contribution and of the signal part which the Allied and Chinese forces under his direction played in the Burma campaign and in the building of this road."[56]

The Ledo Road was concrete evidence of Stilwell's contribution to the war. Stilwell's battle-weary, leech-bitten ground troops, fighting in hand-to-hand combat, had had a spectacular impact on the Hump airlift. In fact, by clearing the Japanese out of Burma, Stilwell's armies had made the lower southern route of the Hump possible. When the southern route was opened, tonnage quickly increased above that being delivered over both the Stilwell and the Burma roads. Many of Stilwell's critics said that the overland roads had been a waste and were an obsolete way to move military supplies.[57]

7

Victory over Japan — 1945

The Allies won a hard-fought victory in 1945. This would be the year of the Big Storm, the Big Airlift Offensive, Victory in Europe, the Big Bomb, Victory over Japan, Closing the Hump, and the Big Rush to go home. In January, no one suspected these events. Flights over the Hump continued, day and night, India-to-China, China-to-India. Tonnage . . . storms . . . death.

The war in China seemed to stagnate in a series of political conflicts. Time on the Hump was not moving—there was no past and no future. Life was a series of "now" events, a constant crisis, and the flight crew's overwhelming desire just to get through the next flight. Air crewmen continued to challenge the weather. Nothing could change the weather.

Radio operator Irving Wagner, McFarland, California, recalls "leaking gasoline barrels over the Hump" in early 1945. "On one trip we got into a real storm. Lightning . . . St. Elmo's fire. The antenna melted as if it had been cut with a torch. Snow on the radar; no radio contact. We eventually got a radio fix. Our crew chief, Red Hession, was hanging onto a doorway, saying this flight was going to make a Christian out of him."[1]

Pilot Lou Reinig wrote, "The winter months presented probably the worst flying conditions that any pilot ever encountered anywhere in the world. I may have been fortunate as the majority of my trips were at night and I missed at lot of the violence." Reinig felt his greatest problem was at the landing fields. Planes often were "stacked" every five hundred feet and had to hold for two to three hours before starting to let down.

In Reinig's log was this report: "I was holding over Chanyi when the tower called for the unidentified aircraft in the pattern to turn on its lights. He did and it was a Jap who let go with cluster bombs and wiped out a 4x4 [truck] and its men waiting on the end of the runway." He logged another incident when a Japanese pilot reported that it was too dark to bomb and he would return when the moon was up. He did.[2]

After three years of Hump flying, weather reporting was still primitive. Dependence on Indian and Chinese weather stations was not successful, and ATC often complained about inadequate weather forecasting. Chinese stations were more adept at spotting enemy aircraft than reporting weather.[3] Pilots crossing the Hump exchanged the latest information on weather they had encountered in the air, but weather moved quickly and these reports were not always accurate.

The Tenth Weather Squadron, with headquarters at Hastings Mill near Calcutta, controlled weather stations throughout India, Burma, and China and tried reconnaissance flights to predict the weather. Army weather officers serving in the CBI were meteorologists trained in American universities and were familiar only with "frontal" weather encountered in the continental United States. Tropical and Asiatic weather were great mysteries, and little was known or even suspected about the violence of weather over the Hump. The storms that ravaged the Hump often had their breeding grounds in the Soviet Union, and Russians stations refused to share information until late in the war.

I went to the Hump in early 1945 as a weather pilot for the Tenth Weather Squadron at Barrackpore, India. My crew and I were a part of a team of four experienced weather crews sent to India to make reconnaissance flights. In 1944, we had flown weather recon across the North Atlantic from Presque Isle, Maine, to Stornoway, Scotland, reporting the icy and stormy weather over the North Atlantic ferry and supply routes. At that time, ships at sea kept radio silence and could not send weather reports, and flying weather crews were used to report weather. In the latter part of 1944, we flew hurricane reconnaissance from Morrison Field, Florida, across the South Atlantic and the Caribbean. We flew the angry violence of eight Atlantic hurricanes that year.

In the CBI, we patrolled the Bay of Bengal to locate storms moving from the south across the Hump. We also flew reconnaissance mis-

C-87 maintenance at Dinjan, India. The C-87 was a cargo version of the B-24. Weather and the searing heat were constant problems. All maintenance was done outdoors—there were no hangars early in the war. *Courtesy Richard "Sahib" Foster*

sions over the Hump from Calcutta to Kunming. Our planes were modified B-25s with extra fuel tanks and all armament removed. Often we flew C-47s and C-46s and combined weather reconnaissance with supply flights to weather stations in China. Operations never considered weather reconnaissance important unless we carried supplies over the Hump. The Hump was geared for supply. Period. Tonnage. Period.

Compared to the hurricane-tossed South Atlantic, the Bay of Bengal was calm and peaceful, with plenty of wind and rain but no storms. On the long recon flights, we were always on instruments, but there was no turbulence. Over the mountains, the weather changed. Wind and rain that, just the day before, had been quietly moving in from Bengal became a raging monster over the Himalayas. The winds from the bay would deflect against the mountains and create terrific wind shear.

Our crews came to the Hump with confidence based on weather

experience. Pilots had green instrument cards, indicating over one thousand hours of pilot time and over one hundred hours of actual instruments. Although we had flown the storms across the North Atlantic and the hurricanes of the South Atlantic, after flying the Hump we were as humble and fearful of the next storm as the most experienced Hump pilots.

The worst and most tragic storm in the history of the Hump was on the night of 6–7 January 1945, when a Siberian cold front moved down across the mountains and mixed with warm moist air from the Bay of Bengal. In that one wild and terrible night, the ATC lost seven aircraft with thirty-one crewmen and passengers. The China National Aviation Corporation (CNAC), whose pilots were the best in the world at flying weather, closed down operations completely after losing three aircraft and nine crewmen. Other commands lost four planes. This tragic night was known as "Black Friday."[4]

Although the official total was fourteen aircraft lost, many historians and researchers think that the losses for "Black Friday" were more than fourteen. Rumors among the pilots reported as many as fifty to sixty planes were lost. According to accident researcher Chick Marrs Quinn, eighteen aircraft were lost in the big storm, with forty-two crewmen and passengers.

Lt. Thomas M. Sykes, Jackson, Massachusetts, reported his experience with the Big Storm, as he and his crew "departed from Chabua in a C-46 to Kunming with twenty-three drums of fuel. Buildups over the first ridge went to 30,000 feet with heavy turbulence . . . to correct for a wind of 100 miles per hour, a thirty-degree drift was made . . . heavy sleet, snow, hail and extreme turbulence caused variations in altitude as much as 2,000 feet up and down."

After Sykes passed Paoshan, all radio frequencies were MAYDAY. His C-46 hit a violent downdraft, which threw the plane on its side. Descending 4,000 feet per minute with full throttle, they recovered at 14,000 feet—below the minimum safe altitude. Sykes's report continues: "All gyros and the artificial horizon were inoperative . . . only the needle and ball were left . . . air speed went from 300 miles per hour to 40 miles per hour . . . rate of climb went to 4,000 feet per minute and we were on our backs, blown skyward like a leaf in a wind . . . hanging on the safety belt with dirt from the floor falling all around . . . [we] finally became level at 21,000 feet."

When normal flight was resumed, Sykes found his heading had changed 180 degrees and they were flying toward Assam. Since he was closer to China, he returned to the original course. Several drums of fuel had broken loose while the aircraft was upside down and had hit the ceiling. They were tied down, and a quick inspection showed no damage to the aircraft.[5]

This was not an isolated experience. Many pilots flew through a turbulent icy hell. Lt. Don Downie, flying over the Hump on that stormy night, cannot forget the panic on the radio: "'Mayday' calls split the radio waves. 'We are at 12,000 feet and still dropping. Our left engine is dead . . . we are bailing out at 10,000 feet. I'll tie the key down and hope you can get a bearing. So long.' A steady tone took the place of his voice. The tone stopped, and there was only static."[6]

Robert H. Nicholas, Stuart, Florida, pilot on a C-87, was flying from Kunming to Tezpur on the afternoon of 6 January. He saw a great buildup near Yunnanyi and tried to go around it. The storm extended as far as he could see — there was nothing to do but head right through, and it was the worst storm he had ever been in. "I'd been in some doozies in Texas and Arkansas. Never had I seen anything like this.

"Updrafts, downdrafts, hail, with the rate-of-climb to the peg in both directions, and, finally, a long updraft, took us up at 3,000-feet-per-minute until we broke out at 32,000 feet, the highest I had ever been. Everything was so bright and clear with Mt. Liki sparkling to the north and the snowy undercast ahead and to the south."

As Nicholas headed toward Chabua, signals on the ADF came in clear, but the needles rotated like propellers at low RPM. They flew for hours. Finally it was dark and they had seen nothing to show where they were. Soon they began to pick up Assam and got a good fix on Chabua. Over Tezpur, they made a letdown in a normal first-class thunderstorm and landed with only fumes in the tank.[7]

On major bases, operations officers were pilots who flew regular Hump missions and worked in flight operations when they were not in the air. This gave crews in trouble an experienced pilot on the ground to talk to. Raymond Woodford, Phoenix, Arizona, was base operations officer at Chabua the night of the Big Storm. Woodford finished a tour of operations duty just after daylight and took a plane to Kunming. He saw the storm moving up through Burma, but it was quite a way off. It appeared to be at least thirty thousand feet high. The air was calm but this solid wall of oily black clouds was moving slowly toward the crowded air lanes.

When Woodford and his crew left Kunming to return to Chabua, it was raining and there was severe turbulence and icing. He was not able to maintain nineteen thousand feet after passing Mount Tali because of icing, and even with full power, on the last third of the trip the aircraft was slowly losing altitude. At ten thousand feet, over Chabua, the ice began to come off the props and it sounded like the plane was being hit by machine guns. "We finally got to the ground," Woodford recalls, "and I was immediately called to the radio room. Chabua was the central plotting station for lost aircraft."

All stations were jammed, and there was never a time when there were fewer than fifteen aircraft waiting for LORAN plots. A C-87 at twenty-four thousand feet was at full power and losing altitude. His plot showed the plane to be flying among the twenty-four-thousand-foot peaks of Bhutan; fifteen minutes later he was at eighteen thousand feet and still losing altitude, but he had cleared the peaks and Woodford hoped he was safe.

Some planes calling would suddenly go silent. Tension mounted as one C-46 flew up and down the valley in Burma for two and a half hours following LORAN plots. Part of the cargo was an X-ray machine and the crew had thrown out everything else. They were told not to throw the X-ray out because there was only one other in China. After three hours, the pilot had burned enough fuel to get back over the ridge to Chabua.

"We reported fourteen ATC planes down," Woodford wrote. "The whole experience was frightening, not only in the ice and rough air, but also on the ground giving instructions to lost aircraft. I tried to tell people how much ice I could see on the plane I had flown that morning. . . . Not many believed . . . four feet thick and running from the nacelle to the fuselage, with just a dip in between. The C-46 was a good workhorse."[8]

In his 1968 article in *Air Progress Magazine*, Lieutenant Downie confirmed what more pilots knew, that the ghost of General Hardin's "there is no weather over the Hump" still remained as a guiding rule. After that deadly night of "Black Friday," investigators from Washington talked with all crews that had survived the story night. On 8 January new rules required pilots who carried passengers to have more than one thousand hours of flying time. Later, no passengers were carried on any flight across the Hump at night and pilots were permitted to make delays because of weather, although they had to file a detailed report about the delay.[9]

To the experienced pilot, flying was almost automatic. To "make it" from flight to flight, day to day, pilots adopted a Zen-like fatalism. Flying high-octane gasoline, live ammunition, bombs, or dynamite through the fury of a storm—whatever will be will be. There was no other way to face the danger day after day on the Hump. Death flew with us each day; the empty cot was the pilot you flew with last week, who now lies in the green jungles of Burma without a grave or a mark on the earth. Eric Sevareid wrote, "The boys who fly the Hump would say, that misleading casual tone I have heard so many times, 'Hannah got his today.'"[10]

Bliss K. Thorne, ATC pilot from Sookerating and later Chabua, wrote in his personal history of the Hump, "We [pilots] acquired a common characteristic—we were all loners." Eating together, living together, and flying for a common purpose, pilots often refused to make close friends because of the pain of loss over the Hump. "I looked around the basha I had been living in for months and saw pilots within a few yards of me, to whom I had hardly ever spoken, whose names I had never heard. . . . We all got used to operating as individuals."[11]

Thomas W. Auner, Jacksonville, Illinois, remembers "getting a fine bottle of scotch to celebrate my birthday. We made our usual trip to China. . . . That night five of my friends who were expected to celebrate my birthday did not make it back."[12]

One of the constant battles in flying was against pilot error, as the following story illustrates. In mid-1945, two pilots of the Tenth Weather Squadron were flying along a riverbed in China, trying to stay under low clouds and land on a small field near Chungking. The clouds kept getting lower until the pilots were flying down the river below the banks. Early in the war, the Chinese had strung cables across the river to keep Japanese planes from attacking the field by flying in between the riverbanks. When the C-47 pilots saw the cable, they had to choose instantly whether to go under the cable or pull up into the clouds and risk hitting the mountains. They decided to duck under, but not quickly enough.

The cable scraped along the top of the C-47, cutting off the radio antennas and half of the vertical stabilizer and rudder. The pilots were not able to see the damage to their plane, and without radio, the tower at the field could not tell them. All they knew was that the plane was difficult to control. After two passes at the field, they made a good landing. When they climbed out of the plane, they saw their C-47 without a rudder.[13]

In August 1945, after repairs were made, flight engineer John Terrell, copilot John Grant, and I were sent from India to bring the plane to Calcutta. Sergeant Terrell made a careful examination of the repairs and decided the plane was airworthy. In the cockpit, I checked the controls, and Terrell, outside the plane, confirmed that the controls were working. After a bizarre takeoff, I discovered that the control cables for the rudder had been rigged backward—when I applied right rudder the plane skidded right.

How did we miss the crossed cables in the ground inspection? Dur-

Tenth Weather Squadron C-47-256 lost its rudder and radio antenna when pilots flew under cable along a Chinese river bed. The plane made a safe landing and was repaired and back in the air in one week. *Courtesy Don Carlson*

ing the ground checkout, as I sat in the cockpit and moved the controls, Sergeant Terrell confirmed that the rudder was moving—he didn't know if I was moving the rudder right or left, so we didn't catch the error. A stupid mistake like that could have cost us our plane or even our lives.

Once in the air, low clouds around the field made a landing dangerous, and after the initial panic, the C-47 was flying so smoothly and the weather to Kunming was good that my copilot and I decided to go on to Kunming, about three hours away.

After a long, wide circle into the Kunming approach and some concern from the control tower, an acceptable landing was made. Overnight, the cables were rerigged, and we were back over the Hump to India the next day. Two experienced pilots had made reckless mistakes in the same plane and the stable old C-47 reaffirmed its ability to fly, and to allow its pilots to fly again.

Defeated in Burma, the Japanese began intensifying their attacks in China and continued their march toward Kunming. The Japanese "last stand" was an attempt to close down the Fourteenth Air Force. This was the only chance for a Japanese victory. On 29 January, Suichuan fell to the Japanese; Kanchow was taken on 7 February; and Laohokow fell on 25 March—all bases of Chennault's Fourteenth Air Force.

On 14 March, Hump transports of the ATC, the Northern Combat Area Command, and the China Theater Command began moving troops into China to try to stop the Japanese. The MARS task force and troops of the Thirtieth, Thirty-eighth, and Fiftieth Chinese divisions were flown over the Hump into China—a movement of 6,235 troops, completed on 14 May. The ROOSTER movement, in April, airlifted 25,136 troops, 2,178 horses, and 1,565 tons of equipment within China to defend the Fourteenth Air Force base at Chihkiang—a total of 1,648 trips.[14] ATC planes always flew overloaded—forty troops in a C-47, sixty in a C-46, and eighty in a C-54.[15]

War is not always a game of out-shooting the enemy. The Japanese were masters at trickery. In the mountains of the Hump, planes were directed by radio signals, and the Japanese often sent deceptive signals. These false navigation signals were blamed for several lost aircraft over the mountains. English-speaking Japanese had flown into Allied flight patterns, asked for instructions, and bombed the runways. Frank Kovach, Combat Cargo flight engineer from Elizabeth, New Jersey, believes that his crew almost became a victim of a Japanese trick in early 1945.

"After two missions into Burma on February 19, we looked forward to an early quit. . . . But, no! The British had called in an urgent request for guns, gasoline and ammunition and our crew was scheduled for the mission . . . to land at an unlighted airfield after dark."

British fields were not lighted. Kovach and his crew were to fly to the intersection of the Chindwin and Irrawaddy rivers, turn to ninety degrees, fly ten minutes, and start flashing their landing lights. They thought that seemed strange because the British were supposed to be far south of there. But, "Ours is not to question . . . ," Kovach thought.

"After circling and flashing, the field lights came on . . . Larry Muckey, pilot, Clearlake, California, made a beautiful landing on a paved runway. Sitting between the pilot and copilot, I had a good view of the field. I yelled at Larry, 'Turn this damned thing around!' 'Why?' he asked. 'Take a look!' Lined up along the runway were Zeros with the unmistakable red balls. Fortunately, the Japs were as confused as we were."

The pilot made a quick U-turn and started a takeoff back down the runway. The takeoff was too slow! The end of the runway was coming up fast. Muckey's copilot happened to be a former P-47 pilot, and P-47s had the same engines as the C-46. He quickly turned the prop controls to high pitch and got an instantaneous surge of power. Muckey gave the "thumbs-up" sign. Kovach pulled the gear, "milked" the flaps up, and the plane took to the air. The pilot flew on the treetops until they reached the Chin Hills — all lights out.

There are numerous personal stories about flying Chinese troops. Len Reinig wrote, "In March 1945, I was assigned to the evacuation of the Chinese Second Army out of Burma. . . . the airport was an unimproved rice paddy . . . the real problem was taking off, loaded with fifty-five Chinese and all of their equipment . . . the first plane took off upwind and uphill . . . plowed into the bamboo and caught fire . . . Chinese troops pouring out of the window over the wing."

Reinig took off downhill and downwind with full power and a little flap. They hit an old rice paddy dike, which bounced the plane into the air. The copilot quickly spun the trim tab back and the aircraft kept its flying speed. This group of Chinese troops was airwise and, knowing that the crew had 'chutes and they had none, stationed a soldier at the door with a Thompson (machine gun) to make sure the crew didn't leave if there was trouble.[16]

On many flights there was turbulence along the route, and the Chinese troops didn't understand this. One plane load of Chinese troops thought that the pilot and copilot had given them a rough ride on purpose. As the crew stepped out of the plane after landing, they were surrounded by angry soldiers, shouting and threatening. Two of the soldiers, with bayonets fixed to their rifles, backed the pilot and copilot up against the plane. They were about to kill them when an English-speaking Chinese officer ran to investigate. It took some explaining before the angry soldiers put up their bayonets.

In 1945, world events changed quickly. Death came to President Franklin Delano Roosevelt on 12 April, at Warm Springs, Georgia. On 30 April, Germany's Adolf Hitler committed suicide in Berlin. A week later, 7 May, Germany surrendered, and on the following day, President Harry S. Truman proclaimed Victory-in-Europe Day.

For Roosevelt China had been a losing battle and a personal disappointment.[17] The United States often felt alone in China.[18] No troops of any Allied nation except the United States participated in any combat against Japan within the Chinese theater.[19] Other Allied troops fought in Burma, yes; India, yes; Indochina, yes; China, no. The British did not want to fight in China, and they did not want the Chinese fighting in Burma.

President Roosevelt had been a friend of the Hump, and he was completely committed to keeping China in the war. He had kept in constant communications with his friend Generalissimo Chiang Kai-shek. One of the reasons, possibly, that Roosevelt agreed to the recall of Gen. Joseph Stilwell was that Stilwell had embarrassed Roosevelt in his relationship with Chiang. Chiang, and his advisor General Chennault, and the President, had believed in air power as a way to win wars. General Arnold, in a tribute to the President, said, "Franklin Roosevelt was . . . one of the best friends the Air Force ever had."[20]

After the war in Europe ended, Allied military might was suddenly shifted to China and dedicated to the defeat of the Japanese as quickly as possible. President Truman wrote Chiang Kai-shek on 5 July, "On this the eighth anniversary [7 July] of your country's heroic stand against the Japanese aggressor, I desire to reaffirm to the Chinese people our deep friendship and admiration of the valiant struggle which China has waged . . . the full weight of Allied might is gathering momentum to be hurled against the Japanese. . . ."[21]

En route to Europe when the war ended, unbelievable amounts of equipment, men, and supplies were diverted to the CBI. General Stratemeyer learned that a new fleet of C-54s was on its way to India. He also learned that he was to become the commanding general of the air forces in China. This was unexpected.

Southeast Asia Commander Lord Louis Mountbatten was planning to increase Allied support of China, to make General Chennault's job more effective. There were also plans for new bases to be built near Myitkyina so that the ATC could get more supplies over the Hump; and additional bases were to be built in India. Bomber groups from the Tenth Air Force were scheduled to support the ATC if additional transport planes were needed for the Hump.

General Wedemeyer had proposed that Chennault be given Stratemeyer's position, but this had been turned down in Washington. Denied this new command, General Chennault, on 6 July, in anger, requested and received permission to retire. The Tenth and Fourteenth

Air Forces, on 23 July, were placed under the command of General Stratemeyer with headquarters in Kunming.[22]

The end of Gen. Claire Lee Chennault's military career in China was painful, completely unexpected, and, apparently, not a consensus of top commanders. On the second anniversary of the Fourteenth Air Force, 10 March 1945, Chennault had issued an "Order of the Day" that outlined the successes of his command, "born out of the early, hard-fighting, tight-pinched days of the American Volunteer Group and the China Air Task Force." His airmen had accounted for eight enemy planes for every American combat plane lost. Chennault looked forward to the end of the war before the "Fourteenth Air Force marks another anniversary."

On 16 May, General Wedemeyer was told that General Chennault would be replaced, and on 17 June, Stratemeyer was on his way to China with a letter from General Arnold to Wedemeyer: "General Chennault has been in China for a long time fighting a defensive air war with minimum resources. The resulting guerilla type of warfare must change to a modern striking, offensive air power. I firmly believe that the quickest and most effective way to change air warfare in your theater, is to change commanders. I would appreciate your concurrence in General Chennault's early withdrawal."[23]

Claire Chennault was nearly fifty-two years old,[24] deaf, and battle-scarred from eight years of active combat. Against his will, he was being retired for a second time, and his second air force career was ending. He made a month-long tour of China, saying goodbye to military units and to his friends Generalissimo and Madame Chiang Kai-shek. He was awarded China's highest honor, the Order of the Blue Sky and Star, at a farewell dinner. On 8 August, he boarded a C-47 at Kunming and left China, over the Hump, through India, to the United States.[25]

The Air Transport Command in the CBI still had a war to support. In May the ATC, whose mission had been in the air, asked for permission to take a convoy of supplies by land over the Burma Road—an unusual request for an airborne unit. Because of a shortage of heavy vehicles in China to handle the cargo being flown over the Hump, ATC wanted to take a one-time trip over the Burma Road to transport the vehicles needed.

Getting the large vehicles over the Hump by air had been impossible. ATC had tried cutting trucks into pieces for transport in the C-46 aircraft, but because of bad weather and other reasons, planes

Elephant carrying block of teak, Rangoon, Burma. Elephants were taught to bend their fore knees, put their tusks under a block, and wrap their trunks over the top. The same technique was used by elephants to load drums of gasoline on ATC planes. *Courtesy Stereograph, Keystone View Co.*

often had to land at alternate fields and the pieces never seemed to get together.

Now ATC wanted to go overland to China. Capt. Edwin C. Frost, automotive maintenance officer at Chabua, volunteered to take the convoy over. Captain Frost was alone in his volunteering—air force officers were reluctant to get involved in the overland Burma Road project.

It was decided that Captain Frost would take one hundred 2½-ton cargo trucks, twenty-four weapons carriers, twelve jeeps, one four-ton wrecker, and an ambulance, plus six officers and 150 enlisted men.

It would be a twelve-day trip during the monsoon season, beginning on 1 June. The convoy was called "The Battle of Ledo." As Frost made plans, various requests came in: "Could you tow one-ton trailers behind the trucks?" "Could you take ¼-ton trailers behind the weapons carriers?" Refueling trucks, tankers, and personnel carriers were needed in Myitkyina. "Could you take these?" In total, three hundred pieces of equipment, plus personnel, were scheduled to be taken over the Burma Road to China by ATC.

Military red tape held the convoy up several times at various checkpoints. The Army Motor Transport Service (AMTS), which had control of the Burma Road convoys, made objections. AMTS was amazed that anyone would consider a convoy of that size over the road. "Are the drivers certified?" "Who will be responsible?" After many inspections, days of paper work, and many radio communiques at ATC headquarters, the convoy was approved and moved out at 1100 hours 1 June, on schedule. A light rain was falling.

A few miles out, a trailer slid into a ditch and another truck had a burned bearing—they were left to be picked up by the wrecker. It continued to rain. On the downgrades, with compression and low gears being used to slow the trucks, valves began to give trouble. Mechanics were working overtime, and it still rained. For miles the convoy passed derelict trucks, mangled, rusted, and stripped of usable parts, along the roadside—victims of bombings and strafing raids. One truck in the convoy needed a new engine, and in a few hours an ATC plane, on a home-bound cargo flight, brought in the engine.

Twelve days after leaving Ledo, the two-mile convoy moved into Kunming. Traffic was blocked and crowds of grinning and shouting Chinese gave their "ding hao" salute. Captain Frost wrote, "The job was done without guidance, assistance or recognition, and, very probably, without any official report. This may be the only record of the project." Captain Frost retired in 1965 as a lieutenant colonel.[26]

Accidents over the Hump continued. Base commanders worked overtime to find ways to fly more freight, maintain a better safety record, and lose fewer aircrews. This was an impossible position. General Stratemeyer was concerned that the Hump accident rate, on paper, seemed higher than combat operations. He proposed that Hump accident statistics be based on flying hours rather than the actual number of accidents—a relative standard of accidents per one thousand hours.[27]

A very common cause of accidents unique to the Hump was aircraft and birds trying to occupy the same airspace. Milton Miller, edi-

The author in "Betsy," Tenth Weather Squadron C-47. "Betsy" was a squadron name, not a personal one.

tor of the Fourteenth Air Force newsletter and a historian for the Hump, writes, "Birds could be as much a hazard as enemy fighters, flak, mountains, ice, fog, or the maps used in China. The birds nesting on the Himalayan crags were a vicious lot. They seemed to have a kamikaze death-wish that insured them a special niche in bird Valhalla if they died attacking a DC-3, B-25 or B-24."

Almost every pilot in the CBI had a bird story, but Miller's story concerns a nameless chaplain. Chaplains were well respected, except for this one. Miller explains, "This chaplain was a goof-off and a gold-brick to end all goof-offs and gold-bricks. . . . a religious service seemed to be an onerous duty [that he] raced through like a quarter horse . . . at briefings, he was in the sack and his one visit to the hospital was to call on a crew member who owed him fifty bucks from a poker game."

Miller remembered, "When he received orders to go home, crews drew lots for the honor of flying him out of China. On this bright day, the padre was sitting fat and happy in a top turret, dreaming of how he could impress the bishop with his lies. Then it happened!

"There was no warning. A dull plop, broken glass and the turret was full of blood and guts . . . the engineer thought they had been attacked. The chaplain was covered with . . . guts, feathers, bone and yucch! 'It's a friggin boid,' said the radio man. 'That's boid crap all over the padre's head! It's boid justice!'"

Carl Fritch, 492nd Bomb Squadron, was in India when the plane landed. He will never forget the vacant stare in the chaplain's eyes as he was helped from the plane to a shower, and to the infirmary.

"You wouldn't believe the change in the man," Fritch writes. "He was convinced that he had received a special message. He now preached love and his voice was loud, clear and sincere. He loved life. He loved his fellow man. Life was beautiful. Life was great."[28]

Crew chiefs took a special pride in their aircraft. They worked to keep them clean and operational. On 1 August 1945, for Armed Forces Day, three crews of the Tenth Weather Squadron had planned a demonstration of tight formation flying in B-25s stationed at Barrackpore. I was flying the lead aircraft, and with two other B-25 crews, we were making low-level passes across the field. Suddenly the oil pressure on the right engine dropped to zero. The copilot quickly feathered the propeller and we were flying at treetop level on one engine. The right wingman peeled off and landed, but the left wingman hung in tighter than ever. He thought the feathered prop was part of the show.

We had enough speed to make a long circling approach and landed with one engine; the left wingman hung in formation and landed with us. As we taxied to the hardstand, I saw the crew chief's face drop as he threw his oily rag to the ground. We had hit a Bengal sea gull. The leading edge of the wing between the engine and fuselage was completely torn open. Oil and fuel lines were ruptured, and bird guts, feathers, and a bright yellow beak were squashed into the wing.

No one except the right wingman, who could see the oil streaming out of the wing, knew we had hit a bird. The pilot on the left thought we were grandstanding and flew right with us to the ground. On the ground, we were commended for a good air show, but the B-25 was out of commission for three weeks.

July 1945 was the all-time record month for supplies over the Hump, with 71,042 tons flown into China.[29] Still the demands increased for more tonnage—more trips per plane, per crew, per day. This was big business in the air. From the day the India-China Wing of ATC began Hump flights, in December 1942, until V-J Day, 721,700 tons were flown into China—76 percent, or 551,288 tons, in the final eight months. That was three-fourths of the tonnage in one-fourth of the time.[30]

Crews almost always flew overloaded, and it brought problems. The following incident happened to Ed Butler, crew chief with the Eleventh Combat Cargo Squadron, in the summer of 1945 on a grassy field near the Burma border. Dangerously overloaded, they were flying troops back to Kunming. Butler warned the young, inexperienced pilot, "Sir, we've got to lighten the load or you will never clear the trees." "No sweat," said the pilot. "Don't worry." But Butler did worry. The pilot stood on the brakes, revved the engines to full power, and let go. The plane slowly gained speed; the trees loomed closer.

Butler started throwing out duffle bags. "We were at the end of the runway; I was out of duffle bags and I bailed out holding the last bag." He landed hard but had no broken bones. The C-47 cleared the runway, clipping trees. "The plane was gone, I was alone and the Japs might show up any minute." Butler gathered up the duffle bags, piled them neatly, and sat on top to wait for whatever fate had to offer. He didn't know if it would it be better to be captured by the Japanese or the Communists. Hours later, he saw a speck in the sky.

Yes, it was the pilot, having deposited his load, returning for his crew chief. Butler was afraid he would be chewed out. "The pilot said that if it had not been for my quick action in lightening the load, he would have never cleared the trees."[31]

Near the end of July, air force commander General Arnold asked each command to "participate in some way" in the celebration of Armed Forces Day on 1 August—something like an open house, a parade, a party, or a reception. General Tunner was in no mood to celebrate. Victory was near, and the invasion of the Japanese islands would cost thousands of lives. He ordered the India-China Wing of ATC to work as usual on Armed Forces Day and make a special effort to fly more freight over the Hump in that twenty-four hour period than ever before.[32]

On that special Armed Forces Day, on ATC bases, from 0001 to 2400, everyone went all out for twenty-four hours—no one slept. "From cooks, clerks, Chinese coolies, to the chaplain, there was a spirit that made the day more fun than work," Tunner said. The general, personally, flew two round trips over the Hump; every available plane averaged two round trips, and one C-54 flew three round trips, being in the air twenty-two hours and fifteen minutes. A plane crossed the Hump every seventy-two seconds, taking four tons a minute into China.

On that one day, 1 August 1945, ATC reached its operational peak, with 1,118 trips over the Hump and 5,327 tons into China—more than twice the tonnage of any one month in 1943.[33]

On a fateful day in history, 16 July 1945, at Alamogordo, New Mexico, the world's first atomic bomb was exploded—a sound heard fifty miles away and a light seen for two hundred miles. With this awesome "big bang" the new universe of atomic power was born.

On the next day President Truman, Prime Minister Churchill, and Marshall Stalin met at Potsdam, Germany, to plan the final stages of the war. During the conference, Clement Attlee succeeded Churchill as prime minister and Churchill returned to London. The conditions for Japan's surrender were detailed by the world leaders, and on 26 July, Japan received the ultimatum to surrender.

The "Potsdam Declaration" issued by the United States, Britain and China (Russia was not yet at war with Japan) promised "prompt and utter destruction" if Japan continued the war. Two days later, Radio Tokyo and the Domei News Agency replied that Premier Kantaro Suzuki and the Japanese cabinet would "ignore" the ultimatum.[34] It was not known until after the war that, at the same time this ultimatum was given, Japanese civilian leaders, with the permission of the emperor, were planning to negotiate for peace.[35]

What followed instead of negotiation was a quick and deadly end to the war. On 6 August, the B-29 *Enola Gay* dropped the first atomic bomb on Hiroshima; Russia declared war against Japan on 8 August, and one day later, the second atomic bomb was dropped on Nagasaki. Two cities lay in ruins, over 100,000 people had died, and Russia was moving troops into Manchuria.

Japan had had enough war and—everyone thought—on 10 August the Japanese offered to surrender "without prejudice to the Emperor's position."

Flying stopped; no one wanted to take a mission. Tensely, we waited. It was not true. Perhaps the Chinese Communists had announced a false surrender on 10 August hoping to upstage Japan's formal surrender. Maybe they were attempting to have Japanese units surrender to them so they could capture their arms and supplies. The real surrender came five days later.

The end of the war brought an anxious lull for the Hump crews — a sort of giddy stupefied exhilaration that followed years of intense effort. I remember the feeling, "Hold your left one — we could still get killed." We adopted a don't-give-a-damn attitude — "I am still alive — the war is over — what the hell." I remember the announcement of the atomic bomb on Hiroshima. We could not understand what this meant; the atomic bomb was a new, unknown weapon. In the CBI, you were out of touch with what was going on in the world.

The formal "Instrument for the Surrender of Japan" came from President Truman on 15 August as "General Order No. 1" to Gen. Douglas MacArthur, Supreme Commander of the Allied Powers in the Pacific: "The Imperial General Headquarters by direction of the Emperor, . . . hereby orders all of its commanders in Japan and abroad to . . . surrender unconditionally . . ."[37]

One gigantic Hump-sized party erupted throughout the CBI that night — a sudden release of tension, hope, fear, and anticipation of going home. I can speak only for the base at Barrackpore, but the story was the same at all Allied bases. Army regulations prescribed that the flight surgeon should give every flight crew member two ounces of 100-proof bourbon liquor for each mission over the Hump, in addition to eight ounces of canned grapefruit juice. Flight-ration liquor had been stockpiling as it kept coming in. When V-J was announced, the flight surgeons decided to distribute the liquor rations to all crews. So, depending on missions over the Hump, we each received several bottles of Old Crow bourbon, along with several forty-eight-ounce cans of grapefruit juice.

The party that followed equaled any battle of the war. There is no reason that we should have survived. We went from tent to tent, shouting, hugging, crying, shooting at beer cans in the air, shooting at anything that moved on the ground — kicking over anything that was standing — drunken jeep races up and down the runways.

No one was flying. The flight line was quiet and for the first time since 1942, there was no sound of aircraft engines being "run-up" for the day's flying. The silence was eerie and wonderful!

All I can remember now is that about daybreak the next day, we were exhausted, zombie dead, clothes torn off except for our belts with the pockets of our pants — people running around with nothing on except a belt with pockets — that's the way it was. I woke up later that day on my cot, mosquito-bitten, tired, with a monstrous headache and memories of the Chinese army marching through my mouth barefooted. The aches and pains of the Hump rolled into one night—the war was over!

We listened to the ceremony of surrender over the radio on 2 September—there was no television. Tokyo Rose, bless her little black heart, was silent. Crews still flying over the Hump heard the two-minute address by Gen. Douglas MacArthur as he faced the Japanese representatives of the emperor on the battleship USS *Missouri*: "It is for us, both victors and vanquished, to rise to that higher dignity which alone befits the sacred purposes we are about to serve. . . . A better world shall emerge out of the blood and carnage of the past." The eloquence of MacArthur's words crackled through the air. We could hear his obvious emotion as he invited the Japanese to sign the surrender document. Suddenly it came to us. Indeed the war was over. But there was no celebration this time.

Gen. Joseph Stilwell, as ranking U.S. Army officer, had been first to board the *Missouri*, unofficial recognition for his long years in China. In character, writing in his diaries, Stilwell continued to display his acerbic nature. He described the men at the surrender ceremonies: "Except for the American admiral and the Japanese, they looked a 'scratchy-looking crowd,' the Englishman 'a fat red dumpling,' the Australian 'a tub of guts,' the Canadian 'an elderly masher of the gigolo type,' the Frenchman 'rather trim' but with a pair of 'dirty apaches' as aides, the Dutchman 'fat and bald.' . . . What a crew of caricatures in the eyes of the Japs."[37]

General Stilwell, who had been prohibited by President Truman from going on Chinese soil, presided over the separate surrender of Japan to China at Ryukyu on 7 September. One hundred navy fighters and sixty B-29s flew over. Stilwell made another request to visit old friends in China but was turned down by Chiang Kai-shek.[38]

Troops stationed in China still had to be supplied until they could be brought out from the hundreds of small detachments in all parts of China. In August and September, forty-seven thousand troops were flown from China into India and on to Karachi, from there to return by ship and air to the United States.[39]

ATC and the Tenth Air Force were called on to move Chinese troops into areas previously occupied by the Japanese. By 22 September, over forty thousand troops had been moved from Luichow to Shanghai and Chihkiang to Nanking. By 1 November, four Chinese armies numbering over 140,000 men and equipment were transported to various parts of China.

After a long Hump flight, Chinese crews unload author's C-47 at Kunming, in 1945. Flight engineer John Terrell checks manifest. How the old trucks kept running was a mystery.

The first American flights into Shanghai, on 20 August, were volunteer missions by two crews of the Eleventh Combat Cargo Squadron from Luichow to bring aid to Allied prisoners of war in Shanghai. Crews were asked to volunteer because the flights would be over occupied China into an airfield still held by the Japanese. Although the war was over, no one was sure if the Japanese in the remote areas would respect the surrender or even allow flights into Shanghai. No one was ready to trust the Japanese. Because of the humanitarian nature of the flights, two crews were quickly assembled. Arrangements were made through the Swiss consulate. Representatives of the army air force, army, navy, and marines, including radio technicians, doctors, and Chinese civilians, were on the flights. They carried jeeps, medical and radio equipment, and other items to help the prisoners.

Jack Corns, Strasburg, Ohio, was on the Shanghai mission. In his research on the Eleventh Combat Cargo, Corns found that the Japanese did not give up easily. As the Allied planes approached Shanghai, the first airstrip was not suitable. The second strip, Tachang, appeared to be in better condition, and the Japanese were waving a large white flag. The pilot landed, and this was the first time that Allied soldiers had set foot in Shanghai since the Japanese occupation.

At Tachang field, when the planes were parked, well-armed Japanese soldiers approached. An angry Japanese lieutenant colonel informed the group that for personal protection, they would be taken to Japanese barracks. The belligerent attitude of the colonel did not reflect the Japanese high command's acceptance of Potsdam. An interpreter insisted that we be taken to the Swiss consulate. The enraged colonel tried to assault the interpreter but was restrained by his subordinate officers. After bitter argument, the colonel agreed to take the members of the flight to the consulate. Two trucks with six to eight armed Japanese soldiers came.

Although the war was over, the intrigue and fear continued. Corns wrote, "We drove through dark Shanghai streets . . . stopping many times by armed troops with fixed bayonets . . . After an hour and a half, we arrived and were interned in the consulate and could leave only with the permission of General Yohamura, Supreme Japanese Commander of occupied China. The next morning, we received permission to return to Luichow, with precise directions as to route and altitude."[40] The group was not permitted to see the Allied prisoners of war.

With the end of the war, the Hump airlift declined rapidly. The record of 71,042 tons was carried in July; August dropped to 53,315 tons; September, 39,775 tons; October, 8,646 tons; and November, 1,429 tons. In November, the Hump was officially closed.

Stopping the war was difficult. Suddenly we realized that we could not just go home and abandon all of the Allied soldiers, aircraft, guns, and bases. We also knew that it would be impossible to return to the United States all of the materiel that had been delivered over the Hump during the last three years. Most of the military equipment from lend-lease was given to the Chinese Nationalists on recommendation of the adjutant general's office.[41]

The last few months of flying were uneasy. To die in combat is a tragedy, but to die after the war, trying to clean up the mess of battle and marking time until you can go home, is a story of even greater anguish. One such story probably never made the official history of the war but has been told in letters written by many air crewmen to

On the night of 6 January 1945, the Hump's worst storm brought down four-teen aircraft, and forty-two crewmen and passengers were lost. On the ground there was also damage, as this scene at Dinjan, India shows. *Courtesy Jack Corns*

the publications of their postwar groups and to their families back home.

In November 1945, pilots of the 311th Fighter Group of the Four-teenth Air Force were at Lung Hwa field, near Shanghai, waiting to go home. Three squadrons of the 311th were ordered to fly to Cal-cutta to ferry P-51s back to Shanghai to be turned over to the Chinese Air Force. The British would not permit Chinese pilots into India to fly the planes back. The squadrons were the 528th, 529th, and 530th. Two squadrons made it back; the 530th did not—eleven of the twenty-two planes were lost during a thunderstorm over China, or had over-flown the coast and crashed at sea.

Col. Ewing Kinkead reported the disaster, blamed on weather, air-craft not in the best mechanical condition, and demands from the Chinese to have the planes brought to Shanghai.

The 530th had picked up the P-51s in India and made it back to Kunming. Maj. Homer Smith was commanding officer. From Kunming to Shanghai, the squadron hit a storm too late to turn back. David Rust writes, "We got to Kunming with no problems and twenty-two P-51s. Shanghai was reported clear. There was a front in central China, but no one knew much about it; most of the weather stations were closed."

As the flight approached the front, the P-51s kept above the clouds, but slowly the cloud deck kept rising. About three and a half hours out they were at 37,000 feet and climbing to stay out of the soup. One pilot dropped behind with supercharger problems, and another was low on oxygen and was forced to turn back. Smith, the flight commander, saw reflections in the cloud deck and thought it was a lake region and told the flight to break up singly and go down. Smith lost radio contact, and Rust, seeing his mistake, reversed his order to break up. Major Smith's flight went down singly, but the rest stayed together as long as possible.

Rust recalled, "The stuff was solid from 37,000 to the deck. I took the flight down to about 3,500, but when we had not broken out, went back to 10,000 and set course for Shanghai. . . . In about an hour . . . picked up the Lung Hwa homer and broke out. Shanghai was clear and sunny. Of the twenty-two, we lost eleven planes and four pilots, including Smitty . . . it was a hell of a shame."[42]

Chinese headquarters continued to request ATC to move more supplies, especially medical and food supplies to internees who had decided to remain in internment camps. The camps of internment were more comfortable than Chinese living conditions. General Stratemeyer, disenchanted with the constant requests of the Chinese, decided that the air force had done enough. After the initial shipment of humanitarian supplies, no further flights were made. "The Air Force feels that it has done its job with respect to civilian internees," Stratemeyer said.[43]

Many pilots believed that the war could not have been won and our planes could not have been kept in the air without the ingenuity and loyalty of our enlisted crew members. Their skill at "moonlight requisitioning" and "interpretation" of army regulations was greater than that of any pilot. They kept us flying.

After many years, George Argyris, Torrance, California, tells a story of the loyalty of his flight crew to their commander. This was after V-J day, in Shanghai:

> I was flight engineer on C-54 #605—a rare airplane; everything worked so well that Brig. Gen. Charles Lawrence decided to take it as his personal staff plane with its crew, Capt. Robert Pickhart,

Chinese soldier guarding captured Japanese planes at Kiangwan Air Base, Shanghai, October, 1945. A Japanese Zero fighter is in front, and a trainer-observation is at rear. *Courtesy Jack Corns*

> pilot; Lt. Milo Muggard, copilot; myself as engineer; Pvt. Julian Aulicino, assistant engineer; Sgt. Ernest Meinbresse, radio operator; and Pvt. Britton Blazerit, clerk.
> We stopped in Shanghai for a few days. There General Wedemeyer's staff C-54 was parked along side our C-54. Be aware that General Wedemeyer was the four-star commanding general of all U.S. Army Air Forces in the CBI. Wow!

General Wedemeyer's C-54 was plush in every respect. It was completely carpeted with a beautiful set of lounge seats. Argyris was embarrassed for his commander, because "our 'poor little' C-54 had only the regulation, GI-issue, green aluminum bucket seats. General Lawrence had asked for better seats and carpeting, but none was available." Engineer Aulicino thought, as Argyris reports, "Why should they not help themselves to some of General Wedemeyer's luxurious surroundings? It didn't seem fair that the general's plane should be so deluxe."

So, during the night, Argyris admits,

> We removed our plain bucket seats and put them in one of the hangars. Then we stole the lounge seats from General Wedemeyer's

plane and installed them into ours, along with the carpeting.

Next morning at 0600, General Lawrence and our pilots arrived for takeoff. The general was pleased and impressed with the ingenuity of his crew in managing to "requisition" such scarce items. We let him think that they came from "supply."

Looking back, I wonder what would have happened if General Wedemeyer had come out to see off General Lawrence? . . . I wonder now if General Lawrence had any suspicion as to the origin of the seats and carpet. . . . Yes, you certainly do things "beyond the call of duty" when you are twenty years old![44]

There were painful stories of aircraft being destroyed rather than risk having them taken over by the Communists. The Chinese government was extremely unstable at the end of the war, and the Communists were ready to take over. Surplus aircraft in India, not wanted by the British, were destroyed at a special "junking facility" at Panagarh, India. Fighters, bombers, and transport planes were cut into pieces and reduced to scrap metal.

Fred Poats, Annandale, Virginia, in India to ferry a P-51 to China, tells of seeing planes being cut to pieces and "grinding compound mixed with the engine oil, and engines revved up until they coughed, rattled, wheezed, clanked and finally died in agony."[45] To a pilot who has lived by his aircraft and prayed that the engines would keep running, this was the ultimate indignity.

After November, ATC planes flew airmen from China bases to Shanghai for the trip back home, rather than risk a Hump flight back to India. I was a pilot for one of dozens of crews working to deactivate weather stations in all parts of China, from Lanchow and Sian to the north to Kunming in the west and south to Canton. All men and equipment were flown to Shanghai. We made several trips back to India, but not over the Hump. From Shanghai we flew to Canton (the British would not allow us to land in Hong Kong); then to Bangkok, Thailand; then to Rangoon, Burma and on to Calcutta, India. It was a long and beautiful trip.

Until the end of 1945, the Tenth Weather Squadron continued evacuating weather stations throughout China. Many times we took off with twenty to twenty-five weathermen, their personal gear, and instruments for an entire weather station. On some bases, we left complete stations to the Chinese. It was too expensive to pack and ship the equipment back.

As we evacuated the military bases, we took many chances, struggling to get the heavy planes into the air. We usually took off at daybreak, when the air was cool and heavy, to get the best lift. After long, slow, mushy takeoffs, we often had to fly for over an hour, dodging peaks and clouds to gain altitude to ten thousand feet to make the trip to Kunming or on to Shanghai. We learned again to respect the C-47 for its ability to get into and out of short fields at high altitude.

As we left town after town, our love for the simple Chinese people came back to us. Abandoning a small Chinese city was a touching experience. In true character, the Chinese smiled and laughed, even as we were taking from them the American servicemen and the town's economic livelihood. They thronged along the streets throwing fire crackers and shouting—children running back and forth in front of the truck.

Most servicemen in China were souvenir gatherers at heart, and we were often able to buy rare and exotic Chinese art and crafts. However, we usually bought the trashy "cheap john" trinkets. Prices were high, but as we were leaving, the best souvenirs could be bought at near their real value. Many poor people brought us gifts. One small-shop owner came to me. He was the one that, just that morning, I had fought a haggling battle with, trying to buy an ebony-wood elephant with ivory tusks for CN 2000. He would not sell. Now, as we were leaving, he brought the elephant smiling, "For you—no money." I gave him CN 2000, just as he knew I would. His smile was sincere as he gave a deep bow and the Chinese handshake.

Was the Hump airlift successful? What good did it do? Thousands of young men died and hundreds of aircraft were lost—the exact number will never be known. Greater numbers of men were scarred for life. A higher price was paid in men and aircraft than military commanders were willing to admit and much more than historians have been able to count. To have kept accurate records would have been an admission of defeat for the military.

Wesley Craven and James Cate, military historians, make this assessment: "What good end was served by the emergency delivery of 650,000 tons of this and that into China? . . . little went directly to the aid of the Chinese people . . . little to the Chinese armies . . . the regime of Chiang Kai-shek would have collapsed without the support of General Chennault's command . . . Chennault's men were wholly dependent on the Hump lift. . . . it may have speeded up somewhat the conclusion of hostilities against Japan."[46]

No Hump crew would admit that they had carried "this and that." Vital military supplies went to the Chinese armies, or they could not have survived. Chiang Kai-shek's regime did collapse, long before the end of the war. Chennault and the valiant ground forces of Stilwell kept China fighting, because of the Hump's supply. Thousands of Japanese soldiers were kept out of the war because of Hump supplies to the Chinese.

The fact was that the Allies did win the war against Japan, with Hump supplies and not with supplies from over the Burma Road. The Chinese did lose the war against the Chinese Communists; two new Chinas were created, one on Formosa (Taiwan), and old mainland China was changed forever. Japan did go down in defeat but, with the help of the Allies, has made its place in the new world.

General Arnold, commander of the U.S. Army Air Forces, proved that air power was the new way to fight a war, if wars have to be fought. "When I thought about the Chinese situation . . . it occurred to me that, in November 1944, we put 34,000 tons over the Hump—more than the Generalissimo had ever thought of asking for; more than Stilwell had hoped for! Thirteen thousand tons more than ever started over the Burma Road! . . .

"Air travel, air power, air transportation of troops and supplies have changed the whole picture [of war]. We must think in terms of tomorrow."[47]

General Tunner, commander of the Hump airlift from August 1944 until the end of the war, felt that the Hump perfected a new idea in warfare and, more important, in life: How to airlift men and supplies on a grand scale. What was learned by flying the transports over the Himalayas saved Berlin with its airlift and taught the army how to move troops and evacuate the wounded in Korea. "From the Hump on, airlift was an important factor in war, in industry, [and] in life."[48]

Barbara Tuchman, China historian, was more critical: "The Joint Chiefs considered abandoning the line over the Hump, [but believed] . . . that this would have such a bad effect on China's morale and give the Japanese so much to talk about, that the United States could not afford it." Tuchman felt that the long effort to supply Chennault over the Hump was wasted and probably cost the Allies, as Stimson wrote, "an extra winter in the main theater of war."[49]

How many lives would have been lost if the thousands of Japanese soldiers, bottled up in China by Chiang Kai-shek, had been free to fight in the Southwest Pacific? The Hump supplied the Chinese soldiers who kept the Japanese in China.

Chick Marrs Quinn in The Aluminum Trail: "My God! The price was too high!"[50]

This has been a personal history of the men and their aircraft that fought the battle of the Hump. On a personal level, the Hump was successful, even if the experts feel that it failed on the abstract or corporate level. If war is inevitable, as it seems to be; if men must fight, as they always have; then it was best that young men, and women, who were called on to fight the war and fly the missions of supply were taught a skill that would help mankind, and themselves, in future years of peace.

We could not stop the enemy action and we could not keep men from dying, but I was thankful for the chance to learn to fly a transport plane, in weather, on instruments, over mountains, under pressure, with both skilled and dedicated, inept and stupid leadership. If I had to fight a war, I shout for joy that I learned a skill that would help me make the peace. The Hump taught us that.

Thousands of young pilots, navigators, maintenance men, operations officers, and weather forecasters, all with priceless experience and uncommon courage, helped the airlines establish air travel and build a postwar economy that would never have been possible without worldwide air travel. The Hump helped to do that.

As young pilots who flew over the Himalayas, my fellow crewmen and I learned three lessons, beyond price, as rules of living, not dying:

One: It is honorable to fight and (if need be) to die for your country, as long as good men, right or wrong in their honest actions, feel that it is necessary to push back a tyrant who seeks to enslave free men.

Two: Anything can be done when men set their minds and hearts to it. Nothing is impossible.

Three: There are better ways to settle disputes than war.

Notes

PREFACE

1. Theodore White, Annalee Jacoby, *Thunder Out of China*, p. 154.
2. Herbert F. Feis, *The China Tangle*, p. 18.
3. Gen. T. H. Loh, speech to the reunion of the Hump Pilots Association, Little Rock, Arkansas, 28 Sept. 1986. General Loh was president of the Chinese Air Forces Veterans Association of the Sino-American Forces of World War II. His speech was published in the *Newsletter* of the Hump Pilots Association (HPA), Autumn 1986, p. 6. The HPA, with over 3,500 members, has made an invaluable contribution to the history and lore of the Hump. Three large books have been published to record the experiences of the pilots and their crews. The association's quarterly newsletter prints any story or picture that a former crew member submits. In sheer volume, there is probably no other military history as complete as the publications of the HPA.

PROLOGUE

1. In training, instrument flying was taught in the air by blocking the student pilots' visual reference to the ground with a hood. The instructor, outside the hood, could instruct the student and provide a safety factor. On the ground, student pilots were taught instrument flying with a flight simulator called a Link trainer. All weather phenomena could be simulated in the trainer with no danger. Flight in actual weather was rarely a part of training. Flight instruments are often called "gauges."

CHAPTER 1. CHINA'S STRUGGLE FOR AIR POWER

1. "Hump," in *Operations of the Air Transport Command, December 1942–August 1945*. Contrary to these figures, Chick Marrs Quinn, as independent researcher from Lake City, Florida, has a record of over three thousand deaths over the Hump, and five hundred bailouts. Her records include the date, aircraft by number and type, crews by name and serial number, and details of each accident. Quinn spent nine and one-half years of research, reading over sixty thousand government documents and every publication she could find about the Hump. The research was a dedication to her husband, Lt. Loyal Stuart Marrs, who was killed over the Hump on 27 February 1945. In her research, Quinn found that few reports were filed for accidents before June 1943, and reports were not kept for all aircraft lost. It took over forty years for Quinn to get the details of the death of her husband.

2. Dr. John G. Martin, Ashland, Kentucky, personal correspondence, 5 Aug. 1989. Dr. Martin is president of the Hump Pilots Association.

3. James F. Sunderman, ed., *World War II in the Air: The Pacific*, pp. 1–2.

4. David J. Lu, *From the Marco Polo Bridge to Pearl Harbor: Japan's Entry into World War II*, p. 1.

5. Eric Larrabee, *Commander in Chief: Franklin Delano Roosevelt, His Lieutenants and Their War*, p. 568.

6. *Foreign Relations of the United States: Diplomatic Papers*, 1937, vol. 4, p. 18. Telegram: The Ambassador in China (Johnson) to the Secretary of State, Peiping, 15 Dec. 1937. NOTE: Subsequent references to *Foreign Relations of the United States, Diplomatic Papers* will be listed as *FRUS*.

7. Olga S. Greenlaw, *The Lady and the Tigers*, p. 148.

8. Ibid., p. 149.

9. *FRUS*, 1940, vol. 4, p. 697. Memorandum of Conversation, by the Secretary of State, Washington, 26 Nov. 1940.

10. *FRUS*, 1937, vol. 3, p. 90. Letter from the Ambassador in China (Johnson) to the Secretary of State, Peiping, 11 May 1937.

11. *FRUS*, 1941, vol. 5, p. 546. The Ambassador to China (Gauss) to President Roosevelt, Chungking, 19 Nov. 1941.

12. Claire Lee Chennault was born in Commerce, Texas, on 6 September 1893. At a 1954 Flying Tiger reunion in New York City, Chennault told Jack Cornelius, former AVG member, who also lived in Commerce, why he was born in Texas. In August 1883, shortly before Claire's birth, his father got into an argument with a prominent citizen of Louisiana. Mr. Chennault ended the argument by shooting the man's hat off. He decided it would be wise to leave Louisiana until tempers cooled, and the family moved to Texas, where baby Claire was born. In about six weeks, the Chennaults moved back to Louisiana, where Claire was raised in the rural atmosphere of Cajun country. In court, Mr. Chennault was able to prove to the jury that he was a good enough pistol shot that he could shoot a man's hat off without having to kill him, that being enough warning that something more serious might follow. Later,

in China, Chennault encouraged his men to do a lot of pistol practice, saying, "If you are a good enough shot, it might keep you from having to kill somebody." This information is contained in a letter from Jack Cornelius to the Hunt County Historical Survey Committee, dated 21 February 1985. The original letter is in the archives of the Walworth Harrison Library, Greenville, Texas.

13. John Toland, *But Not in Shame*, p. 50.

14. Clare Booth Luce, "The A.V.G. Ends its Famous Career," *Life*, 20 July 1942, pp. 2–7.

15. Don Moser and the editors of *Time-Life* Books, *China-Burma-India*, p. 36.

16. Joseph W. Stilwell, *The Stilwell Papers*, edited and arranged by Theodore H. White, pp. 183–84.

17. William J. Koenig, *Over the Hump: Airlift to China*, p. 3.

18. Frank Fisher, "Vinegar Joe's Problems," *Harper's*, Dec. 1944, p. 66.

19. *FRUS*, 1933, vol. 3, p. 604. The Minister in China (Johnson) to the Secretary of State, Peiping, 27 July 1933.

20. Koenig, *Over the Hump*, p. 30.

21. *FRUS*, 1933, vol. 3, pp. 455–56. The Consul General at Nanking (Peck) to the Secretary of State, Nanking, 14 Nov. 1933.

22. Charles R. Bond, Jr., and Terry H. Anderson, *A Flying Tiger's Diary*, p. 8. This is a personal story of the AVG (Flying Tigers) by a member of the group.

23. *FRUS*, 1937, vol. 3, p. 87. The Ambassador in China (Johnson) to the Secretary of State, Nanking, 11 May 1937.

24. Elmer T. Clark, *The Chiangs of China*, p. 97.

25. Sterling Seagrave, *The Soong Dynasty*, p. 361.

26. Malcolm Rosholt, *Flight in the China Air Space, 1910–1950*, p. 102. Rosholt was a newspaper man in China for many years before and during the war, and worked in U.S. Intelligence. He is one of the on-the-scene historians of the Sino-Japanese air war.

27. Pickler, "United States Aid to the Chinese Nationalist Air Force, 1931–1949," p. 28.

28. Ibid., pp. 29ff.

29. Ibid., p. 30.

30. Ibid., p. 36.

31. *FRUS*, 1941, vol. 5, p. 540. Memorandum by John P. Davies, Jr., of the Division of Far Eastern Affairs, Washington, 22 Oct. 1941.

32. Bond and Anderson, *A Flying Tiger's Diary*, p. 5.

33. "Chiang's War," *Time*, 26 June 1939, pp. 29–32.

34. Greenlaw, *The Lady and the Tigers*, p. 34.

35. Ernest Hauser, "China's Soong," *Life*, 24 Mar. 1941, p. 91.

36. Franklin D. Roosevelt radio address, 15 Mar. 1941. *New York Times*, 16 Mar. 1941.

37. James A. Huston, *The Sinews of War: Army Logistics, 1775–1953*, p. 450.

38. *FRUS*, 1938, vol. 4, p. 451. Secretary of State to the Ambassador in Japan (Grew), Washington, 25 Aug. 1938.

39. William M. Leary, Jr., *The Dragon's Wings*, p. 126; Greenlaw, *The Lady and the Tigers*, p. 27. The success of the Hump airlift was dependent on the experience and leadership of the China National Aviation Corporation (CNAC). *Dragon's Wings* is the story of this important airline and its pioneering leadership of the Hump airlift. Dr. Leary is an expert in early Chinese aviation.

40. *FRUS*, 1940, vol. 4, p. 672. The Ambassador in China (Johnson) to the Secretary of State, Rangoon, 15 Nov. 1940.

41. Seagrave, *The Soong Dynasty*, p. 365; Leary, *The Dragon's Wings*, p. 134.

42. Pickler, "United States Aid to the Chinese," p. 71. Quoting *North China Herald*, 23 Oct. 1940.

43. *FRUS*, 1940, vol. 4, p. 693. The Consul at Rangoon (Brady) to the Secretary of State, Rangoon, 15 Nov. 1940.

44. Raymond Callahan, *Burma, 1942–1945*, p. 58.

45. Seagrave, *The Soong Dynasty*, p. 369.

46. Ibid., p. 370.

47. Bond and Anderson, *A Flying Tiger's Diary*, pp. 18–19.

48. *FRUS*, 1941, vol. 5, p. 675. The Consul at Rangoon (Brady) to the Secretary of State, Rangoon, 14 July 1941.

49. Edward Jablonski, *Airwar*, vol. 2, book 2, p. 2.

50. Greenlaw, *The Lady and the Tigers*, p. 32.

51. *Newsletter* of the China-Burma-India Hump Pilots Association (HPA), Autumn 1986, p. 10. Subsequent citations will be listed as *HPA Newsletter*.

52. Leslie Anders, *The Ledo Road, General Joseph W. Stilwell's Highway to China*, pp. 28–29.

53. Pickler, "United States Aid to the Chinese," p. 109.

54. Leary, *The Dragon's Wings*, p. 135.

55. Clayton Knight, *Lifeline in the Sky, The Story of the Military Air Transport Service*, p. 31.

56. Leary, *The Dragon's Wings*, p. 136.

57. Ibid., p. 135.

58. Ibid., pp. 138–39.

59. Ibid.

60. Ibid.

61. Ibid., pp. 129–40.

62. Edmund Townsend, "Over the Hump and Into China," *Australian Daily Telegraph*, 21 July 1945.

63. *HPA Newsletter*, Winter 1987, p. 6.

64. Ibid., p. 8.

65. Bob Riley, "The Highest Peak", *jing bao Journal*, Oct.–Nov. 1988, p. 17. The *jing bao Journal* is the official publication of the Flying Tigers of the Fourteenth Air Force Association. All stories and sightings of a mountain higher than Everest seem to center in the Amne Machin range in China's Tsinghai Province. In 1954, remembering the stories I had heard while flying

the Hump, I researched the possibility of a mountain higher than Everest. Since 1922, when Amne Machin was first sighted by a British explorer, reputable explorers from France, Germany, the United States, and other countries have tried to measure the peak. All attempts have failed and most expeditions have ended in disaster. There is no official recognition of Amne Machin being higher than Everest.

66. Bond and Anderson, *A Flying Tiger's Diary*, p. 52.

67. Harold Sweet, "Whistling Willie, the Flying Sieve," in *The Air Forces Reader*, pp. 226–27.

68. H. H. Arnold, "Report of the Commanding General of the Army Air Forces to the Secretary of War," in *The Air Forces Reader*, p. 25. General Arnold's report was made 4 January 1944.

69. Bruce Bodie, "Flying Tigers," *Soldier of Fortune*, Mar. 1984, p. 37.

70. Theodore White, "Background Letters to *Time-Life* Editors," Feb. 1943; reprinted in *jing bao Journal*, various issues.

71. Ibid.

72. Jablonski, *Airwar*, p. 32.

73. Bond and Anderson, *A Flying Tiger's Diary*, pp. 60–61.

74. "Flying Tigers," *China at War*, vol. 9, no. 3, Sept. 1942, pp. 12–13.

75. Don Van Cleve, former American Volunteer Group (AVG) flight crewman, interview with author, Irving, Texas, 27 Mar. 1989.

76. Jablonski, *Airwar*, p. 34.

77. Grace Person Hayes, *The History of the Joint Chiefs of Staff in World War II,—The War Against Japan*, p. 79.

78. Pickler, "United States Aid to the Chinese," p. 116.

79. Moser, *China-Burma-India*, p. 17.

80. *China at War*, vol. 9, no. 3, Sept. 1942, p. 12; Greenlaw, *The Lady and the Tigers*, pp. 136–37.

81. Greenlaw, *The Lady and the Tigers*, p. 187.

82. Larrabee, *Commander in Chief*, p. 569.

83. Leary, *The Dragon's Wings*, p. 149.

84. H. H. Arnold, *Global Mission*, p. 279.

85. Arnold, "Report of the Commanding General," p. 23.

86. Arnold, *Global Mission*, p. 279.

CHAPTER 2. THE HUMP BEGINS

1. Bernard Grun, *The Timetables of History*, p. 518.

2. Mary H. Williams, *Chronology, 1941–1945, United States Army in World War II, Special Studies*, p. 11.

3. Arnold, "Report of the Commanding General," p. 23.

4. Larrabee, *Commander in Chief*, p. 556.

5. *FRUS*, 1942, The Far East, p. 57. Memorandum of Conversation, by Mr. Calvin H. Oakes of the Division of Northeastern Affairs, Washington, 26 May 1942.

6. Leary, *The Dragon's Wings*, p. 149.

7. Wesley Frank Craven and James Lea Cate, eds., *Services Around the World*, vol. 7 of *The Army Air Forces in World War II*, p. 114. Craven and Cate have edited the most infinitely detailed history of the Sino-Japanese war. The Office of Air Force History considers this to be the definitive history of the total operation, on land and in the air.

8. "Ancient Cultural Contacts Between China and India," *China Institute Bulletin*, vol. 6, nos. 6–7, Mar.–Apr. 1942, p. 6.

9. *FRUS, 1942, The Far East*, pp. 600–601. The First Secretary of the British Embassy (Hayter) to the Assistant Chief of the Division of Far Eastern Affairs, Washington, 10 July 1942.

10. *FRUS, 1942, The Far East*, p. 626. Telegram: The Secretary of State to the Ambassador in China (Gauss), Washington, 3 July 1942.

11. *FRUS, 1942, The Far East*, p. 604. Telegram: The Ambassador in China (Gauss) to the Secretary of State, Chungking, 19 Aug. 1942.

12. Bernard A. Millot, *The Battle of the Coral Sea*, p. 27n.

13. Norman Carlisle, "The First Raid on Japan, 18 April, 1942," in *The Air Forces Reader*, pp. 163–68.

14. Moser, *China-Burma-India*, p. 65.

15. Larrabee, *Commander in Chief*, p. 366.

16. Hayes, *The History of the Joint Chiefs*, pp. 202–203.

17. Robert W. Coakley and Richard M. Leighton, *Global Logistics and Strategy, 1943–1945*, p. 501.

18. Patrick McMahon, "Over the Hump," *Douglas Air Review*, Mar. 1944; reprinted in *HPA Newsletter*, Spring 1988, pp. 22–23.

19. Greenlaw, *The Lady and the Tigers*, pp. 249–51.

20. Bodie, *Soldier of Fortune*, p. 37.

21. Joseph Stilwell, "The Army Air Forces Section of the Report of General Stilwell to the Secretary of War on his Mission in China-Burma-India," *China-Burma-India, Theater History, 1941–1945*. Microfilm Index 940, Roll A8155. Headquarters, United States Air Force Historical Research Center, Maxwell Air Force Base, Alabama, 1988. Unfortunately, many of these documents were reproduced so poorly on 16-mm microfilm that they are impossible to read. The documents are also poorly organized, with many page numbers omitted, making accurate reference difficult.

22. Greenlaw, *The Lady and the Tigers*, pp. 136, 302, 310.

23. "Pappy" Boyington, *Baa Baa Black Sheep*, p. 116.

24. Rosholt, *Flight in the China Airspace*, pp. 112–13.

25. Moser, *China-Burma-India*, p. 70.

26. *China at War*, vol. 9, no. 3, Sept. 1942, p. 17.

27. *HPA Newsletter*, Spring 1986, p. 3.

28. "Detonation" is a severe loss of engine power because low-octane gasoline prefires before the pistons of the engine reach normal firing position. This results in an engine running extremely rough (shaking in the mount), and the power of the gasoline firing tries to push the piston backward instead of forward. This results in loss of power and possible engine failure.

29. *HPA Newsletter*, Autumn 1988, p. 15.

30. Ibid., Spring 1986, p. 22.

31. Ibid., Summer 1987, p. 27.

32. Craven and Cate, *Services Around the World*, p. 117.

33. Leary, *The Dragon's Wings*, p. 151.

34. Craven and Cate, *Services Around the World*, p. 32.

35. Joseph Stilwell, "History of the India-China Division, Air Transport Command, December 1942 to October 1944," *China-Burma-India, Theater History, 1941–1945*, p. 1.

36. Theodore White, "'The Hump,' The Historic Airway to China was Created by U.S. Heroes," *Life*, 11 Sept. 1944, p. 82.

37. Koenig, *Over the Hump*, p. 33.

38. *HPA Newsletter*, Summer 1985, p. 12.

39. John T. Foster, "How Did We Ever Win the War?" *jing bao Journal*, Dec. 1984–Jan. 1985, p. 33.

40. Craven and Cate, *Services Around the World*, p. 118.

41. Ibid.

42. William H. Tunner, *Over the Hump*, pp. 129–30.

43. Koenig, *Over the Hump*, p. 51.

44. Craven and Cate, *Services Around the World*, p. 118.

45. Charles F. Romanus and Riley Sunderland, *Stilwell's Mission to China*, vol. 1 of *United States Army in World War II: China-Burma-India Theater*, p. 167; Leary, *The Dragon's Wings*, p. 155.

46. Leary, *The Dragon's Wings*, p. 155.

47. Romanus and Sunderland, *Stilwell's Mission to China*, p. 167; Leary, *The Dragon's Wings*, p. 157.

48. Barbara W. Tuchman, *Stilwell and the American Experience in China, 1911–1945.* p. 222.

49. Larrabee, *Commander in Chief*, p. 531.

50. Anders, *The Ledo Road*, p. 75.

51. *FRUS*, 1942, China, p. 57. Memorandum of Conversation by Mr. Calvin H. Oakes of the Division of Far Eastern Affairs, Washington, 26 May 1942.

52. *FRUS*, 1942, China, pp. 49–51. Memorandum by the Advisor of Public Affairs (Hornbeck), Washington, 27 June 1942.

53. *FRUS*, 1945, vol. 7, the Far East—China, p. 57. The acting secretary of state to the chargé in China (Atcheson), Washington, 28 Feb. 1945. The *New York Times*, 28 Feb. 1945.

54. *FRUS*, 1942, China, pp. 90–91. Memorandum prepared in the Department of State, Washington, 27 June 1942.

55. Tunner, *Over the Hump*, p. 129.

56. Townsend, "Over the Hump into China"; reprinted in *HPA Newsletter*, Autumn 1986, pp. 19–20.

57. Richard "Sahib" Foster, Venice, Florida, letter to the author, 12 Nov. 1988. Foster said that in India he had trouble remembering names, so he called everyone "Sahib." In turn, he received that nickname, which has stayed with him over the years since his Hump duty.

58. Tunner, *Over the Hump*, pp. 55, 59.

59. *HPA Newsletter*, Summer 1987, p. 8.

60. "Follow-up Memories of Phil Hageman," *jing bao Journal*, June–July 1983, p. 29.

61. The relief tube is a necessary piece of equipment in military aircraft. Before the days of designer fixtures, it was simply a funnel with a tube extending to the outside. The purpose, as its name implies, was for relief. On long flights, and during periods of stress, we praised the inventor for wonderful foresight.

62. *HPA Newsletter*, Summer 1985, p. 22.

63. Reginald M. Cleveland, *Air Transport at War*, p. 213.

64. Joseph Stilwell, "History of the India-China Division, Air Transport Command, December 1942 to October 1945," *China-Burma-India, Theater History, 1941–1945*, p. 13.

65. Ibid., p. 14.

66. Romanus and Sunderland, *Stilwell's Mission to China*, p. 188.

67. Don Van Cleve, former American Volunteer Group (AVG) flight crewman, interview with author, Irving, Texas, 27 Mar. 1989.

68. Milton Miller, "Stolen: One Fighter Squadron," *jing bao Journal*, Mar.–Apr. 1977, pp. 10–11.

69. Joseph Stilwell, "History of the India-China Division, Air Transport Command, December 1942 to October 1945," *China-Burma-India, Theater History, 1941–1945*, pp. 15–16.

70. Tuchman, *Stilwell and the American Experience*, p. 337.

71. Craven and Cate, *Services Around the World*, p. 14.

72. Ibid., p. 120.

73. *HPA Newsletter*, Summer 1986, p. 18.

74. Dr. John Martin, Ashland, Kentucky, telephone conversation with author, 4 Aug. 1989. Dr. Martin is historian for the Hump Pilots Association.

75. Wallace H. Little, "Stupid Is as Stupid Does," *jing bao Journal*, Apr.–May 1985, pp. 7–8.

76. Richard Rhodes, "The Toughest Flying in the World," *American Heritage* 37 (Aug.–Sept. 1986): 68.

77. Anders, *The Ledo Road*, pp. 237–38.

78. Jim Stark, "Stark the Hustler," *jing bao Journal*, Aug.–Sept. 1988, p. 19.

79. Richard Foster, Venice, Florida, letter to the author, 6 Aug. 1989.

80. Knight, *Lifeline in the Sky*, p. 30.

81. McMahon, "Over the Hump"; reprinted in *HPA Newsletter*, Spring 1988, pp. 22–23.

82. *HPA Newsletter*, Summer 1987, p. 28.

83. Robert T. Boody, *Food-Bomber Pilot, China-Burma-India: The Diary of the Forgotten Theater of World War II*, p. 29.

84. Bliss K. Thorne, *The Hump, The Great Military Airlift of World War II*, p. 61.

CHAPTER 3. THE HUMP MATURES

1. "Casa Blanca Conference and its effect on the CBIT," *China-Burma-India, Theater History, 1941–45*, p. 21.

2. Koenig, *Over the Hump*, p. 96.

3. Arnold, *Global Mission*, p. 442.

4. Tunner, *Over the Hump*, p. 62.

5. *China-Burma-India, Theater History, 1941–1945*, p. 27.

6. Ed Ballenger, "How Did We Win the War?" *jing bao Journal*, June–July 1977, pp. 16–17.

7. *China-Burma-India, Theater History, 1941–1945*, "Casa Blanca," p. 12.

8. Arnold, *Global Mission*, p. 415.

9. Claire Lee Chennault, *Way of a Fighter*, p. 216.

10. *China-Burma-India, Theater History, 1941–1945*, "Casa Blanca," p. 23. When Bissell and Chennault were promoted, Stilwell gave Bissell his new rank one day earlier than Chennault.

11. Ibid.

12. Ibid., p. 24.

13. Ibid., p. 22, Memo from Marshall to Leahy, 4 Jan. 1943.

14. Ibid.

15. Feis, *The China Tangle*, p. 57; Arnold, *Global Mission*, pp. 417–19.

16. Milton Miller, "Mosquito Chasers," *jing bao Journal*, Apr.–May 1978, p. 19.

17. *FRUS*, 1943, China, p. 500. Memorandum of Conversation by Mr. Alger Hiss, Assistant to the Advisor on Political Relations (Hornbeck), Washington, 12 Feb. 1943.

18. *FRUS*, 1943, China, p. 502. Telegram: The Chargé in China (Vincent) to the Secretary of State, Chungking, 20 Mar. 1943.

19. Craven and Cate, *Services Around the World*, p. 114.

20. Tunner, *Over the Hump*, pp. 61–62.

21. Arnold, *Global Mission*, p. 357.

22. Michael Parfit, "The Only Substitute for an Old DC-3 is Another Old DC-3," *Smithsonian*, June 1988, pp. 145–68.

23. Richard Rossi, ed., *A Brief History of the China National Aviation Corporation*, vol. 5 of *Wings Over Asia*, p. 10.

24. *HPA Newsletter*, Summer 1987, p. 16.

25. Sweet, "Whistling Willie," p. 229. The question is often asked, "When is a Japanese a 'Jap'?" William J. Dunn gives this answer on page 40 of *Pacific Microphone:* "When he is flying an enemy plane, occupying an enemy bunker, pacing the bridge of an enemy warship, or merely trying to eliminate you from this earth."

26. Ibid.

27. Leary, *The Dragon's Wings*, pp. 147–48.

28. Sweet, "Whistling Willie," p. 229.

29. Arnold, *Global Mission*, p. 417.

30. *HPA Newsletter*, Autumn 1987, p. 12.

31. Ibid., Spring 1988, p. 14.

32. Ibid., Autumn 1985, p. 26.

33. Ibid., p. 51.

34. Milton Miller, "Over the Road with Sweeze," *jing bao Journal*, Oct.–Nov. 1988, pp. 8–10.

35. *FRUS*, 1943, China, p. 663. Telegram: Memorandum by the Advisor on Political Relations (Hornbeck) to the Assistant Secretary of State (Berle), Washington, 27 Feb. 1943.

36. *HPA Newsletter*, Winter 1988, pp. 18–19.

37. Craven and Cate, *Services Around the World*, p. 116.

38. Ivan Ray Tannehill, *Weather Around the World*, p. 51.

39. Tunner, *Over the Hump*, p. 73.

40. C. J. Rosbert, "Only God Knew the Way," *Saturday Evening Post*, 12 Feb. 1944, pp. 12ff.

41. Paul Quinnett, "It Seemed a Lifetime," in *China Airlift—The Hump*, p. 179.

42. *HPA Newsletter*, Spring 1985, p. 15.

43. Leary, *The Dragon's Wings*, p. 160.

44. Craven and Cate, *Services Around the World*, p. 119.

45. Tunner, *Over the Hump*, p. 63.

46. Craven and Cate, *Services Around the World*, p. 132.

47. *HPA Newsletter*, Autumn 1978, p. 10.

48. John Matheis Jones, "The Burma Road of the Air," *Travel Magazine* 83 (May 1944): 14.

49. *HPA Newsletter*, Summer 1986, pp. 10–11.

50. Tom Barnard, San Clemente, California, personal letter to the author, 27 Nov. 1989. Barnard was a pilot for the American Airlines Project 7-A.

51. *HPA Newsletter*, Summer 1988, p. 13.

52. Jones, "The Burma Road of the Air," p. 16.

53. *HPA Newsletter*, Summer 1986, p. 11.

54. Cleveland, *Air Transport at War*, p. 215.

55. Jones, "The Burma Road of the Air," p. 34.

CHAPTER 4. WORKING OUT THE PROBLEMS

1. *HPA Newsletter*, Spring 1985, p. 19.

2. Ibid., Summer 1985, pp. 10–12.

3. I was a student at Barksdale, Louisiana, in December 1942, when the instrument landing system was being taught to army pilots flying B-25 medium bombers. On some landings, on a good approach, pilots actually few into the runway. Although that sounds dangerous, the approach angle to the runway was so shallow that the touchdown was usually no more than a hard landing. It was an experience that taught respect for the instruments and the aircraft.

4. *HPA Newsletter*, Autumn 1987, p. 10.

5. Don Downie, "The First Real Airlift," *Air Progress Magazine*, Nov. 1968; reprinted in *HPA Newsletter*, Summer 1987, p. 28.

6. Edgar D. Crumpacker, Kailua, Kona, Hawaii, unpublished personal memoir, used with permission. Crumpacker was a pilot for the Thirteenth Combat Cargo Squadron and the Tenth Weather Squadron.

7. Downie, "The First Real Airlift," p. 28.

8. Eric Sevareid, *Not So Wild a Dream*, p. 260.

9. Ibid., p. 265.

10. Ibid., pp. 252–54, 282–83.

11. Ibid., pp. 283–84.

12. Chick Marrs Quinn, *The Aluminum Trail*, p. 73.

13. Ibid.

14. *HPA Newsletter*, Winter 1988, p. 9.

15. Ibid.

16. Tunner, *Over the Hump*, pp. 82–83.

17. "More on Ransom to Community," *jing bao Journal*, April–May 1988, p. 13.

18. *FRUS*, 1945, The Far East, China, p. 14. Representative Michael J. Mansfield of Montana to President Roosevelt, Washington, 3 Jan. 1945.

19. Boody, *Food-Bomber Pilot*, p. 43.

20. Knight, *Lifeline in the Sky*, p. 43.

21. Koenig, *Over the Hump*, p. 71.

22. Won-loy Chan, *Burma, The Untold Story*, pp. 41–42.

23. *HPA Newsletter*, Summer 1987, p. 19.

24. Boody, *Food-Bomber Pilot*, p. 38.

25. *HPA Newsletter*, Autumn 1985, pp. 25–26.

26. Wesley Frank Craven and James Lea Cate, eds., *Men and Planes*, vol. 6 of *The Army Air Forces in World War II*, p. 446.

27. Ibid., pp. 446–48.

28. Tunner, *Over the Hump*, p. 63.

29. *HPA Newsletter*, Summer 1987, p. 26. The author went to the CBI in March 1945, just after the "no weather" edict had been lifted. General Tunner had rescinded the rule, but it was not officially discarded until after the Big Storm of January 1945, by orders from Washington.

30. Koenig, *Over the Hump*, p. 115.

31. *HPA Newsletter*, Summer 1987, p. 5.

32. Joseph Stilwell, "Operations Report, December 1942 to October 1944," *China-Burma-India, Theater History, 1941–1945*, p. 6.

33. Craven and Cate, *Services Around the World*, p. 129.

34. Ibid., p. 132.

35. Knight, *Lifeline in the Sky*, pp. 42–43.

36. *HPA Newsletter*, Spring 1988, p. 13–14.

37. Tunner, *Over the Hump*, p. 106.

38. Ibid.

39. Arnold, *Global Mission*, p. 463.

40. Tuchman, *Stilwell and the American Experience*, p. 403.

41. Williams, *Chronology*, p. 150.

42. Larrabee, *Commander in Chief*, p. 529.

43. Tuchman, *Stilwell and the American Experience*, pp. 394–95.

44. Craven and Cate, *Services Around the World*, pp. 129–30.

45. Joseph Stilwell, "India-China Division, Air Transport Command during General Stilwell's Command, December 1942 to October 1944," *China-Burma-India, Theater History, 1941–1945*, p. 6.

46. Tunner, *Over the Hump*, p. 40.

47. Bob Cowan, "Fragments of the Past," *jing bao Journal*, Oct.–Nov. 1986, pp. 21–22, 40.

48. Boody, *Food-Bomber Pilot*, p. 28.

49. We learned quickly that the term "Chinaman" is considered one of racial disrespect.

50. Chan, *Burma*, p. 15.

51. Menu from Billie's Cafe, Kunming, China, 1943, courtesy of Don Van Cleve, Irving, Texas.

52. Crumpacker, unpublished personal memoir.

53. Richard Foster, Venice, Florida, letter to the author, 7 July 1989.

54. Bob Mongell, "Pinwheel Annie," *jing bao Journal*, Oct. 1975, pp. 1–3.

55. Richard Foster, letter to the author, 7 July 1989.

56. Paul Brock, "Green Death," *jing bao Journal*, Aug.–Sept. 1980, p. 11.

CHAPTER 5. A NEW CHALLENGE TO THE HUMP

1. Craven and Cate, *Services Around the World*, p. 24.

2. Ibid.

3. Tuchman, *Stilwell and the American Experience*, p. 352.

4. Craven and Cate, *Services Around the World*, pp. 24–25.

5. H. L. Buller, "The C-46 and C-47 in CBI Operations," *Aerospace Historian* 22 (Summer–June 1975): 82.

6. Craven and Cate, *Services Around the World*, p. 25.

7. Tuchman, *Stilwell and the American Experience*, p. 375.

8. Knight, *Lifeline in the Sky*, p. 31.

9. Craven and Cate, *Services Around the World*, p. 127.

10. Buller, "The C-46 and C-47," p. 82.

11. *HPA Newsletter*, Summer 1985, pp. 15–16.

12. Ibid., Autumn 1986, p. 16.

13. Crumpacker, unpublished personal memoir.

14. The first C-46 planes, delivered in 1940, cost $341,831. The price declined until, in 1945, the cost was $221,550 — still nearly three times the price of a C-47. There were 3,144 C-46s delivered during World War II.

15. Pearl S. Buck, *China as I See It*, p. 170.

16. *HPA Newsletter*, Summer 1985, pp. 23–24.

17. Tunner, *Over the Hump*, pp. 129–30.

18. Arnold, *Global Mission*, pp. 172–73.

19. Williams, *Chronology*, p. 163.

20. Craven and Cate, *Services Around the World*, pp. 90–91.

21. Wesley Frank Craven and James Lea Cate, *The Pacific: Matterhorn to Nagasaki*, vol. 5 of *The Army Air Forces in World War II*, pp. 18–19.

22. Larrabee, *Commander in Chief*, p. 580.

23. Arnold, *Global Mission*, p. 245.

24. Foster Hailey, "This Is the Superfortress," in *The Air Forces Reader*, p. 190.

25. Larrabee, *Commander in Chief*, p. 580.

26. Walter McCallum, "America's No. 1 Eagle," in *The Air Forces Reader*, p. 183.

27. Williams, *Chronology*, p. 171.

28. James Stewart, "How 430,000 Chinese Built the B-29 Bases," *Reader's Digest*, Aug. 1944, p. 74.

29. Mauer Mauer, *Air Force Combat Units of World War II*, pp. 452–53.

30. Winton R. Close, "B-29s in the CBI—A Pilot's Account," *Aerospace Historian* 22 (Mar. 1983): 6–14.

31. *HPA Newsletter*, Spring 1987, p. 24.

32. Craven and Cate, *The Pacific: Matterhorn to Nagasaki*, p. 140.

33. Ibid., p. 141.

34. Stilwell, "India-Burma Sector, China Burma India Theater, August 1944," *China-Burma-India, Theater History, 1941–1945*, p. 11.

35. Keith Wheeler and the editors of *Time-Life* Books, *Bombers Over Japan*, p. 71.

36. Carl Berger, *B-29: The Superfortress*, p. 97; "B-29s over Hankow," *jing bao Journal*, Feb.–Mar. 1988, pp. 12–13.

37. Chennault, *Way of a Fighter*, p. 330.

38. *FRUS*, 1945, vol. 7, The Far East, China, p. 110. The Ambassador in China (Hurley) to President Truman, Chungking, 20 May 1945.

39. Coakley, *Global Logistics and Strategy*, p. 622.

40. Craven and Cate, *Services Around the World*, p. 131.

41. John G. Martin, *It Began at Imphal: The Combat Cargo Story*, p. 49.

42. Tunner, *Over the Hump*, p. 55.

43. White and Jacoby, *Thunder Out of China*, p. 155.

44. Charles F. Romanus and Riley Sunderland, *Stilwell's Command Problems*, vol. 2 of *United States Army in World War II: China-Burma-India Theater*, p. 99.

45. Arnold, *Global Mission*, p. 433.

46. Martin, *It Began at Imphal*, pp. 7ff.

47. Dr. John Martin, letter to the author, 4 Aug. 1989.

48. Mauer, *Air Force Combat Units*, pp. 32, 34.

49. Martin, *It Began at Imphal*, p. xi.

50. Romanus and Sunderland, *Stilwell's Command Problems*, p. 175.

51. Craven and Cate, *Services Around the World*, p. 134.

52. Ibid., p. 190.

53. Martin, *It Began at Imphal*, p. 5.
54. Ibid., p. 15.
55. Sevareid, *Not So Wild a Dream*, p. 230.
56. Crumpacker, unpublished memoir.
57. This story was verified to me by a CBI pilot in 1945. I never saw a Chinese soldier thrown to his death. However, the story was told, as truth, so many times that I believe that it did happen.
58. *HPA Newsletter*, Summer 1988, p. 13.
59. Ibid., Summer 1986, p. 11.
60. Ibid.
61. Tunner, *Over the Hump*, p. 126.
62. *HPA Newsletter*, Summer 1987, p. 23.
63. Arnold, *Global Mission*, p. 437.

CHAPTER 6. WINGATE TO TUNNER

1. Larrabee, *Commander in Chief*, p. 548; Shelford Bidwell, *The Chindit War: Stilwell, Wingate, and the Campaign in Burma: 1944*, p. 37.
2. Moser, *China-Burma-India*, p. 96.
3. B. H. Liddell-Hart, *History of the Second World War*, p. 366.
4. B. E. Fergusson, *The Trumpet in the Hall*, p. 180.
5. Larrabee, *Commander in Chief*, pp. 551–52.
6. Ibid.
7. Ibid., p. 556.
8. Bidwell, *The Chindit War*, p. 39.
9. Larrabee, *Commander in Chief*, pp. 551–52.
10. Stilwell, "Army Air Forces, India-Burma Sector," *China-Burma-India, Theater History, 1941–1945*, pp. 19–20.
11. *HPA Newsletter*, Summer 1986, p. 12.
12. Don Van Cleve, interview with the author, 27 Mar. 1989.
13. Craven and Cate, *Services Around the World*, p. 135.
14. Boody, *Food-Bomber Pilot*, p. 43.
15. Stilwell, "India-Burma Sector," *China-Burma-India, Theater History, 1941–1945*, pp. 9–10.
16. Williams, *Chronology*, p. 239; Bidwell, *The Chindit War*, p. 280.
17. *FRUS*, 1945, vol. 7, The Far East China, p. 6., Rep. Michael J. Mansfield, of Montana, to President Roosevelt, Washington, D.C., 3 Jan. 1945.
18. Bidwell, *The Chindit War*, p. 280.
19. *FRUS*, 1944, vol. 4, China, p. 260, Memo by the Chief of the Division of Chinese Affairs (Vincent) to the Division of Far Eastern Affairs (Grew), Washington, 2 Oct. 1944.
20. Bidwell, *The Chindit War*, p. 19.
21. Milton Miller, "How Inflation Came to Woochow," *jing bao Journal*, Dec. 1979–Jan. 1980, pp. 10–11.
22. Tuchman, *Stilwell and the American Experience*, p. 1.

23. *FRUS*, 1944, vol. 6, China, pp. 157–58. President Roosevelt to Generalissimo Chiang Kai-shek, Quebec, 16 Sept. 1944.

24. *FRUS*, 1944, vol. 6, China, p. 265. Memorandum by the Ambassador in China (Gauss), Chungking, 3 Oct. 1944.

25. *FRUS*, 1944, vol. 6, China, p. 165. President Roosevelt to Generalissimo Chiang Kai-shek, Washington, 5 Oct. 1944.

26. Sevareid, *Not So Wild a Dream*, p. 331.

27. Milton Miller, "Hao! Boo Hao!" *jing bao Journal*, June–July 1982, pp. 1–5.

28. Tunner, *Over the Hump*, pp. 50–51.

29. Leary, *The Dragon's Wings*, p. 171.

30. Craven and Cate, *Services Around the World*, p. 140.

31. Tunner, *Over the Hump*, p. 50.

32. Ibid., pp. 56–57.

33. Ibid., p. 86.

34. Ibid., pp. 87, 113.

35. *HPA Newsletter*, Spring 1985, p. 19.

36. Tunner, *Over the Hump*, p. 91.

37. Tunner, *Over the Hump*, pp. 101ff.

38. Martin, *It Began at Imphal*, p. 249.

39. Craven and Cate, *Services Around the World*, pp. 140–41.

40. Jones, "The Burma Road of the Air," p. 16.

41. Tunner, *Over the Hump*, p. 111.

42. *FRUS*, 1944, vol. 6, China, p. 163. President Roosevelt to Maj. Gen. Claire Chennault, Washington, 2 Oct. 1944.

43. Feis, *The China Tangle*, pp. 194–95.

44. Craven and Cate, *Services Around the World*, p. 139.

45. Ibid., p. 27.

46. Tunner, *Over the Hump*, p. 71.

47. A "split-S" is a maneuver in which an aircraft follows a flight pattern similar to the bottom half of a capital "S." Rolling on its back, the plane describes an arc toward the ground. Tremendous speeds are reached, and pull-out at the bottom puts tremendous stress on the aircraft and its crew—the wildest roller coaster ride in the world.

48. *HPA Newsletter*, Summer 1987, p. 11.

49. Ibid., Spring 1985, p. 13.

50. Ibid., Autumn 1986, p. 28.

51. *FRUS*, 1944, vol. 6, China, p. 292. Mr. Donald M. Nelson to President Roosevelt, Washington, D.C., 20 Dec. 1944.

52. Martin, *It Began at Imphal*, p. 10.

53. *HPA Newsletter*, Winter 1988, p. 19.

54. Lou Minella, "An Incredible Tale," *jing bao Journal*, Apr.–May 1979, p. 14.

55. Williams, *Chronology*, pp. 375, 379, 386, 392.

56. Tuchman, *Stilwell and the American Experience*, p. 511.

57. Ibid., p. 484.

CHAPTER 7. VICTORY OVER JAPAN

1. *HPA Newsletter,* Summer 1986, p. 2.
2. *HPA Newsletter,* Autumn 1986, p. 16.
3. Craven and Cate, *Services Around the World,* pp. 424–25.
4. Knight, *Lifeline in the Sky,* p. 41.
5. *HPA Newsletter,* Spring 1987, p. 20.
6. Don Downie, "The Wildest Night," *Flying Ace Magazine,* Oct. 1945.
7. *HPA Newsletter,* Summer 1989, p. 20.
8. Ibid., Summer 1988, pp. 11–12.
9. Downie, "The First Real Airlift."
10. Eric Sevareid, "The Flying Humpty Dumpties," *Reader's Digest,* May 1944, p. 41.
11. Bliss K. Thorne, *The Hump, The Great Military Airlift of World War II,* p. 64.
12. *HPA Newsletter,* Spring 1985, p. 17.
13. Crumpacker, unpublished memoir.
14. Craven and Cate, *Services Around the World,* p. 149.
15. Tunner, *Over the Hump,* p. 126.
16. *HPA Newsletter,* Autumn 1986, p. 16.
17. Tuchman, *Stilwell and the American Experience,* p. 491.
18. *FRUS,* 1945, vol. 7, The Far East, China, p. 108. Telegram: The Ambassador in China (Hurley) to President Truman, Chungking, 20 May 1945.
19. Ibid., p. 113.
20. Arnold, *Global Mission,* p. 548.
21. *FRUS,* 1945, vol. 7, The Far East, China, pp. 126–27. President Truman to President Chiang Kai-shek, Washington, 12 Aug. 1945.
22. Charles F. Romanus and Riley Sunderland, *Time Runs Out in CBI,* vol. 3 of *United States Army in World War II: China-Burma-India Theater,* pp. 357–58.
23. Craven and Cate, *The Pacific: Matterhorn to Nagasaki,* pp. 170–71.
24. There has been a question about General Chennault's age. Two separate major biographies of Chennault have listed his birth in different years —1890 and 1893. A historical marker in Commerce, Texas, the town of his birth, lists his birthdate in 1890. His grave marker in Arlington National Cemetery lists his birthdate in 1893. Chennault's daughter explained that when her father went to get his marriage license, he was younger than his bride. So he listed his birthdate as September 6, 1890, so that he would be older. A letter from his father, John S. Chennault, in the archives of the Commerce (Texas) Public Library, gives his birth year as 1893.
25. Rosholt, *Claire L. Chennault: A Tribute,* p. 14.
26. Edwin C. Frost, "China Convoy," *Aerospace Historian* 22 (Mar. 1983): 15ff.
27. Craven and Cate, *Services Around the World,* p. 143.
28. Milton Miller, "It's a Boid," *jing bao Journal,* Feb.–Mar. 1980, pp. 23–24.
29. Craven and Cate, *Services Around the World,* p. 143.

30. *"Hump" Operations of the Air Transport Command, December 1942–August 1945*, p. 3.

31. Ed Butler, "Bailout on the Runway," *jing bao Journal*, June–July 1979, p. 18.

32. Tunner, *Over the Hump*, p. 131.

33. Ibid., 133.

34. For an interesting and significant sidelight to the Potsdam ultimatum, see William J. Coughlin, "The Great Mokusatu Mistake," *Harper's*, Mar. 1953, pp. 31ff.

35. Romanus and Sunderland, *Time Runs Out in CBI*, p. 389.

36. *FRUS*, 1945, vol. 7, The Far East, China, p. 530. Directive by President Truman to the Supreme Commander for the Allied Powers (MacArthur), Washington, 15 Aug. 1945.

37. Tuchman, *Stilwell and the American Experience*, p. 522.

38. Ibid., 523.

39. Craven and Cate, *Services Around the World*, p. 150.

40. *HPA Newsletter*, Spring 1988, pp. 8–10; Jack Corns, Strasburg, Ohio, letter to the author, 30 Jan. 1990. This experience is from Corns's unpublished history of the Eleventh Combat Cargo Squadron.

41. *FRUS*, 1945, vol. 7, The Far East, China, p. 1124. Telegram: The Ambassador in China (Hurley) to the Secretary of State, Chungking, 18 Aug. 1945.

42. Ewing Kinkead, "Postlude to War," *jing bao Journal*, Aug.–Sept. 1978, pp. 8–10.

43. *FRUS*, 1945, vol. 7, The Far East, China, p. 574. Telegram: The Chargé in China (Robertson) to the Secretary of State, Chungking, 29 Sept. 1945.

44. *HPA Newsletter*, Autumn 1986, p. 18.

45. Fred Poats, "Don't Tell Wedemeyer," *jing bao Journal*, Feb.–Mar. 1983, p. 11.

46. Craven and Cate, *Services Around the World*, p. 151.

47. Arnold, *Global Mission*, pp. 539, 615.

48. Tunner, *Over the Hump*, p. 135.

49. Tuchman, *Stilwell and the American Experience*, pp. 499–500.

50. Quinn, *The Aluminum Trail*, p. 476.

Bibliography

AAF, The Official World War II Guide to the Army Air Forces. New York: Bonanza Books, 1988.

"Ancient Cultural Contacts Between China and India." *China Institute Bulletin,* vol. 6, nos. 6–7, March–April 1942, p. 6.

Anders, Leslie. *The Ledo Road, General Joseph W. Stilwell's Highway to China.* Norman, Oklahoma: University of Oklahoma Press, 1965.

Arnold, H. H. *Global Mission.* New York: Harper & Brothers, Publishers, 1949.

———. "Report of the Commanding General of the Army Air Forces to the Secretary of War." In *The Air Forces Reader,* 15–36. Indianapolis: The Bobbs-Merrill Company, 1944.

"The ATC at its Best Hops Dangerous 'HUMP.'" *Newsweek,* 11 June 1945, pp. 52–53.

"B-29s over Hankow," *jing bao Journal,* February–March 1988.

B-29 Program Chronology, 9 September 1950. Historical Archives, The Boeing Company, Seattle, Washington.

Ballenger, Ed. "How Did We Win the War?" *jing bao Journal,* June–July 1977, pp. 16–17.

Berger, Carl. *B-29: The Superfortress.* New York: Ballantine Books, 1970.

Bidwell, Shelford. *The Chindit War: Stilwell, Wingate, and the Campaign in Burma: 1944.* New York: The Macmillan Publishing Co., 1979.

Bodie, Bruce. "Flying Tigers." *Soldier of Fortune,* March 1984, p. 37.

Bond, Charles R., Jr. and Terry H. Anderson. *A Flying Tiger's Diary.* College Station: Texas A&M University Press, 1984.

Bonham, Frank. *Burma Rifles.* New York: Thomas Y. Crowell Co., 1960.

Boody, Robert T. *Food-Bomber Pilot, China-Burma-India: The Diary of the Forgotten Theater of World War II.* New York: Robert T. Boody, 1989.

Boyington, "Pappy" (Col. Gregory Boyington, USMC-Ret.). *Baa Baa Black Sheep.* New York: G. P. Putnam's Sons, 1958.

Brewer, James F., Harry G. Howton, Janet E. Thies, editors. *China Airlift—The Hump.* vol. 2. Poplar Bluff, Missouri: Hump Pilots Association, 1980.

Brock, Paul. "Green Death." *jing bao Journal,* August–September 1980, p. 11.

Buck, Pearl S. *China As I See It,* New York: The John Day Co., 1970.

Buller, H. L. "The C-46 and C-47 in CBI Operations." *Aerospace Historian* 22 (Summer/June 1975): 80–83.

Butler, Ed. "Bailout on the Runway," *jing bao Journal,* June–July 1979, p. 18.

Byrd, Martha. *Chennault: Giving Wings to the Tiger.* Tuscaloosa: University of Alabama Press, 1987.

Caldwell, Oliver J. *A Secret War: Americans in China, 1944–1945.* Carbondale: Southern Illinois University Press, 1972.

Callahan, Raymond. *Burma, 1942–1945.* Newark: University of Delaware Press, 1978.

Carlisle, Norman. "The First Raid on Japan, 18 April 1942." In *The Air Forces Reader,* edited by Norman Carlisle, pp. 163–68. Newark: University of Delaware Press, 1978.

Casey, Gene. "With the India-China Wing of the U.S. Air Transport Command." *Collier's,* 12 February 1944, pp. 8, 51.

Chan, Won-loy. *Burma, The Untold Story.* Novato, California: The Presidio Press, 1986.

Chennault, Anna. *A Thousand Springs: The Biography of a Marriage.* New York: Paul S. Eriksson, Inc., 1962.

Chennault, Claire Lee. *Way of a Fighter.* New York: G. P. Putnam & Sons, 1949.

Chennault, John S. Letter in the archives of the Commerce (Texas) Public Library, dated 9 July 1942.

"Chiang's War." *Time,* 26 June 1939, pp. 29–32.

China at War, vol. 9, no. 3, September 1942.

China-Burma-India, Theater History, 1941–1945. Microfilm Index 940, Roll No. A8155. Headquarters, United States Air Force Historical Research Center, Maxwell Air Force Base, Alabama.

China Institute Bulletin, vol. 6, nos. 6–7, March–April 1942.

Churchill, Winston Spencer. *The Hinge of Fate.* vol. 4 of *The Second World War.* Boston: Houghton Mifflin Company, 1950.

———. *Triumph and Tragedy,* vol. 6 of *The Second World War.* Boston: Houghton Mifflin Company, 1953.

Clark, Elmer T. *The Chiangs of China.* New York: Abingdon-Cokesbury Press, 1953.

Cleveland, Reginald M. *Air Transport at War.* New York: Harper & Brothers, 1946.

Close, Winton R. "B-29s in the CBI—A Pilot's Account." *Aerospace Historian* 22 (March 1983): 6–14.

Coakley, Robert W., and Richard M. Leighton. *Global Logistics and Strategy, 1943–1945*. Washington, D.C.: The War Department, 1968.

Contemporary China, A Reference Digest, vol. 2, no. 1, 1 June 1943.

Cornelius, Jack. Letter to the Hunt County Historical Survey Committee, dated 21 February 1968. Original letter in the archives of Walworth Harrison Library, Greenville, Texas.

Coughlin, William J. "The Great Mokusatsu Mistake." *Harper's*, March 1953, pp. 31ff.

Courtney, W. B. "The Ferry Service, An Important Wartime Function." *Collier's* 107, 5 April 1941, p. 6.

———. "The Great Lift." *Collier's* 116, 29 September 1945, pp. 21–30.

Cowan, Bob. "Fragments of the Past." *jing bao Journal*, October–November 1986, pp. 21–22, 40.

Craven, Wesley Frank, and James Lea Cate, editors. *Men and Planes*. vol. 6 of *The Army Air Forces in World War II*. Chicago: University of Chicago Press, 1955.

———. *The Pacific: Matterhorn to Nagasaki, June 1944 to August 1945*. vol. 5 of *The Army Air Forces in World War II*. Chicago: University of Chicago Press, 1953.

———. *Services Around the World*. vol. 7 of *The Army Air Forces in World War II*. Chicago: University of Chicago Press, 1958.

Davis, Luther. "The 'B'-40 Over Burma." In *The Air Forces Reader*, edited by Norman Carlisle, pp. 130–233. Newark: University of Delaware Press, 1978.

Donald , W. H. "Twelve Peace Offers Spurned by Chiang." *New York Times*, 28 February 1945.

Downie, Don. "The First Real Airlift." *Air Progress Magazine*, November 1968.

———. "The Wildest Night." *Flying Ace Magazine*, October 1945.

Dunn, William J. *Pacific Microphone*. College Station: Texas A&M University Press, 1988.

Dupuy, Trevor Nevitt. *Asiatic Land Battles: Allied Victories in China and Burma*. vol. 10 of *The Military History of World War II*. New York: Franklin Watts, 1963.

Feis, Herbert F. *The China Tangle*. Princeton, New Jersey: Princeton University Press, 1953.

Fergusson, B. E. *The Trumpet in the Hall*. London: Collins, 1973.

Fisher, Frank. "Vinegar Joe's Problems." *Harper's*, December 1944, p. 5.

"Flying Tigers." *China at War*, vol. 9, no. 3, December 1942.

"Follow-up Memories of Phil Hageman," *jing bao Journal*, June–July, 1983.

Foreign Relations of the United States, Diplomatic Papers. 1931, vol. 3, The Far East. Department of State Publication 2476. Washington, D. C.: U.S. Government Printing Office (GPO), 1946.

———. 1933, vol. 3, The Far East. Department of State Publication 3508. GPO, 1948.

———. 1937, vol. 3, The Far East. Department of State Publication 5453. GPO, 1954.

————. 1937, vol. 4, The Far East. Department of State Publication 5545. GPO, 1954.

————. 1938, vol. 4, The Far East. Department of State Publication 5697. GPO, 1955.

————. 1940, vol. 4, The Far East. Department of State Publication 5916. GPO, 1955.

————. 1941, vol. 5, The Far East. Department of State Publication 6325. GPO, 1956.

————. 1942, vol. 1, The Far East. Department of State Publication 6995. GPO, 1956.

————. 1943, vol. 3, The Far East. Department of State Publication 7601. GPO, 1957.

————. 1944, vol. 6, China. Department of State Publication 8229. GPO, 1967.

————. 1945, vol. 7, The Far East, China. Department of State Publication 8451. GPO, 1969.

Foster, John T. "How Did We Ever Win the War?" *jing bao Journal*, December 1984–January 1985, p. 33.

Frost, Edwin C. "China Convoy." *Aerospace Historian* 22 (March 1983): 15ff.

Goodenough, Simon. *War Maps: World War II*. New York: Crescent Books, 1988.

Gordon, John W. *Wings: From Burma to the Himalayas*. Memphis, Tennessee: Global Press, 1987.

Greenlaw, Olga S. *The Lady and the Tigers*. New York: E. P. Dutton & Co., 1943.

Grun, Bernard. *The Timetables of History*. New York: Simon and Schuster, 1979.

Hailey, Foster. "This Is the Superfortress." In *The Air Forces Reader*, edited by Norman Carlisle, pp. 188–91. Newark: University of Delaware Press, 1978.

Hauser, Ernest. "China's Soong." *Life*, 24 March 1941, p. 91.

Hayes, Grace Person. *The History of the Joint Chiefs of Staff in World War II—The War Against Japan*. Annapolis: Naval Institute Press, 1982.

Heiferman, Ron. *Flying Tigers: Chennault of China*. New York: Ballantine Books, 1971.

Hotz, Robert B. *With General Chennault: The Story of the Flying Tigers*. New York: Coward-McCann, 1943.

Howton, Harry, David J. Orth, and Janet M. Thies, editors. *China Airlift—The Hump*. vol. 2. Poplar Bluff, Missouri: China-Burma-India Hump Pilots Association, 1983.

"The Hump: A Picture Story of ATC's India-China Division." *Flying Magazine* 37, November 1945, pp. 35–38.

"Hump" Operations of the Air Transport Command, December 1942–August 1945. Maxwell AFB, Alabama: Office of Air Force History, n.d.

Hump Pilots Association. *Roster: January 1988*. Poplar Bluff Missouri: CBI Hump Pilots Association, 1988.

————. *HPA Newsletter*, official quarterly publication of the CBI Hump Pilots Association, Poplar Bluff, Missouri.

Huston, James A., *The Sinews of War: Army Logistics, 1775–1953*. Washington, D.C.: United States Army, 1966.

Jablonski, Edward. *Airwar*. vol. 2, book 2. New York: Doubleday & Co., 1979.

jing bao Journal, official bimonthly publication of the Flying Tigers of the Fourteenth Air Force Association, New York.

Jones, John Matheis. "The Burma Road of the Air." *Travel Magazine* 83 (May 1944).

Kinkead, Ewing. "Postlude to War." *jing bao Journal*, August–September 1978, pp. 8–10.

Knight, Clayton. *Lifeline in the Sky, The Story of the Military Air Transport Service*. New York: William Morrow and Company, 1957.

Koenig, William J. *Over the Hump: Airlift to China*. New York: Ballantine Books, 1972.

Larrabee, Eric. *Commander in Chief: Franklin Delano Roosevelt, His Lieutenants and Their War*. New York: Harper & Row, 1987.

Leary, William M., Jr. *The Dragon's Wings*. Athens: University of Georgia Press, 1976.

Lee, Shirley. "Pappy Boyington and the Black Sheep Boys." *Collectibles Illustrated*, January–February 1984, p. 40.

Leighton, Richard M., and Robert Coakley. *Global Logistics and Strategy, 1940–1943*. Washington, D.C.: The War Department, 1955.

Liddell-Hart, B. H. *History of the Second World War*. New York: G. P. Putnam's Sons, 1971.

Little, Wallace H. "Stupid Is as Stupid Does." *jing bao Journal*, April–May 1985, pp. 7–8.

Lopez, Donald S. *Into the Teeth of the Tiger*. New York: Bantam Books, 1986.

Lu, David J. *From the Marco Polo Bridge to Pearl Harbor: Japan's Entry into World War II*. Washington: Public Affairs Press, 1961.

Luce, Clare Booth. "The A.V.G. Ends Its Famous Career," *Life*, 20 July 1942, pp. 2–7.

Lui, Chih-pu. *A Military History of Modern China, 1924–1949*. Princeton, New Jersey: Princeton University Press, 1956.

Martin, John G. *It Began at Imphal: The Combat Cargo Story*. Manhattan, Kansas: Sunflower University Press, 1988.

————. *Through Hell's Gate to Shanghai*. Athens, Ohio: The Lawhead Press, 1983.

Mason, Herbert Mason, Jr. *The United States Air Force: A Turbulent History*. New York: Mason Charter, 1976.

Mauer, Mauer. *Air Force Combat Units of World War II*. Washington, D.C.: Office of Air Force History, 1983.

Miller, Milton. *Tiger Tales*. Manhattan, Kansas: Sunflower University Press, 1948.

————. "Hao! Boo Hao!" *jing bao Journal*, June–July 1982, pp. 1–5.

———. "How Inflation Came to Woochow." *jing bao Journal*, December 1979–January 1980, pp. 10–11.

———. "It's a Boid." *jing bao Journal*, February–March 1980, pp. 23–24.

———. "Mosquito Chasers." *jing bao Journal*, April–May 1978, p. 19.

———. "Over the Road with Sweeze." *jing bao Journal*, October–November 1988, pp. 8–10.

———. "Stolen: One Fighter Squadron." *jing bao Journal*, March–April 1977, pp. 10–11.

Millot, Bernard A. *The Battle of the Coral Sea*. Annapolis: Naval Institute Press, 1974.

Mims, Sam. *Chennault of the Flying Tigers*. Philadelphia: Macrae-Smith Company, 1943.

Minella, Lou. "An Incredible Tale." *jing bao Journal*, April–May 1979, p. 14.

Mohair, Annie Laurie, and Doris Benardete. *American Expression of the War and the Peace*. New York: American Book Company, 1943.

Mongell, Bob. "Pinwheel Annie." *jing bao Journal*, October 1975, pp. 1–3.

"More on Ransom to Community." *jing bao Journal*, April–May, 1988, p. 13.

Moser, Don, and the editors of *Time-Life* Books. *China-Burma-India*. New York: *Time-Life* Books, 1978.

Murthy, Nagid Krishna. *Mahatma Gandhi*. Columbia, Missouri: Journal Press, 1948.

McCallum, Walter. "America's No. 1 Eagle." In *The Air Forces Reader*, edited by Norman Carlisle, pp. 181–87. Newark: University of Delaware Press, 1978.

McMahon, Patrick. "Over the Hump." *Douglas Air Review*, March 1944.

"The New Army." *Time*, 4 June 1945, pp. 40–43.

Parfit, Michael. "The Only Substitute for an Old DC-3 is Another Old DC-3." *Smithsonian*, June 1988, pp. 144–68.

Pickler, Gordon K. "United States' Aid to the Chinese Nationalist Air Force, 1931–1949." Ph.D. diss., Department of History, Florida State University, 1971.

Poats, Fred. "Don't Tell Wedemeyer." *jing bao Journal*, February–March 1983, p. 11.

Quinnett, Paul. "It Seemed a Lifetime." In *China Airlift—The Hump*, edited by Harry Howton, David J. Orth, and Janet Thies. Poplar Bluff, Missouri: Hump Pilots Association, 1980.

Quinn, Chick Marrs. *The Aluminum Trail*. Lake City, Florida: The Sequin Press, 1989.

Rawlings, Edwin W. "The Evolution of Air Logistics." *Air University Quarterly* 2 (Spring 1959): 2–15.

Rhodes, Richard. "The Toughest Flying in the World." *American Heritage* 37 (August–September 1986): 66–73.

Riley, Bob. "The Highest Peak." *jing bao Journal*, October–November 1988, p. 17.

Romanus, Charles F., and Riley Sunderland. *Stilwell's Command Problems*. vol. 2 of *United States Army in World War II, China-Burma-India Theater*.

Washington, D.C.: Office of the Chief of Military History, Department of the Army, 1956.

————. *Stilwell's Mission to China.* vol. 1 of *United States Army in World War II, China-Burma-India Theater.* Washington, D.C.: Office of the Chief of Military History, Department of the Army, 1953.

————. *Time Runs Out in CBI.* vol. 3 of *United States Army in World War II, China-Burma-India Theater.* Washington, D.C.: Office of the Chief of Military History, Department of the Army, 1959.

Roosevelt, Franklin D. Address, 15 March 1941.

Rosbert, C. J. "Only God Knew the Way." *Saturday Evening Post,* 12 February 1944, pp. 12ff.

Rosholt, Malcolm. *Flight in the China Airspace, 1910–1950.* Rosholt, Wisconsin: Rosholt House, 1984.

————. *Claire L. Chennault: A Tribute.* New York: Flying Tigers of the Fourteenth Air Force Association, 1983.

————. *Annual Pictorial Magazine.* New York: Flying Tigers of the Fourteenth Air Force Association, 1989.

Rossi, Richard, ed. *Wings over Asia.* vol. 1, *A Brief History of China National Aviation Corporation.* The China National Aviation Association Foundation, 1971.

————. *Wings over Asia.* vol. 4, *Memories of C.N.A.C.* The China National Aviation Association Foundation, 1976.

————. *Wings over Asia.* vol. 5, *A Brief History of China National Aviation Corporation.* The China National Aviation Association Foundation, 1986.

Sampson, Jack. *Chennault.* New York: Doubleday, 1987.

Scott, Robert Lee, Jr. *Flying Tiger: Chennault of China.* Garden City, New York: Doubleday & Company, 1959.

Seagrave, Sterling. *The Soong Dynasty.* New York: Harper and Row, 1985.

Sevareid, Eric. "The Flying Humpty Dumpties." *Reader's Digest,* May 1944, pp. 41–43.

————. *Not So Wild a Dream.* New York: Alfred A. Knopf, 1946.

————. "Our Good Friends, the Head-Hunters." In *The Air Forces Reader,* edited by Norman Carlisle, pp. 305–16. Newark: University of Delaware Press, 1978.

Silsbee, Nathan F. "A Brief History of the Army Air Force." In *The Air Forces Reader,* edited by Norman Carlisle, pp. 43–50. Newark: University of Delaware Press, 1978.

Sinclair, Boyd. *Confusion Beyond Imagination.* Coeur D'Alene, Idaho: Joe F. Whitley, 1988.

Smith, R. T. *Tale of a Tiger.* Van Nuys, California: Tiger Originals, 1986.

Spector, Ronald A. *Eagle Against the Sun: The American War with Japan.* New York: Vintage Books, 1985.

Spencer, Otha C. "Higher Than Everest?" *Coronet,* August 1954.

Stark, Jim. "Stark the Hustler." *jing bao Journal,* August–September 1988, p. 19.

Stewart, James. "How 430,000 Chinese Built the B-29 Bases." *Reader's Digest,* August 1944, p. 74.

Stilwell, Joseph W. *The Stilwell Papers.* Edited and arranged by Theodore H. White. New York: William Sloan Associates, 1948.

———. "The Army Air Forces Section of the Report of General Stilwell to the Secretary of War on His Mission in China-Burma-India." *China-Burma-India, Theater History, 1941–1945.* Microfilm Index 940, Roll No. A8155. Headquarters United States Air Force Historical Research Center, Maxwell Air Force Base, Alabama.

Stowe, Leland. *Soldier of Fortune,* March 1984.

Strong, Anna Louise. *One Fifth of Mankind.* New York: Modern Age Books, 1938.

Sulzberger, C.L., and the editors of *American Heritage. American Heritage Picture History of World War II.* New York: The American Heritage Publishing Co., 1966.

Sunderman, James F., ed. *World War II in the Air: The Pacific.* New York: Van Nostrand, Reinhold Company, 1963.

Swanberg, W.A. *Luce and His Empire.* New York: Charles Scribner's Sons, 1972.

Sweet, Harold. "Whistling Willie, the Flying Sieve." In *The Air Forces Reader,* edited by Norman Carlisle, pp. 226–29. Newark: University of Delaware Press, 1978.

Tannehill, Ivan Ray. *Weather Around the World.* Princeton, New Jersey: Princeton University Press, 1952.

Thomas, Lowell. "Out of this World, A Journey to Lhasa." *Collier's* 11, 18 February 1950.

Thorne, Bliss K. *The Hump, The Great Military Airlift of World War II.* Philadelphia: J. B. Lippincott, Co., 1965.

Toland, John. *But Not in Shame.* New York: Random House, 1961.

Townsend, Edmund. "Over the Hump and Into China." *Australian Daily Telegraph,* 21 July 1945.

Tuchman, Barbara W. *Stilwell and the American Experience in China, 1911–1945.* New York: The MacMillan Company, 1970.

Tunner, William H. *Over the Hump.* Washington, D.C.: Office of Air Force History, United States Air Force, 1985.

U.S. War Department. *Merrill's Marauders—February–May 1944.* Washington, D.C.: U.S. Government Printing Office, 1945.

Wagner, Ray. *American Combat Planes.* Garden City, New York: Doubleday & Company, 1982.

Webster's American Military Biographies. Springfield, Massachusetts: G. & C. Merriam Company, 1978.

Wheeler, Keith, and the editors of *Time-Life* Books. *Bombers Over Japan.* Alexandria, Virginia: *Time-Life* Books, 1982.

White, Theodore. "'The Hump,' The Historic Airway to China Was Created by U.S. Heroes." *Life,* 11 September 1944, pp. 81–88.

————. "Background Letters to *Time-Life* Editors," February 1943. Printed in *jing bao Journal*, various issues.

White, Theodore, and Annalee Jacoby. *Thunder Out of China*. New York: William Sloan Associates, 1946.

Williams, Mary H. *Chronology, 1941–1945, United States Army in World War II, Special Studies*. Washington, D.C.: Office of the Chief of Military History, Department of the Army, 1958.

Yang, Richard, and Edward J. Lazzerini. *The Chinese World*. Arlington Heights, Illinois: The Forum Press, 1978.

Ziden, Wu. "The Hump and the Hump Airlift." *People's Daily*, 17 July 1975.

Index